Power Moms

Also by Joann S. Lublin

Earning It: Hard-Won Lessons from Trailblazing
Women at the Top of the Business World

Power Moms

How Executive Mothers
Navigate Work and Life

Joann S. Lublin

HARPER
BUSINESS

An Imprint of HarperCollins*Publishers*

HarperCollins books may be purchased for educational, business, or sales promotional use. For information, please email the Special Markets Department at SPsales@harpercollins.com.

FIRST EDITION

Designed by Bonni Leon-Berman

Library of Congress Cataloging-in-Publication Data has been applied for.

ISBN 978-0-06-295490-9

21 22 23 24 25 LSC 10 9 8 7 6 5 4 3 2 1

To my mother, Betty Lublin:

She was always my biggest critic—and

biggest supporter—of my role as a working mom.

Contents

Introduction

In my late thirties, I was a well-regarded reporter for the *Wall Street Journal* in Washington, DC, when it named me second in command to the female chief of its important London bureau. For the first time, women would run a bureau of the United States' premier business newspaper.

I was thrilled about joining management and becoming a pioneer for fellow female journalists. Abra, my four-year-old daughter, was not thrilled.

She and seven-year-old Dan would stay with my parents for two weeks while I arranged child care, schools, and housing in London. On a dark, wintry evening, our kids and their grandmother accompanied me to Washington Dulles International Airport for my overseas flight. I hugged them good-bye at the gate before I walked toward the plane.

Suddenly Abra rushed over and locked herself to my left ankle. I could barely walk. "Mommy, don't go! Mommy, don't go!" she screamed hysterically. She panicked because she couldn't fathom when she would ever see me again. Guilt filled me. A guilt that many working mothers know well.

I pried Abra loose, then stumbled aboard the aircraft. Tears streamed down my face. "Oh, my God, how can I do this?" I asked myself between sobs. "How can I leave my children with my parents?" I worried that my wrenching decision meant I might value my job more than my kids. I felt horribly inadequate as a mother. I also was depressed that I didn't know how I might have handled the situation better.

That painful departure was the low point of a persistent tug-of-war between my commitments to my family and my career. I later advanced to management news editor, inaugurated the *Journal*'s career advice column, and shared its 2003 Pulitzer Prize. Abra and Dan are now grown, and he's a married father of three.

My experiences as a working parent gave birth to this book. Reflecting on the years I spent raising children while a highly driven journalist, I wondered whether things have changed much for today's executive mothers.

Do women of the GenX generation tackle the daunting challenges of parenthood any differently than my generation of baby boomers did decades ago? I suspected that GenXers handle the conundrums of work and family better because more of them occupy influential positions and face less social stigma. I decided to explore the unusual world of Power Moms, whom I defined as experienced female business executives with successful careers and children.

I spoke to eighty-six such mothers from the previous generation and the present one. All have worked for sizable U.S. companies in a wide swath of industries such as food, media, technology, financial services, retail, cosmetics, management consulting, and advertising. They divulged heartfelt stories about their illustrious lives.

My yearlong exploration of both generations helped me forgive my own shortcomings as a working mother. Their coping strategies at home and work offer useful guideposts to aspirational women everywhere—with or without offspring. Using their playbook, you can flourish both on and off the job.

I discovered a profound cultural shift between the two waves of Power Moms. Amid greater societal acceptance of their dual roles as caregivers and business leaders, contemporary executive mothers pursue ambitious paths that were uncommon only a few decades ago. The risky entrepreneurial ventures launched by many illustrate this change.

Emboldened to pursue their lofty career goals more aggressively, the current crop of Power Moms manages work/life conflicts with far more aplomb and dexterity than I had expected. But I was disappointed to see that they often still lead stressful lives and haven't completely overcome working-mother guilt. It's a troublesome sign that America must further improve its treatment of employed parents.

Baby boomers, who were born between 1946 and 1964, were the first wave of mothers to reach the higher echelons of American business. They usually concealed their parenting problems from colleagues because they felt pressured to leave their authentic selves at home. They often lacked female role models, rarely insisted that their spouses be hands-on parents, and enjoyed few family-friendly perquisites. Those trailblazer women were typically in their sixties when we chatted.

I also interviewed twenty-five adult daughters of boomers who shared gripping accounts about their tight though occasionally tense ties with their mothers. Their average age was about thirty years old. Some daughters vowed never to follow in Mom's weary footsteps because she had toiled long hours and fought to defy her era's constrictive social norms.

Younger executives make up the second wave of Power Moms. Born between 1974 and 1985, they were under forty-five when I began meeting them in late 2018. Nearly two-thirds are GenXers; the rest are millennials.

Second-wave women navigate working parenthood with less angst because they assertively bring their authentic selves to the office. They benefit from advanced technology, involved husbands, and more supportive employers. Thanks to gutsy breakthroughs by the initial cadre of executive mothers, a number of present ones held important management positions by the time they began their families. Their elite job status and financial resources give them greater control over their work schedules. And they can rely on a growing network of managerial moms like them.

In fact, a significant proportion of women in charge of major U.S. corporations have children. That's true for 63 percent of the female chief executives at the biggest businesses, including the heads of General Motors, The Hershey Company, Ulta Beauty, and Best Buy. Those nineteen moms were among the thirty women steering companies in the S&P 500 index as of early March 2020, according to Catalyst, a nonprofit organization that conducts research about topics related to women.

Executive mothers also thrive better at work and home now because the overall ranks of senior female leaders have grown. Women held 21 percent of executive suite positions in 2020, concluded a study by McKinsey & Company and Lean In, founded by Sheryl Sandberg, the chief operating officer of Facebook. The management consultancy and nonprofit group tracked women's progress based on data from 317 U.S. and Canadian companies. They separately surveyed more than 40,000 employees about their workplace experiences. The percentage of women at the top rung of the corporate ladder was a marked increase from 17 percent just five years before.

By comparison, women accounted for only about 10 percent of corporate officers in Fortune 500 companies as of 1996, according to a Catalyst census. No comprehensive data exist about the prevalence of mothers in upper levels of business decades ago, however. In 2013, a majority of roughly twenty thousand members of the National Association for Female Executives reported having children, according to a survey by the professional group.

Corie Barry epitomizes the way second-wave Power Moms reap career gains based on breakthroughs and sponsorship by the first wave. The mother of an eight-year-old daughter and twelve-year-old son turned forty-four the same week in April 2019 that Best Buy announced her imminent ascension to CEO.

Barry had been one of three mothers on the top executive team at the electronics retailer. She had won her elevated status by progressing from an initial position of financial analyst two decades earlier. Barry had been promoted to finance chief in 2016. Her female predecessor actively sponsored her for the prestigious position.

There's another sharp distinction between present and previous generations of executive mothers: the contemporary cohort practices the new concept of "work/life sway." They deliberately move back and forth between the professional and personal sides of their digital-centric lives, accepting inevitable and aggravating disruptions such as taking their youngsters to medical checkups during the workday.

Such Power Moms view a job task interrupted by their children's needs as a well-deserved work break. In other words, they go with the flow. Mothers who sway know when to say no. Nor do they hesitate to request help from their spouses and supervisors.

Work/life sway is a far cry from work/life balance, an impossible ideal that boomers often pursued but never achieved. Creating balance assumes that we can simultaneously fulfill every demand of our separate spheres. It's the equivalent of a shaky yoga pose.

I first learned about work/life sway when I visited Vanessa Hallett, a GenXer who is the worldwide head of photographs at Phillips, a boutique auction house. The thirty-eight-year-old executive adorns the walls of her Manhattan skyscraper office with pictures of her two young sons and their colorful art projects. A pair of photo montages features bright red hearts. She grabbed a thick notebook to show me her detailed calendar of daily schedules for the boys and their nanny.

Late one afternoon several years ago, Hallett was busy working past 5:00 p.m. when she paused to watch her eleven-month-old elder son take his first steps at home via an instant video from the nanny. "My eyes teared," she recalled. "I left work immediately and rushed home," she continued. "I still feel sad I missed the moment. But I try to look at the bigger picture."

For Hallett, the bigger picture means having a fulfilling career plus swaying for regular peeks at her boys' activities—"everyday moments that allow me to feel more connected."

Certain second-wave mothers I met run a global work team from their master bedroom. Some order groceries online as they march into a business boardroom. Others escaped corporate America by forming their own business. Female entrepreneurs frequently devise family-friendly environments rather than expect mothers and fathers to work as if they weren't parents, too. Unfortunately, that approach remains infrequent at companies led by men.

Consider Katia Beauchamp, the CEO of Birchbox. The former bank analyst cofounded the online beauty business in 2010 right after completing her MBA at Harvard Business School. Every month, Birchbox sends subscribers a box of samples from cosmetics, skin care, and hair care brands. Customers can then buy full-sized items from the firm. By 2014, the start-up was valued at nearly $500 million.

Creating a company "allowed me to think about building a culture that works for me and that I think can change things for other women, too," the thirty-six-year-old entrepreneur told me during her third week back at Birchbox following the late-2018 birth of her fourth child. We talked in the sun-drenched conference room of its

Manhattan headquarters. I noticed deep bags under her eyes, which she kept wiping wearily.

Moments before my arrival, Beauchamp had conducted a conference call as she pumped breast milk for her infant daughter in the headquarters nursery. She lacks a private office. The nursery, filled with a couch, fruit basket, flowers, and refrigerator, was being used regularly because mothers make up about 10 percent of Birchbox's largely female U.S. workforce.

Beauchamp insists that a woman's career trajectory need not slow upon her return from maternity leave. "There's kind of this implicit bias [that] once you are going to be a mom, you can't handle as much," she pointed out. "I just want Birchbox to have the ability to support you as a mom."

Among other things, Beauchamp requires extra training for Birchbox operational managers about how to "onboard" returning new mothers and fathers. "We allow you to come back to work on a very different schedule of your choice as you're easing back in," she explained. "We just make that work."

But like many start-ups, Birchbox subsequently hit a rough patch. An extensive layoff announced in January 2020 affected forty-four of the ninety-four staffers at its headquarters.

The pioneering first wave of executive mothers faced different obstacles as they sought to radically reshape the U.S. business landscape. They battled sexist workplace practices, the gender pay gap, and stereotypes about female corporate leaders—an odd oxymoron at that point in U.S. history.

About 30 percent of interviewed boomer moms are present or past chief executives of public companies. (Private companies aren't required to publish data about their top officers.) I heard compelling career tales from Carol Bartz, the first woman to command Autodesk and Yahoo! I also interviewed Hershey Company CEO

Michele Buck, DuPont's former CEO Ellen Kullman, ITT's retired CEO Denise Ramos, WW International CEO Mindy Grossman, and Betsy Holden, a former co-CEO of Kraft Foods (now The Kraft Heinz Company).

"Mine was the first generation to say, 'We're going to find a way to have both a career and a family,'" remembered Holden, who coled Kraft when it was the biggest U.S. food company. The problem was "finding the time to do it all."

A veteran of the consumer goods industry, Holden bore a son and daughter after she reached upper middle management at Kraft. The company makes popular items such as Jell-O and DiGiorno pizza. She became pregnant for the second time while a Kraft vice president of strategy and new products. "No one has ever done this [VP job] with two children," her male boss said. In reality, no Kraft *mother* had ever done so.

"How many children do you have?" Holden asked her boss.

"Two," he replied.

So "someone has done this before with two kids," she noted. A different senior executive elevated Holden to vice president of marketing two months before her daughter, Julie, arrived in June 1991. She was the first woman to land the powerful post at Kraft.

At the time, Holden and a female colleague had recently organized an internal Working Moms Exchange Group, largely because they lacked higher-level role models within Kraft. "We talked about it being the sisterhood," Holden recollected. As working mothers, "you weren't alone in some of the things that you were going through."

Members of the unconventional support network met monthly to swap solutions to their common issues, such as unsuitable nannies. Holden led an entire session on spending quality time with your kids.

She treasured memorable moments with her own progeny, which she sometimes arranged spontaneously. "Do you have to go to work today?" four-year-old Julie inquired one Friday morning in December 1995. Holden was president of Kraft's cheese division and lived with her family in Winnetka, an affluent Chicago suburb.

The executive checked her calendar. No deadlines loomed. "You know, I don't have to go to work today," she told her delighted child. Mother and daughter spent the bitterly cold day in downtown Chicago, where they toured the children's museum, dined out for lunch, and rode a Ferris wheel.

Seeing her mom skip work just for her made Julie feel special. The adventurous day "meant a lot to her," Holden said. She left Kraft in 2005 and is now a McKinsey & Company senior adviser.

Younger working moms continue to bear a bigger burden of juggling job and Junior than do working dads due to the persistence of overall gender bias and employment discrimination known as the "motherhood penalty." Despite women's considerable gains in the workplace, "I'm nowhere near to doing a victory lap," said Melanie Steinbach, the chief talent officer of McDonald's at the time we spoke. (She subsequently became its U.S. chief people officer and left in August 2020.)

I chatted with the forty-four-year-old mother of two daughters in a windowless conference room at the Chicago headquarters of the big fast-food chain. In the same room several months earlier, a male colleague had objected to Steinbach's planned promotion of an expectant manager. He had suggested postponing the increased duties for the mother-to-be until her maternity leave ended.

"We will promote her now," Steinbach retorted, staring hard at the man. "Her pregnancy has nothing to do with it."

A panoply of work/family challenges confronts second-wave executive moms at home as well because social norms still hold mothers ultimately responsible for the domestic domain. The thirtysome-thing head of a high-tech start-up wished that her husband would share household chores such as preparing meals and washing clothes for them and their baby. "But he never thinks of initiating these things," she complained. As a result, she would run a load of laundry rather than "tell him to do it and wait for him to do it."

Not long after our interview, however, she stopped washing her husband's dirty clothes. "Something needed to get off my plate," she explained. That CEO and ten other second-wave executive moth-ers have experience leading a start-up or a publicly held company. Among the latter is Marissa Mayer, a former Yahoo! CEO.

I spoke with almost every mother face-to-face, traveling to eight states from coast to coast. I often describe how they looked and reacted so you can imagine being in the room with me and fully appreciate their inspirational stories. Sixteen of those interviewed are women of color.

Every executive has or had a husband except for two with male domestic partners and a third with a wife. Several divorced Power Moms raised their offspring alone. Some came from modest back-grounds, never envisioning themselves as future business leaders. Margaret Keane, the CEO of Synchrony Financial, the biggest U.S. issuer of store credit cards, certainly didn't aim high during her youth.

The mother of two was born into an Irish American family in 1959. Keane's father worked as a New York City police officer. He and his wife raised their seven kids near John F. Kennedy Interna-tional Airport in Queens.

"I used to see the planes go all the time, and I'd be like 'Well, I want to go on a plane someday,'" Keane told me. We conversed in her expansive corner office at Synchrony headquarters in suburban Stamford, Connecticut. Following her first flight at age sixteen, she said, she had briefly yearned to become a stewardess "so I could fly around the world."

Other women welcomed me into their homes and hearts. Ten executives cried or choked up while sharing certain intensely poignant moments. They turned tearful when recounting ugly quarrels with an estranged husband, spiteful treatment on the job, remorse over frequent business trips, or their youngster's painful medical condition.

Among the lachrymose was Inhi Cho Suh, a GenX mom. The then head of a multibillion-dollar software business for IBM shed tears while describing the sacrifices her mother had made for Suh's career. "It's a little bit emotional," she said, grabbing a tissue to dab her eyes in her office in downtown San Francisco.

The forty-four-year-old executive wore a fancy black dress and checked jacket that morning because she would address a major conference for women in technology hours later. A native of Seoul, South Korea, Suh moved to the United States at age five with her family. Her parents spoke no English, she recalled. "They only had a couple of bags and a little bit of cash."

Suh's parents settled in Spartanburg, South Carolina, and eventually excelled as owners of small businesses. Her father opened a martial arts school. Her mother had to learn to sew before she could open a seamstress shop.

Suh joined IBM as a marketing assistant in 1998. Moving up rapidly, she became the youngest ever vice president of the computing giant—at age thirty-two. In 2011, she considered leaving Durham, North Carolina, where she was working. She and her husband, a fellow IBM executive, wanted to accept attractive assignments at company headquarters in suburban New York.

Suh worried about finding good child care for their toddler and infant sons because she lacked immediate family near the new locale. She called her parents for guidance. They promised to sell their businesses, come live with her family in Ridgefield, Connecticut, and spend several years caring for their grandsons. Repeating her mother's rationale for this radical change made Suh cry.

"My sun is setting," her mom told Suh in Korean. "Yours is rising."

Working mothers such as Suh's affect their daughters' career prospects, but they have no significant impact on their sons' employment, a large-scale study showed. The study, which was published in 2018, reflects two surveys covering more than a hundred thousand men and women in twenty-nine countries between 2002 and 2013. The researchers didn't explain why the sons had failed to get career benefits but did find that those men held much more egalitarian gender attitudes than women with stay-at-home moms.

Adult daughters of employed mothers are more likely to work themselves, hold supervisory responsibility, work more hours, and earn higher incomes than women whose mothers remained home full-time, the study showed. That's especially the case for women raised by mothers with extensive education and higher-skilled jobs.

Our mothers influence us profoundly at every age. For women, the mother-daughter connection undoubtedly represents the most important human bond. We remain strongly linked throughout our lives. For instance, the portion of the brain that regulates emotions is more similar in mothers and daughters than in any other pairing of generations, according to a small study published in 2016.

Yet relationships between first-wave executive moms and their grown daughters can become complicated and heated. The daughter sometimes resists her mother's informal career coaching because she wants to succeed on her own terms—even though her Power Mom knows what it takes to succeed in business.

That happened after twenty-two-year-old Melanie Herscher finished Smith College in spring 2014 with a mathematics degree. Her mother, Penny, was then the CEO of FirstRain, a business analytics company, and had chosen the same college major. Penny had previously been one of the first women to run a U.S. semiconductor business.

Melanie said that her mother had urged her to imitate her by obtaining an entry-level job in computer science. Penny opened doors for the new graduate through her contacts at high-tech companies.

But only a handful of the 113 companies where Melanie applied gave her a phone interview, and those were firms where staffers knew her mom. None offered the young woman a job.

"With every rejection, I felt like I was dying a bit inside," Melanie recollected. "I had not lived up to expectations." She stopped job hunting. She spent the late summer stretched out on her parents' couch, "watching television and petting the dog."

Penny alerted her FirstRain colleagues about her daughter's hard job search, and the company's head of sales offered her a temporary internship. Melanie said the stint helped her "figure out what I wanted to do with the rest of my life." She worked elsewhere before joining Snowflake, a data storage firm, as a data analyst in December 2016.

Yet she doesn't aspire to be a high-powered executive mother like Penny, who suffered multiple strokes during Melanie's youth. "I watched how stressful it was for her to be that person. How much was on her shoulders. How much she had to give up," Melanie said sadly.

In subsequent chapters, you'll receive insights from Power Moms about numerous issues that touch working women everywhere—whether it's timing childbirth to minimize career disruptions or leveraging your parenting experiences to become a better boss. You'll also hear how these moms handled difficult dilemmas such as heavy business travel, dual-career clashes, unequal domestic duties, and the high-tech demands of being "always on" in a nation that reveres overwork. I interweave their stories with my own.

Chapter 10, "Ditch Working-Mother Guilt," describes ten highly creative ways to shed the working-mother guilt that both waves of executive mothers weathered. Their offspring and careers benefited greatly. The final chapter examines how several innovative U.S. companies serve working parents well—partly by changing men's assumptions about their role. I also spell out the unfinished agenda for public-sector and private employers.

I nevertheless remain optimistic, especially since the significant shift toward work/life sway dramatizes the strides achieved by Power Moms. Women in the second wave can sway because those in the first one reaped gains for themselves and their employers—as evidenced by studies showing that businesses with the most gender-diverse leadership generate higher profits.

Here's a breakdown of key differences between the waves:

A First-Wave Power Mom Born Between 1946 and 1964:

- Was often the only woman in upper management at her workplace.
- Faced tremendous social pressure to be a hands-on mother while holding low parenting expectations for her spouse.
- Usually didn't tell male colleagues about her pregnancy difficulties, sick youngsters, or work/family conflicts in order to conceal the chaos of motherhood.
- Avoided requesting a reduced schedule because she wanted to be seen as fully committed to her career—in other words, one of the guys.

- Found it hard to leave the office at a reasonable hour due to a lack of sophisticated technology for easily wrapping up work from home later.
- Knew few executive mothers at other companies who could be role models.
- Lacked employee benefits that promote coparenting, such as paid paternity leave and telecommuting.

A Second-Wave Power Mom Born Between 1974 and 1985:

- Is usually one of multiple women in upper management at her workplace.
- Expects her spouse to coparent and share household duties.
- Routinely discusses her work/family conflicts with male colleagues and feels proud to call her youngster's child care provider from the office.
- Brings her authentic self to work in other ways—such as by choosing an employer that will accommodate her parenting needs.
- Achieves work/life sway through technological advances that let her move back and forth seamlessly between home and job tasks.
- Has a sizable external network of supportive executive mothers who also serve as her role models.
- Enjoys senior male leaders' endorsement of using perks such as paid parental leave, work-from-home arrangements, and flexible hours.

The dozens of executives I met belong to an economically privileged and well-educated group. Though they don't represent every woman, I have singled out the high achievers for close scrutiny because they do represent important and influential players in the business world who set the standard for mothers' future success at home and on the job.

I had anticipated that the affluence of Power Moms would allow them to deftly manage the conflicts between their work and family identities. The fact that many female executives still wrestle with these problems today reflects wider societal pressures affecting working moms in every kind of job. The tremendous stress caused by those pressures became evident during the coronavirus pandemic as many women struggled to work from home, educate their youngsters, and run their households. Those social pressures are the focus of the coming chapter.

1

Hard Work for Working Mothers

At age twenty-five, I was committed to being "child free."

I enjoyed my prestigious position as one of the handful of female reporters for the *Wall Street Journal*. None of us had kids. I feared that bringing up a child would wreck my professional progress. I also refused to relinquish journalism for full-time motherhood. I couldn't picture myself doing both.

"Our society has failed to create easy ways for me to combine a family and a career," I complained in a first-person essay that I wrote for the *Journal*'s editorial page about my predicament. Few employers encouraged flexible work arrangements, I noted. And "there are pitifully few adequate and inexpensive day care centers in the U.S."

I penned those words in the late 1970s. Eventually I overcame my ambivalence about parenthood because I didn't want to miss the uniquely female experience of giving birth and, with my husband, Mike, raising a family.

Despite progress in the decades since I decided to have children, American working mothers in the twenty-first century still struggle harder than working fathers to balance their work and family roles. It's not fair. Employed moms live in a nation with a deep tradition of personal responsibility for child rearing, persistent gender stereotypes, and scant institutional support for parents with paid jobs.

U.S. Moms at Work

Toil outside the American home is nothing new for many low-wage women of color. By the 1880s, 35.4 percent of married black women participated in the labor force—irrespective of the presence of children—partly because black men faced such pervasive job bias, according to a 2019 analysis by the Economic Policy Institute, a nonprofit think tank. But "white women typically left the labor force after marriage."

By 1920, African American women were about twice as likely to work as white women, the journalist Amy Westervelt noted in her 2018 book, *Forget "Having It All": How America Messed Up Motherhood—and How to Fix It*.

The overall employment picture for U.S. women began to change during World War II. The mobilization of troops caused labor shortages when companies rushed to produce badly needed military supplies. The shortages assuaged widespread worries about employing women with youngsters under fourteen.

Wartime mothers came to view paid work outside the home as their patriotic duty. However, employers willing to hire moms complained that they didn't show up because they lacked someone to care for their kids. The upshot? "The U.S. government for the first, and still only time in history, saw fit to subsidize childcare for working mothers," Westervelt wrote. "At its peak in July 1944, the system boasted more than 3,000 centers looking after some 130,000 children."

But after World War II ended, many middle-class white women

faced social pressure to relinquish their jobs to returning soldiers. Their exodus caused a slump in the labor force participation of women, as I pointed out in my 2016 book, *Earning It: Hard-Won Lessons from Trailblazing Women at the Top of the Business World.*

The presence of middle-class women in the workplace revived during the 1960s, thanks to the launch of the modern women's movement, the introduction of the birth control pill, and landmark federal legislation outlawing sex bias on the job. The proportion of women with jobs or pursuing them exceeded 40 percent by 1966, a postwar high.

Economists estimate that a significant portion of the growth in work productivity between 1960 and 2008 reflected the removal of barriers that had prevented many white women from realizing their economic potential. Indeed, by the dawn of the twenty-first century, the United States boasted one of the highest labor force participation rates for women among major wealthy countries.

Mothers came to occupy a more sizable presence in U.S. workplaces as well. About seven in ten women with children under eighteen years old have held jobs or sought work outside the home every year since 1994, the U.S. Bureau of Labor Statistics (BLS) reported. The 71.5 percent level reached in 2018 was the highest since 2000.

Moms with white-collar positions have made even more impressive gains. In 2017, 47 percent of U.S. mothers held jobs in management, professional, and related occupations—far more than the 40 percent of fathers. That's up from about 45 percent for moms and 38 percent for dads four years earlier, BLS data show.

Overall labor force participation by U.S. adults aged twenty-five to fifty-four, which had slipped for years, turned around between 2016 and 2018. Women in their late twenties and early thirties accounted for much of the recovery, the *Wall Street Journal* reported. "The recent expansion of parental benefits at many American companies may have helped to reverse the decline in female work-force participation." The reversal followed a sixteen-year slide in the proportion of women in the labor force.

However, the United States' prominent international standing disappeared as nations elsewhere enlarged state-financed parental leave policies and child care programs. Countries such as Germany, Australia, and the United Kingdom overtook the United States, according to data compiled by the Organisation for Economic Co-operation and Development.

Public intervention alleviates work/family conflicts for mothers outside the United States, the sociologist Caitlyn Collins noted in her 2019 book, *Making Motherhood Work: How Women Manage Careers and Caregiving*. The assistant professor of sociology at Washington University argued that U.S. working moms have a tougher time than their counterparts in any other developed nation, based on her conversations with 135 such women in the United States, Sweden, Germany, and Italy.

The United States "has the least generous benefits, the lowest public commitment to caregiving, the greatest time squeeze on parents, the highest wage gap between employed men and women, and the highest maternal and child poverty rates," Collins wrote. She blames the American ethos of private responsibility for raising children. Not until 1993, for example, did the United States enact a law requiring twelve weeks a year of *unpaid* family leave so parents could care for a newborn without fear of job loss.

This sad state of affairs deeply troubles Lindsay Kaplan, a millennial executive mom who has advocated for better treatment of working parents. I met the thirty-four-year-old at the Manhattan clubhouse of Chief, a private network for powerful female leaders that she and Carolyn Childers founded. Besides its clubhouse, Chief offers speaker series, networking events, and career coaching sessions.

Childers is a former executive at Handy, a small provider of home-cleaning services. She and Kaplan signed up more than seven hundred members within six months of inaugurating Chief in January 2019.

Kaplan had previously been a vice president of Casper Sleep, an online mattress seller. During more than four years with the start-up, she bore her son, Max, and watched Casper's revenue soar to $350 million from nothing. She successfully fought for Casper to provide employees with parental leave and flexible schedules.

"The number one thing I would like as a mother is for America to get its act together and to support working families," she declared vehemently. She was seated in a tiny back room of Chief's elegant, high-ceilinged clubhouse. At the time, about half of Chief members had children. Expanded government services such as comprehensive parental leave and heavily subsidized child care "will allow mothers to concentrate on being good parents and good employees," she argued.

The U.S. private sector also long ignored the needs of working mothers and fathers. That was the harsh reality during the 1980s, when many boomer Power Moms started their families. As of 1988, only 2 percent of full-time women at U.S. companies with at least a hundred staffers could receive any paid maternity leave, the Bureau of Labor Statistics reported. And the proportion of men then eligible for some paid paternity leave at those businesses? A dismal 1 percent.

That picture is brighter for parents from the GenX and millennial generations. About 27 percent of U.S. employers offered paid parental leave in 2019—up from 17 percent in 2016, according to surveys of human resource professionals by the Society for Human Resource Management.

In particular, more businesses recognize fathers' critical contribution in caring for their newborns. About 30 percent of employers covered by the 2019 study provided paid paternity leave, a dramatic improvement from 21 percent in 2016. But new dads these days often hesitate to take their compensated time off, due to worries about career damage and social disapproval.

Men who actively care for their children are teased and insulted at work more than so-called traditional fathers and men without children, concluded research published in 2013. The paper was based on two field studies of workplace mistreatment among middle-class employees. Active dads were considered to be less dedicated to their jobs. It's the same misperception that frequently hurts working mothers.

"Today, women and men both are more likely to ask their employers to do more for working parents than they did in the past," said Shelley J. Correll, a professor of sociology and organizational behavior at Stanford University, in an interview. But "paternity leave usage won't increase until we change our norms about what is acceptable for men and women to do."

The Motherhood Penalty

Correll should know. A leading scholar on gender issues, she documented the "motherhood penalty"—the notion that women fare badly in employment decisions due to their parental status. Employers assume that "mothers are less committed to their jobs because of the competing demands about having children," she said.

As part of a groundbreaking 2007 study, Correll and two fellow researchers submitted 1,276 résumés and cover letters for pairs of fictitious applicants to 638 employers with real job vacancies over an eighteen-month period. Half of the equally qualified candidates were parents. Childless female applicants got 2.1 times as many employer callbacks as mothers did for entry-level and midlevel marketing and business jobs.

The study was "the first to provide causal evidence that mothers experience hiring discrimination," Correll and her coauthors pointed out. They predicted that further investigation would reveal that mothers are held to a harsher standard on the job, such as when bosses decide to bestow raises.

Motherhood does exacerbate the gender pay gap. It's an unfortunate consequence of how employers still perceive moms and the inadequate societal support for their disproportionate caregiving duties. This yawning economic divide has long symbolized American women's slow progress at work. If present trends persist, women will have to wait until 2059 to achieve pay equality, according to a 2019 report from the Institute for Women's Policy Research, a non-profit think tank.

The gap stirs strong emotions, and understandably so. In March 2019, the U.S. women's soccer team sought equal pay for better work. The team sued the U.S. Soccer Federation, alleging that female players make less money than male peers despite their greater victories.

Four months later, the women's team won the World Cup. A deafening chant filled the stadium following its final victory in Lyons, France. "Equal pay! Equal pay!" thousands of fans shouted again and again. The gender discrimination lawsuit sought more than $66 million in damages. In May 2020, however, a federal judge gutted the team's claim of pay bias. He said that the female players hadn't provided sufficient evidence to take the issue to trial.

Yet the extent of the motherhood pay gap has become clear. The

earnings gulf between working moms and dads exceeds the dispar-
ity between all employed women and men, a 2019 analysis by the
National Women's Law Center found. Full-time female employees
with at least one child under eighteen make sixty-nine cents for
every dollar paid to fathers, the advocacy group reported. By comparison, all women working full-time are typically paid eighty cents
for every dollar earned by their male counterparts.

The gap is even wider for women of color. Black women employed
full-time typically make sixty-one cents for every dollar paid to
white, non-Hispanic men. For Latinas, the figure is fifty-three cents.

The arrival of a couple's first baby doubles the pay gap between
husbands and wives, the U.S. Census Bureau stated in a 2017 working paper. The woman's earnings fall at the time of a child's birth.
The gap keeps growing for the next five years, driven by her reduced
income. Her pay doesn't recover until their child reaches nine or ten
years old, Census researchers stated. The paper didn't discuss which
factors depressed a mother's earnings, such as a protracted maternity leave or part-time hours.

Highly skilled white women with high earnings pay the highest
price for parenthood. The finding emerged from a 2016 study tied to
a national survey that followed the same women from youth through
middle age.

The well-paid women occupied largely professional or managerial
positions. They received generous raises and promotion opportunities. "That meant bigger potential losses of raises while out of work
for a protracted period after having a baby," observed Paula England, a sociology professor at New York University and the study's
lead author, in an interview. Those mothers earned 10 percent less
per child than if they had remained child free, she and her three
coauthors estimated.

Sumaiya Balbale, a young executive mom, told me that she had confronted a different type of motherhood pay penalty following the 2014 birth of her son, Zayn. She was working as a general manager for Quidsi, a unit of Amazon.com. She had amassed a sizable stash of stock options from the e-commerce giant.

You can use options to buy shares once they finish vesting years later. Balbale was dismayed when Amazon stopped giving vesting credit for her options during her four-month maternity leave. It didn't explain why.

The suspension upset her because she had worked so hard for the Amazon unit and so much of her compensation came from stock awards rather than cash. "Emotionally, it felt like a very imbalanced relationship—one where the business was happy to take but not give," she recollected. "Practically speaking, the policy failed to provide compensation protection during parental leave," she continued. "The financial impact is significant, especially for mothers who tend to take more time off for paid parental leave than fathers."

When we spoke, the thirty-seven-year-old Balbale was the vice president of e-commerce, mobile, and digital marketing for Walmart in the United States. She soon quit the giant retailer, took a seat on the board of directors of Shake Shack, and began advising start-ups. In June 2020, she became the chief marketing officer of Houlihan Lokey Inc., a global investment bank.

The New Religion of "Workism"

Additional social forces affect the lives of today's employed mothers in different ways from their predecessors. The U.S. college-educated elite worships work as the centerpiece of personal identity. It's a potent religion nicknamed "workism" by *The Atlantic*.

Harvard Business School professor and gender researcher Robin J.

Ely agrees. "What holds women back at work is not some unique challenge of balancing the demands of work and family but rather a general problem of overwork that prevails in contemporary corporate culture," concluded a 2020 *Harvard Business Review* article that she coauthored.

For too many women, this means that we're expected to toil long hours and always be reachable long after the workday officially ends. In a stark sign of the generational fault line, younger executive mothers I interviewed frequently feel compelled to stay connected constantly to their high-powered jobs—especially when they command distant teams. About a dozen present-generation moms sleep close to their smartphones. One tucks her device under her pillow the night before she announces a new product.

It's no wonder that most working women with children feel glum about their chances for job success. Nearly three out of four employed moms "believe they get fewer career advancement opportunities than women who are not mothers," a 2018 survey of 2,143 U.S. adults found. That's because American culture "perpetuates the idea that mothers don't work as hard as their peers or are incapable of managing family and work responsibilities."

An equally disturbing finding: the proportion of polled women who would fear telling their boss that they are pregnant nearly doubled to 21 percent from 12 percent in 2014. Bright Horizons Family Solutions, the largest U.S. provider of employer-sponsored child care, commissioned the surveys.

Though Bright Horizons couldn't explain the increase, the 2018 survey noted that "the motherhood penalty goes beyond their likelihood to be hired for jobs or receive equal pay. It's a nearly invisible hurdle—moms are overlooked for career-advancing opportunities simply because they are mothers." (I couldn't find comparable data about what women with children in the 1970s and 1980s felt about their chances for job success.)

I had expected that life would be much easier for second-wave Power Moms such as Genevieve Roth, an entrepreneur and former magazine executive. They see numerous moms in managerial positions—role models that boomer mothers typically lacked. Yet that doesn't always ease their qualms about having kids.

Roth toiled alongside mothers at *Glamour* magazine between 2004 and 2009. What she witnessed then persuaded her never to have children. Every afternoon at 4:00, her colleagues grew anxious about leaving in time to collect their offspring before the child care center closed or their nanny's shift ended. The then twenty-something journalist saw stress etched on her coworkers' faces as they prepared to dash out the door.

"It just looked like a backwards hustle. Like, what is fun about this?" Roth told me while sipping coffee at The Wing, a women's coworking space in downtown Manhattan. "It wasn't a version of motherhood that I wanted," she recalled, running her hands repeatedly through her very short hair.

In hindsight, she said in a subsequent email, she realized that those hardworking associates were doing their absolute best to parent and lead within a broader culture that didn't always support working mothers.

Roth later quit an executive position at *Glamour* to join Hillary Clinton's unsuccessful presidential campaign. She changed her mind about motherhood after falling in love. Her romance with Jordan blossomed amid her 2017 launch of Invisible Hand, a social impact strategy and events agency whose clients include the Obama Foundation.

Roth gave birth to their daughter, Frankie, in June 2018. She married Jordan thirteen months later. On the day we chatted, the thirty-eight-year-old entrepreneur was operating her small business from an office on the same floor as their loft apartment. They live blocks away from The Wing. She often saw Frankie during the workday.

She takes over from their nanny most evenings before Jordan, a digital communications specialist, returns home from his midtown office. "I have that flexibility, and I'm closer," she remarked. Being able to afford a nanny is among the many things that "make our experience of parenting peaceful and easier than it otherwise would be."

Roth's relative affluence enables her to work productively without worrying about her daughter's care. By comparison, lower-income American women required to work outside the home for economic survival long lacked access to higher-paid jobs.

"Societal constraints dictated the type of work women were 'allowed' to do," such as cooking, housecleaning, laundry, and textile manufacturing, commented Lorraine Hariton, the president and CEO of Catalyst, the research organization. She commenced her career in 1976 as a computer programmer and subsequently led two Silicon Valley start-ups. White-collar women like her "were the first generation taking advantage of the women's movement," she recalled.

Hariton added that female professionals with children faced equally rigid norms during the 1980s, when she bore a son and daughter: "We had to fit into the male-dominated business culture—no maternity leave, dress like a man, [and] no flexibility for work/life balance."

Thirteen of the forty-four executives I interviewed from Hariton's trailblazer generation reached the pinnacle of power by running a public company. Each became the first woman to take charge.

Ten younger mothers besides Roth had created a business when we spoke, striking out on their own in industries such as apparel, toys, sports, and technology. Earlier in their careers, they had worked for companies with revenues of at least $100 million a year. Nearly everyone else in the current cohort continues to be employed by such sizable businesses.

The second wave of executive moms expressed a greater sense of expansiveness about their dual roles than baby boomers did. Compared to the initial wave, "we're not hiding the fact that we have children," said Meredith Bodgas, the editor in chief of *Working Mother* magazine and mother of two young sons. "When our day care provider calls us at the office, we proudly take those calls."

Her bold mind-set reflects her generation's belief in practicing work/life sway, creating modest corporate structural changes, evolving social mores, and capitalizing on the hard-fought battles won by the first wave of Power Moms.

Intensive Parenting

U.S. working moms often work hard at being highly involved parents.

The bar keeps moving higher, however. Helicopter parents emerged during the 1980s. They hovered over everything their youngsters did, typically because they feared for the kids' physical safety.

Starting in the 1990s, helicoptering evolved into intensive parenting. Numerous mothers and fathers decided that they must constantly monitor and teach their children. "This is when parents began filling afternoons and weekends with lessons, tutors, and traveling sports games," the *New York Times* said in a 2019 piece about the practice.

Cultural expectations of intensive parenting weigh heaviest on mothers, even though fathers are now expected to spend more time with their children. "Anytime something goes wrong with a child, it's your fault—not Dad's," contends Correll, the Stanford sociologist. "When moms appear to be putting career before family, they are often viewed negatively."

Intensive parenting may be a leftover consequence of debunked psychological theories about "refrigerator mothers." In the 1950s and 1960s, most experts "believed that autism was caused by mothers who were insufficiently loving and warm," Deborah Tannen wrote in her 2006 book, *You're Wearing That? Understanding Mothers and Daughters in Conversation.* Autism's origin turned out to be biological.

Katia Beauchamp, the youthful CEO and cofounder of Birchbox, exemplifies intensive mothering. She maintained a very close watch on her twin boys after their birth in 2014. The first-time mother resumed running her online beauty start-up ten weeks later. "I kept a journal of the twins' poops and pees for like four months," she confided to me.

"You're just trying to make sure that they're okay," she said. "You're so stressed out, and everything feels so intense."

Parents in Extremis

The most relentless parents these days are dubbed "snowplows" because they spend so much time and money trying to overturn the obstacles confronting their progeny.

Even once the youngsters reach adulthood.

About 74 percent of parents with offspring aged eighteen to twenty-eight have booked appointments for them at doctors' offices and elsewhere, according to a 2019 survey conducted for the *New York Times*. The nationwide poll covered 1,136 such parents and a separate group of 1,508 individuals aged eighteen to twenty-eight. Neither the newspaper nor its pollster divulged whether the parent primarily booking appointments was the mother. Another example of snowplow parenting cited in the *New York Times* piece is the parent who complains to a grown child's employer when an internship doesn't result in a job.

Alexandra Lebenthal, a first-wave executive mom, was still booking doctor visits for her nearly twenty-three-year-old daughter, Charlotte Diamond, when we dined at a stylish Park Avenue restaurant in Manhattan. She had led Lebenthal & Co., her family's municipal bond firm, until 2017. For our lunch, the Wall Street veteran wore a black sweater and leopard-print skirt that matched the thick black rims of her glasses.

Working motherhood "certainly gets a lot easier when your kids are in high school or college or grown up because you don't have that same need to be present," she told me. She also has an adult son and a teenage daughter. She didn't view arranging appointments for Diamond as part of her maternal role, "but I did it anyway." She presently works with female entrepreneurs as a senior adviser for Empire Global Ventures, an investment boutique.

Her elder daughter, a jewelry market assistant at *Vogue* magazine when we spoke, said her mother mainly scheduled initial consultations with health care providers so Diamond could avoid taking work time off for the chore. The young woman now books her own medical appointments because "I haven't seen a new provider for quite some time."

I wonder whether Lebenthal became a snowplow parent for her grown daughter because she regretted some aspects of how she parented years ago. She admits that she didn't get everything right while raising a family and commanding a complex company. She once arrived too late for a mother-daughter lunch at Diamond's elementary school in Manhattan. "I had messed up the time, and then I had to get [uptown] from Wall Street." The CEO sobbed in the street after missing her daughter's school event.

Audience members at Lebenthal's public appearances frequently press her to reveal the secret of work/life balance. The executive urges women to not view their parental shortcomings as defining who they are as mothers.

Lebenthal believes that employed moms grapple with this issue even if they can't afford a full-time nanny and a weekly cleaning woman as she did. The challenges of combining motherhood and work "are emotional and personal issues that each mother faces," she explained.

"Sometimes you're going to be perfect. You're going to throw your hands up in victory," she said, raising her hands high in the air. "And the next day, you may be crying on the street. Neither of these are going to last."

American mothers have greatly expanded their presence in workplaces and influential management roles. Yet they continue to confront societal obstacles, such as entrenched stereotypes about their career commitment and the absence of nationally mandated paid family leave. Workism pressures further complicate matters.

On the positive side, however, second-wave Power Moms enjoy a much wider choice of family-friendly employers than boomers did. GenXers can join a sympathetic corporate giant with generous perks or a start-up whose female chief executive treats working parents fairly—because she has children, too.

2

High Potentials with
High Hopes for Motherhood

Every mother-to-be dreams of a perfect pregnancy.

But my second pregnancy turned into a nightmare. I developed a dangerous high blood pressure condition known as preeclampsia, which can cause fatal strokes.

Blood pressure disorders represent a leading cause of death among new mothers and infants worldwide, according to the Preeclampsia Foundation. Preeclampsia affects at least 5 percent of all pregnancies.

I was then working for the *Wall Street Journal*'s Washington bureau, where I faced daily deadlines and demands to deliver exclusive stories. I worried whether my high-pressure job had triggered my high blood pressure. Researchers later linked preeclampsia to occupational stress.

Five weeks before my due date in 1983, I anxiously awaited relief from preeclampsia via a cesarean section delivery at Washington Hospital Center. I was hooked up to an automated blood pressure cuff that beeped loudly with every frequent reading. A nurse poked my enlarged abdomen roughly shortly before my surgery in the adjoining operating room.

"This [baby] is just a peanut," she announced gruffly. "You should insist on postponing the C-section for at least two weeks so the baby can get bigger."

I started crying hysterically, driving my elevated blood pressure even higher. My hastily summoned obstetrician reassured me that my fetus was big enough to be born. Two hours later, Abra was born, weighing in at four pounds, eight ounces. I proudly nicknamed my preemie "Baby Woman."

Luckily, neither of us suffered lasting ill effects from the preeclampsia. But the scary experience is a major reason why I never got pregnant again.

Stacey Tank, a young executive mother, dealt differently with her two bouts of preeclampsia. Unlike me, she refused to agonize over whether her demanding job might have caused the blood pressure ailment. She told me that a preeclampsia-related seizure had almost killed her just before the birth of her son Jackson in 2009.

Five years later, preeclampsia forced her to be hospitalized for five weeks before the arrival of her second son, Crosby. The nearly thirty-three-year-old Tank was already a senior vice president at Heineken USA, a unit of the big Dutch brewer. She helped manage stressful corporate crises, such as that unit's first ever recall of beer bottles because the bottles might contain small pieces of broken glass.

She said she had worked from her hospital bed in what felt like a twelve-foot-square cell. During one of her numerous conference calls, a participant asked whether the loud beeping noise was a truck backing up outside. "I would put [the phone] on mute and turn down my patient monitors so they couldn't hear," Tank recalled. She was far from unique. I met a number of hard-driving women from both waves who felt driven to work despite all sorts of personal and professional hardships.

Tank lost her eyesight for several days during both bouts of preeclampsia. Even if stress did play a role in triggering the disorder, "I'll be in denial until I catch my last breath," she vowed during our session in her twenty-second-floor office at the Atlanta headquarters of Home Depot. She enjoyed a panoramic view of the distant downtown skyline. She then was an operational vice president for the home improvement chain, running a multibillion-dollar unit whose approximately five thousand employees arrange home renovations and repairs for U.S. customers.

"Work has always been really important to me," Tank noted. "I love to fall into bed and pass out at the end of the night because I gave everything I had that day." In June 2020, she became chief transformation and corporate affairs officer at Heineken N.V.

The Power Moms I interviewed had approached potential parenthood with high hopes for their child and postpartum career trajectory. The women of both generations had usually postponed starting families until they were in their thirties and well established professionally.

The two waves diverged in their efforts to conceive, bear a child, take time off, and resume work, however. Involved husbands and empathetic bosses have lessened some of the burdens of new motherhood for GenXers. By contrast, boomers usually got little assistance from their spouses or employers. They also risked social disapproval unless they sidelined or slowed their careers once a child arrived. Yet neither wave discovered foolproof ways to manage their life-changing journey to unpredictable working parenthood.

Healthy Terms

Women from both eras often struggled to get pregnant. The dilemma affects would-be mothers at every job level. Jana Schreuder spent thirty-eight years moving up at Northern Trust Corporation, a major Chicago bank that serves wealthy individuals and businesses worldwide. She spent almost half those years trying to become pregnant.

Northern Trust initially rejected the recent college graduate for four different low-level jobs in 1980. "I was either overqualified or underqualified, depending on what they were looking for," she remembered when we conversed in a noisy French brasserie in midtown Manhattan.

After the bank turned her down for the fourth time, the twenty-one-year-old business novice approached an internal recruiter. "I really want to work here," she insisted. "I will do anything except accounting." She had performed terribly at accounting in school.

"I hate to tell you, but the only other job I have here is an accounting job," the Northern Trust recruiter replied. "It's called employee benefits accounting."

Lacking an alternative, Schreuder accepted the job of employee benefits accountant. She produced pension plan reports for corporate clients of Northern Trust. The four-foot, ten-inch executive always wore four-inch heels to the office, where she regularly worked fourteen to sixteen hours a day.

She and her husband, Eric, a hotel manager, worked equally hard for fourteen years to produce a child. "I always wanted to be a mother," she explained. "I just thought that was a part of life, a part of my definition of success. A career would not have been enough."

Schreuder's biological clock was winding down at the same time that she was moving up in management. It's a risky path that ambitious women often tread. How do you pursue your lofty career goals without new motherhood slowing your progress? Which likely tough trade-offs can you avoid having to make by choosing a family-friendly workplace? In Schreuder's case, she said she was willing to switch employers if becoming a mother disrupted her Northern Trust career.

She and her husband went through seven treatments for infertility, including in vitro fertilization four times. "Nothing worked," Schreuder said. She felt it was irrelevant to widely discuss the details of those treatments with her predominantly male associates at the bank.

Schreuder and her husband also pursued adoption, but they were rejected because Eric was already middle-aged. The couple abandoned their pursuit of parenthood in 1994.

To her shock, Schreuder soon discovered that she was pregnant. The thirty-eight-year-old vice president gave birth to their daughter, Allison, in 1996. "She's my miracle baby," she declared, beaming.

In 2014, she became the first female chief operating officer of Northern Trust. She retired four years later at age sixty.

Executives from each wave had trouble staying pregnant, too. Several baby boomers I met never revealed their miscarriages to their mostly male coworkers because they wanted to be taken seriously—and not detract from their executive persona. In comparison, GenX women often interact extensively with their colleagues when they lose a pregnancy. They believe in bringing their true selves to their workplace, where they tend to have highly supportive female associates and operate in a transparent corporate culture.

This generational shift is typified by Janelle Bieler, a senior vice president for the U.S. arm of the Adecco Group, a giant staffing firm based in Switzerland. She oversees Adecco's retail operations throughout the United States.

By age twenty-three, Bieler was a branch manager at Enterprise Rent-A-Car, a popular brand whose parent company was steered by a woman. She left Enterprise in 2011 and joined ManpowerGroup because it offered flexible schedules. "I could manage being a [future] mom and having a successful career," she said. Manpower "prioritized the human side of work." The thirty-six-year-old executive bore her daughter, Brie, in 2013.

Recruited by rival Adecco as a regional vice president the following year, Bieler had two miscarriages before she gave birth again in 2016. She received extensive comfort from her boss and coworkers after each failed pregnancy.

Her supervisor, a mother of two, urged Bieler to take as much time off as she needed to recover emotionally and physically from her first miscarriage in 2014. "I know you want to get back into work," her boss said. "But I'm going to make sure that you're okay." An empathetic style ought to be standard behavior today for every boss, irrespective of gender.

Bieler's close-knit cadre of twelve vice presidents—ten of whom were women—reacted in a remarkably caring way as well. She said she had ebulliently told them her good news during the second month of her original pregnancy. Sadly, she miscarried two weeks later.

Fellow executives didn't merely express sympathy over her loss, she recalled. "Colleagues were like 'What do you need? Can I help you with something? With work? If you're going to take time off, what can I take off your plate?'" She stayed home for a week. Meanwhile, several female vice presidents opened up to her about their own miscarriages.

Bieler had a difficult time coping with her second miscarriage, too. Yet the repeated outreach from her peers "made me realize that a lot of those people were friends," she said. "I still get emotional talking about it," she added, choking back tears.

The Adecco executive believes her candor about her failed pregnancies illustrates the recent metamorphosis in workplace conversations, with a bigger focus on employee mental health and well-being. "Some of that openness around self-care comes from younger executive women like me," Bieler said. "We aren't afraid to find and express our voice, making it easier for others to do the same."

Pregnancy problems helped transform Meaghan Schmidt, another younger executive mother, into an outspoken advocate for other working parents. She is a managing director of AlixPartners, a global management consulting firm. She won the senior spot at age thirty-six in 2017, thirteen years after her debut as an entry-level associate. In addition, she serves on the firm's board of directors.

Schmidt carries out high-stakes financial investigations for multinational companies and played an instrumental role in unraveling the alleged $50 billion fraud by money manager Bernard Madoff.

Schmidt was a middle manager with a toddler son named Ryan when she miscarried twice within a few months. Her first miscarriage happened during a 2014 meeting with ten male executives in a client's Manhattan boardroom. She was the sole woman there.

"I wanted to crawl under the table and get out of that room," she recalled during our interview in her narrow office in midtown Manhattan. She somehow powered through the rest of what suddenly had become an incredibly intense client meeting. She stayed because she had fought to prove her value and be accepted by certain older male colleagues, she explained. "I finally had my seat at the table."

Schmidt agreed that Power Moms from both generations have felt compelled to project a certain public image on the job. Hers involved an intense demonstration of strength to men seated at the table with her.

Once the meeting ended, she walked four blocks back to Alix-Partners. The distraught executive locked herself in a bathroom stall. Then she cried. "We had struggled for two-plus years to give our first son a sibling."

Schmidt's traumatic miscarriages helped inspire her to create an employee resource group for working parents at AlixPartners. Launched in September 2015, six months after the birth of her son Owen, the group had grown to 443 members worldwide by the end of January 2020.

The parents' network persuaded AlixPartners to expand family-friendly benefits for staffers. Through the group, Schmidt also connects with coworkers who are concerned about the career impact of future motherhood. "I'm the default person that they call," observed the executive, who delivered her daughter, Casey, in 2016. "That's another benefit of having more females at the firm [and] having my generation of moms."

Her cadre of Power Moms is large enough that women often support and mentor each other on the job. Their work environment is nothing like what first-wave pioneers encountered decades ago, when female executives were a rare breed with almost no women as role models or mentors.

Would-be young mothers at AlixPartners confide to Schmidt that they have fertility difficulties. "Guess what? So did I," she replies. "Let's talk about it." When she counsels them face-to-face, "you [can] instantaneously see the pressure and stress drop off," she told me.

"We say AlixPartners has this family feel," she said, pointing to her offspring's brightly colored artwork on her office walls. "This [parent group] just adds to that."

Expectant on the Job

Ecstatic about expecting my first child in 1979, I never anticipated all of the ways that imminent motherhood might affect my job as a journalist.

Being pregnant did enable me to cover an important news event for the Washington bureau of the *Wall Street Journal*. One hot afternoon close to my July due date, I and a diminutive red-haired man attempted to squeeze into a packed news conference held by Massachusetts senator Ted Kennedy. The congressional hearing room was jammed with TV camera operators, lobbyists, tourists, and reporters. Everyone wanted a glimpse of the prospective Democratic candidate for U.S. president in 1980.

"Press! Press!" the little man beside me squeaked. The crowd barely moved.

"Pregnant press! Pregnant press!" I boomed. The sweaty sea of humanity immediately parted for me.

Unfortunately, I also experienced the dark side of being a pregnant professional. My bulging body turned into public property twice during a single workday. The public relations manager of a medical products manufacturer and another male source each patted my rotund stomach without my permission.

I deeply resented those men's belly pats as an invasion of my personal space. The pats were no more desired nor deserved than if I had stroked their respective rear ends. In the protracted fight for reproductive rights, women long sought greater respect for their bodily autonomy. Expectant mothers lose even more bodily autonomy—as I discovered.

But I stewed in silence. By the late 1970s, sexual harassment had not yet attracted widespread public attention. And pregnancy bias remained rampant in the workplace despite the 1978 passage of a

U.S. statute outlawing it. Employers could still fire, lay off, or refuse to hire pregnant women even though they couldn't single them out for worse treatment.

My distressing experience was hardly out of the ordinary. Baby-boom executives who shared their insights with me recounted how they frequently worried about their treatment at work during pregnancy. Anne Weisberg and Aida Sabo exemplify such women.

Weisberg, a 1985 cum laude graduate of Harvard Law School, commands the women's initiative for Paul, Weiss, Rifkind, Wharton & Garrison. The New York–based law firm recruited her for the new role so she could identify "gender gaps at any point in our [talent] pipeline and design interventions to close them," she said during our interview in her skyscraper office. Her position subsequently expanded to cover the firm's working parents' needs, such as child care.

She came to Paul, Weiss in 2015 following stints as a diversity executive focused on women's advancement at several businesses, including BlackRock, the world's biggest money management company. Along the way, she coauthored a 1994 guide for working mothers.

Weisberg considers herself a professional feminist. "I see everything through a gender lens," she noted, peering at me intensely with dark-rimmed glasses perched atop her head. "Girls Just Wanna Be CEO" blared the slogan painted on a ceramic teabag holder at the edge of her broad desk. Her fierce commitment to gender equity issues partly grew out of her heated confrontation over her second pregnancy with a leader at another New York law firm.

She joined that small firm in 1987 because she had no other offers. Major law firms refused to hire her once they learned about her infant daughter, Sarah. "I needed to be at a place where I didn't have to hide that I had a ten-month-old at home," she explained.

Yet her new employer, which already had about a half-dozen female attorneys, didn't pay big salaries. "I made literally half of what my peers were making a year out of law school," Weisberg said.

With her next child due in June 1989, the thirty-one-year-old lawyer marched into the office of a male managing partner and requested four months of paid maternity leave.

"Well, why should I pay you to go on leave? I'd like a four-month vacation," he snapped. "You chose to have a baby."

"I didn't choose to bear the kid," Weisberg replied with exasperation. "That's why it's called sex discrimination." The law firm ultimately provided her requested paid leave through its disability insurance, and she resumed work afterward.

Weisberg again planned to return after a 1991 leave of absence to write her advice book for working moms. The law firm dissolved during that break, however. By becoming an advocate for women, "I found my true passion and purpose," she said. And her experience as an employed mother "informed my understanding of how gender works in the workplace."

Like Weisberg, Sabo is a veteran diversity leader who battled workplace barriers while expecting years ago. Since 2014, she has been the vice president of diversity and inclusion for Parexel International Corporation, a drug research company headquartered in Waltham, Massachusetts.

Sabo immigrated with her family to Silicon Valley from Mexico when she was three years old. Her father, who sometimes worked as a janitor, set her up for future economic success by encouraging her to excel throughout school.

"My life is always focused on work," she told me when we chatted—ironically, on Equal Pay Day. She viewed hard work as a way to escape "this [crowded] living situation where we all lived together in an apartment." The brisk spring morning that we met, the fifty-eight-year-old Hispanic executive was wearing dangly turquoise earrings that poked out from under her dusty gray baseball hat.

Equipped with an electrical engineering degree, Sabo was hired by Hewlett-Packard Company as a "solution architect" in 1987. She developed expertise about antenna measurements. She hid her subsequent pregnancy for as long as possible in order to keep her career on track at the technology giant.

She believed that new mothers were considered less committed to Hewlett-Packard and feared that she would be accused of caring more about home than work. "It was the big elephant in the room," she recalled. She and a bunch of female colleagues gathered in the ladies' room to secretly rejoice about the debut of their pregnancies.

Sabo even wore a girdlelike band for more than four months so she could conceal her growing belly from male coworkers in their Hewlett-Packard laboratory. No other women toiled in the lab—a vastly different work world from the one GenX women would experience years later. Her son, David, was born in 1991.

Over time, the status of working mothers improved at Hewlett-Packard—as evidenced by the changed occupants of its corner office. Sabo moved up to business development manager and then left Hewlett-Packard in 2000.

That was only one year after Carly Fiorina, who had a stepdaughter, took charge of Hewlett-Packard and became the first woman to lead a Fortune 20 company. Meg Whitman, named the CEO of Hewlett-Packard in 2011, is the mother of two sons.

Positive pregnancy experiences of second-wave executives such as Jennifer Hyman illustrate how radically things have changed since the prior wave of pacesetter boomers. The CEO of Rent the Runway attributes this seismic shift mainly to the fact that "I have a level of openness and transparency with my board of directors and my executive team that I think likely would not have been possible twenty or thirty years ago." A possible reason: deep-pocketed venture capitalists like to play hands-on roles in their portfolio companies. Decades ago, there were few start-ups run by women and backed by venture capitalists.

Hyman cofounded her clothing rental company in 2008 after working as a manager for bigger businesses such as Starwood Hotels and Resorts Worldwide. The dark-haired executive, who is five feet, ten inches tall, was expecting her second child when we conferred in her windowless office at Rent the Runway headquarters in SoHo, a fashionable Manhattan neighborhood. Seated near a white credenza crammed with personal photos, she grabbed a silver-framed picture from her 2017 wedding to Ben Stauffer, a self-employed film and television editor. The newlyweds hold six-month-old Aurora, their first baby, in the photo.

Rent the Runway initially rented pricey gowns before switching to a subscription service. Customers presently pay a monthly fee to borrow everyday items or rent special-occasion dresses. The fast-growing start-up hit $100 million in revenue and turned profitable in 2016.

The thirty-five-year-old Hyman got engaged that spring. Weeks later, she and her seven fellow board members celebrated Rent the Runway's success at L'Artusi, an Italian restaurant in Greenwich Village. During a wine toast for the company, she revealed a highly personal decision: "I just announced to everyone on my board, 'Hey, by the way, I'm going to start trying to have a baby.'"

She felt as though the directors, who were evenly split by gender, deserved to know about important aspects of her private life—especially since none had ever hinted "that becoming a parent was something that I should be fearful of," she said. When you're building a company, "people who invest in you become part of your extended family," she went on. She feels "real friendship and love with people who are on my board."

Indeed, everyone reacted enthusiastically to the chief executive's announcement about her planned conception. "They were cheering, hugging me, kissing me."

Nor did pregnancy impair Hyman's amazing prowess at fundraising for Rent the Runway. She finished raising $125 million in March 2019 while nine months pregnant with her second daughter, Selene. The company's largest ever investment elevated its value to $1 billion. Rent the Runway earned "unicorn" status, reflecting the fact that few start-ups are worth that much money.

Hyman had read horror stories about the difficulties that pregnant entrepreneurs previously faced in raising substantial sums, such as potential investors doubting whether they could manage both a start-up and an infant. "I've not experienced that," she noted. "Because of the level of passion and handwork that I've put into the business, there wasn't a question that that would just somehow stop" with the arrival of her next baby. In other words, she had already proven to prior Rent the Runway investors that she knew how to successfully run a business and mother a child.

Workable Maternity Leaves

Younger executive mothers often stayed home for months after giving birth. Hyman, for example, took four months off in March 2017 to care for Aurora. She trusted her executive team to make decisions and run Rent the Runway during her absence.

"No one had the final say. They collaborated on every decision," she said. She can count on one hand how many times she needed to make the final decision when she held team meetings during the last few years before her first maternity leave. She credits "a dynamic of trust that I've created amongst my team. It was really easy for them to continue that."

At the time we spoke, five women served on Hyman's seven-member team—and every member of the team had children. She stayed home for nearly five months following Selene's birth in April 2019.

Hyman's lengthy maternity leaves are a dramatic difference from those of the prior generation. Boomer executive moms viewed six weeks off as a generous benefit. Some took much briefer breaks because they wanted to demonstrate their dedication to their jobs.

Lynn Zuckerman Gray is an especially dramatic example. Trained as a lawyer, she ascended to upper management at Lehman Brothers Holdings before the once venerable investment bank filed for bankruptcy protection in 2008. She next formed a business called Campus Scout, which assists employers with college recruitment. She runs her enterprise from a bedroom in the Manhattan apartment where she has lived for decades.

Gray, a stocky individual with a heavily creased forehead, was a thirty-two-year-old senior vice president of Integrated Resources, a real estate investment company, while expecting her daughter, Emily, in 1982. Even though she was the company's highest-ranked woman, "all of the guys just assumed I wasn't coming back to work," she said.

Based on their beliefs, those male colleagues stopped bringing her into real estate deals during the final months of her pregnancy. "The more that they didn't take seriously that I wasn't coming back, the more I knew I was coming right back," she explained. "It was almost like 'Okay, I'll show them.'"

So she never requested *any* time off for childbirth. Her draconian decision highlights what it took for some women to have careers and children during the 1980s. They desperately wanted male associates to view them as highly committed to their jobs. And unlike their counterparts today, they usually lacked an empathetic group of fellow female managers.

Gray and three-day-old Emily left the hospital on a Tuesday. The next day, the executive went back to her office, which was two blocks from her apartment. She felt so sore from the baby's delivery that she couldn't sit down without a special postpartum pillow she brought to work.

"I never took maternity leave, which is a terrible thing," she admitted, extending her palms apologetically in front of her chest. "I had to prove something: that I was coming back—and that they should take me more seriously." Though her career was very important to her, she now regrets her decision. "I wish I had taken that special time off to heal physically and to enjoy precious moments with my child."

Gray is unusual, though not unheard of among boomer women. Strong evidence of the generational divide over maternity leaves amid improving social norms showed up in a 2018 survey of 362 tech industry women. Most worked in the San Francisco Bay area. About 44 percent of the women who had taken maternity leave said they had taken off less time than they had been entitled to because they had thought a full leave would hurt their careers. That was true for 53 percent of women over forty-five years old but only 38 percent of those under forty-five, according to Michele Madansky, the research consultant who conducted the poll.

She did the survey as a sequel to a similar 2016 report entitled "Elephant in the Valley," which she had cowritten with the venture capitalist Trae Vassallo.

Where Are the New Dads?

Dorrit J. Bern, a first-generation manager mom, received scant assistance from her husband, Steve, after she bore Chad, their eldest son, in 1979. Bern was a twenty-nine-year-old buyer for a division of Allied Stores in Dallas, where he was the finance vice president for a unit of the Boeing Company.

Steve skipped work only one day following Chad's birth. He refused to request additional vacation time because "he was worried how it would look," Bern remembered. "No one had a working wife." A week later, Steve left her and their newborn for a ten-day business trip to Seattle.

Chad got sick a lot during his first year, and juggling her job and ill baby "took a toll on me," Bern said. She refused to bear more children until Steve was willing to get more involved in parenting. He agreed.

Bern had another two sons while advancing in her retail industry career. When those babies came, her husband "was very supportive, with bottles, diapers, [and] getting up at night." Her eldest son turned eight years old the year she became the first female national merchandise manager at Sears, Roebuck & Company. She left the retail giant in 1995 to take the helm of Charming Shoppes and led the women's plus-size retailer for the next thirteen years.

By contrast, mates of contemporary Power Moms are more likely to take substantial paternity leaves. A good example is Ben Stauffer, the film and TV editor who is married to Rent the Runway CEO Jennifer Hyman. In a sign of the cultural shift among men, he stayed home with infant Aurora as long as she did. "We were able to enjoy this very special new time as a family" during those four months, Hyman recalled. Self-employed fathers such as Stauffer have greater control over their schedules and workplace norms than do dads employed by big businesses, however.

That's one reason new parenthood was much harder for management consultant Mary Hamilton and Paul Sternhagen, her long-time domestic partner. The almost forty-one-year-old Hamilton had twin boys five days after Sternhagen joined McKinsey & Company as a partner in 2016. They already had a two-year-old son.

Hired by Accenture, another global management consultancy, in 1997, Hamilton was promoted to head its research-and-development laboratories for the Americas shortly before we conferred at her suburban home in San Mateo, California.

The twins stayed in a hospital intensive care unit for four weeks. Sternhagen stopped working entirely for only a week—much less than the two months of paid paternity leave that McKinsey offered him. "I'm the brand-new guy. How can I take this [full] leave? No way," he told Hamilton. "I have colleagues that took two days and bragged about it."

Hamilton disagreed. She pointed out that McKinsey had picked him for a good reason. So "he shouldn't start out by feeling like he couldn't take full advantage of the parental benefits." Her partner's resistance suggests that expanded parental benefits don't always go far enough in accommodating the needs of moms and dads. Corporate cultures must adapt as well.

Sternhagen subsequently developed paternal postpartum depression, a disorder that affects as many as 10 percent of men worldwide. He harbored grave doubts about whether he could be a good father, Hamilton recollected. "He would pull back from parenting because he didn't feel like he was competent."

Caring for her partner and their three kids "was such a burden on me," the Accenture executive said, choking back tears. She pressed her clasped hands hard on the glass-topped table where we sat in her dining room. He finally recovered from his deep depression, aided by couples' therapy and a new employer. Just as Janelle Bieler did in choosing Manpower, younger men keen to coparent their children should factor that preference into their choice of a workplace.

New Mom at Work

For my vanguard generation of baby boomers, our return to full-time jobs as working moms carried unexpected occupational hazards. One of the worst was unsympathetic colleagues.

I took a three-month break following Dan's birth by combining paid maternity leave with vacation time. On my first day back at the *Journal*, male coworkers needled me with nasty comments.

"Where do you dump the kid every day?" one fellow asked.

Another man noticed my annoyance as we waited twenty minutes for the bus home. "Well, Joann, you don't *have* to be here," he cracked. "You could be home rocking your baby in the rocking chair."

I quoted their demoralizing remarks in a first-person essay that I wrote for the paper's editorial page. My 1980 piece, published in the pre-PC era, appeared alongside a drawing of a baby frowning at a typewriter. "I didn't realize juggling job and junior would be so difficult, so nerve-frazzling, so filled with guilt," I wrote. "Society still dictates that a working mother must be a lousy mother." That overall stereotype has since faded but not disappeared entirely—especially for women with highly demanding jobs.

Nor was I able to pump and store breast milk on the job. Breast-feeding moms maintain their milk supply by nursing their infant or pumping multiple times a day for as much as an hour each time. Amid tears of frustration over my baby's wasted nourishment, I expressed milk down the toilet at the *Journal*. Portable breast pumps and office lactation rooms didn't exist yet. My daily dumps of breast milk also exacerbated my horrible feelings of lonely isolation. I was the only working mom in the *Journal*'s Washington bureau.

Margaret Keane, the chief executive officer of Synchrony, shared a similar sad saga with me. She was the chief marketing officer for Citibank's real estate business in New York when she gave birth to her son, Brian, in 1989 at age thirty. No one attempted to ease her return to the big bank.

"You had your baby. You came [back] into work. You never talked about it again," she recalled. She never confided in her female supervisor about her exhaustion from repeatedly getting up with Brian every night. That boss "had no children [and] wasn't very supportive," she observed. "There was still a perception back then that when you have kids, you should probably be home. I don't think people think twice about it now."

Other executive mothers I met generally agreed with Keane's viewpoint. A significant minority of Americans do not. Roughly one in five U.S. adults believes that staying home with young children is the ideal situation for women, according to a 2019 survey of 9,834 Americans by the Pew Research Center.

Workplace attitudes toward working new mothers are clearly changing. AlixPartners' Meaghan Schmidt witnessed a significant shift just during the five years between the end of her first and third maternity leaves. That was especially true for her pumping efforts.

The only way that Schmidt could pump milk at the office following her initial 2012 leave was by locking herself inside a staff pantry on the floor above hers because AlixPartners lacked special lactation facilities for staffers. "The firm's general counsel stored his lunch in the pantry refrigerator," she remembered. "From time to time, he would knock on the door and say, 'Meg, how's it going in there?'"

After Schmidt completed her 2017 leave, she had an office with a privacy screen on the door. There, she could work and pump simultaneously. Clients occasionally inquired about the odd noise they heard during their conference calls.

"I'm sorry. That's my breast pump," the executive said. Nevertheless, she emphasized, "I was never embarrassed."

AlixPartners soon began to install "wellness" rooms around the globe, primarily to serve nursing mothers. They feature self-locking doors, stocked beverage coolers, and sinks deep enough for moms to wash pump parts. Twenty of the firm's twenty-three offices worldwide provided wellness rooms as of July 2020, with the rest due for completion in 2021. Such employer efforts carry broader cultural implications. Businesses prove their interest in retaining working moms when they offer comfortable settings to pump milk.

Not every breastfeeding mother these days is so fortunate when she resumes working. A 2010 law requires U.S. employers to give "reasonable break time," so a staffer can express breast milk for a nursing child—and provide a shielded place other than a bathroom where she can do so.

But just 47 percent of expectant women say there's a designated lactation area at their workplace, and 63 percent think there's a stigma attached to women who breastfeed on the job. The findings emerged from a 2018 survey of 774 pregnant American women by Aeroflow Healthcare, a manufacturer of breast pumps.

Similarly, women lost their jobs in nearly two-thirds of legal cases that alleged breastfeeding bias over the past decade, according to a 2019 report by the Center for WorkLife Law at the University of California's Hastings College of the Law. Among the forms of discrimination cited in the report: the denial of pumping break requests "from employees who are in pain and leaking milk."

First-wave Power Moms also infrequently won promotions shortly after childbirth. Such an opportunity came with a catch for Penny Herscher, the tech industry veteran who later led FirstRain. The CEO of Synopsys, a fast-growing maker of design software, asked Herscher to head a division four weeks after the 1993 birth of her son. She was then the company's head of marketing.

The catch? She would have to cut short her six-week maternity leave so she could assist the Synopsys chief in revamping the company's corporate organizational structure. "At week five, I was in the office and I nursed him in the office," she said of her newborn. "It was very shocking at the time."

It's much more common for second-wave executive women to achieve career breakthroughs around the time they become parents. IBM's Inhi Cho Suh, for example, was home with her three-month-old son, Jacob, in November 2007 when she found out she would advance to a vice presidency upon her return.

"I became a new vice president, a first-time mom, and a leader of a global team that varied in expertise, size, and location—all at the age of thirty-two," she recalled. The high-pressure situation forced her to be agile, she noted. She has continued to advance at IBM. In January 2020, she became its general manager of global strategic partnerships, overseeing multibillion-dollar relationships with huge corporate partners.

Dreams for Our Daughters

Several women I interviewed harbored an especially ardent desire for a girl, partly because mothers and daughters often enjoy close bonds. It took four unsuccessful pregnancies before Martha Olson, a thirty-eight-year-old vice president of Playtex Products, gave birth to Megan in 1993. "I wanted a child in the worst way, and I was glad it was a girl," she told me. "I was a girl's girl growing up."

My husband and I also rejoiced when Abra arrived. We already had a healthy, energetic son. I embraced the goal of perpetuating myself by raising a strong-minded woman with high ideals about gender equality.

But Abra later reacted negatively to my career commitment. I realized that girls can be especially adept at guilt-tripping their working moms. Any mom who defies cultural standards risks clashing with her daughter.

Each generation of Power Moms devised different solutions to a host of issues involving new motherhood as they sought fulfilling careers. Boomers took radical actions in order to be taken seriously by their male colleagues, including staying mum about their problems getting pregnant, concealing their growing girths, and resuming work quickly after childbirth.

By comparison, GenXers are more likely to work alongside supportive managerial moms and have an equally understanding boss at a family-friendly workplace. In turn, some current Power Moms champion corporate benefits for their fellow working parents. The effort heightens their internal visibility and chances for further advancement.

Yet U.S. companies could do much more to lessen career trade-offs as employees enter parenthood. Protracted paternity leaves, for instance, will become widely socially acceptable only when men at the top of big businesses routinely take them.

3

When Work and Family Collide

As a hardworking mother of two young children, I never perfected the art of work/life sway. In hindsight, I wish someone had taught me to sway well.

It didn't help that my mom and kids *did* perfect the art of guilt-tripping me about my dueling roles—sometimes through unspoken messages.

Let's turn the clock back to 1986. My husband, Mike, a fellow journalist, and I are raising six-year-old Dan and three-year-old Abra in suburban Bethesda, Maryland. We commute a total of two hours to and from our offices at *BusinessWeek* and the *Wall Street Journal* in downtown Washington, DC. A neighbor named Fanny provides child care for us in her home.

Mike and I push to complete our job assignments by 5:30 p.m., then rush to retrieve our offspring before Fanny's 6:30 p.m. quitting time. We prepare a simple dinner—microwaved hamburgers, anyone?—that we'll eat with Dan and Abra. The phone rings just as I lift my first forkful of food. My mother is checking up on me.

"Did I call you at a bad time?" she inquires. She poses the identical question at 7:00 every work night.

"Yes, you did," I say in a snarky tone. "We're just sitting down to dinner."

Her unspoken message: "What's so important about your job that your children must always eat their dinner so late?"

That same year, Dan and Abra burden me with their subtle guilt trip about having a working mom. I consider applying to be the first journalist to ride on the space shuttle. My voyage to outer space would be much more than a once-in-a-lifetime thrill; blasting off would tremendously boost my career and ego—by landing me in the history books. That imagined scenario gave me goose bumps.

Initially excited about having an astronaut as their mother, Dan and Abra change their minds after hearing that my space ride training would likely keep me far away from them for months. They beg me to not head for outer space.

Their unspoken message was, "We see too little of you already. You work late a lot. We miss you." I never raise my hand for the ride to outer space. I am both disappointed over missing a fabulous professional opportunity and elated that my youngsters want to spend more time with me.

Manager moms often endure greater pressure points than dads when their work and family needs collide. The women move ahead in business because they're star performers. They also set steep standards for their maternal roles—and suffer angst when they don't get home for their children's dinner or bedtime. Fathers usually agonize less because they face lower social expectations for their paternal role. Indeed, some dads earn colleagues' kudos for leaving work early to attend their child's school event.

Work-family conflicts take an especially harsh toll on women, research shows. The conflict causes "increased psychological strain, with higher levels of stress and lower levels of well-being," a large-scale study published in 2019 stated. Its authors analyzed data from 6,025 UK adults covering eleven measures of chronic stress, such as high blood pressure. Chronic stress levels are 40 percent higher in women who are bringing up two children and employed full-time, concluded researchers from the University of Manchester and University of Essex in Great Britain.

Both sets of Power Moms featured in this book devised strategies to reduce the stress of their long work hours and long days away from their families during business trips and long-distance commutes. Their efforts ranged from educating their kids about why they worked so hard to creating imaginative, personalized expressions of their love. Distinct differences emerged between the two waves of executive mothers, however.

Baby boomers broke gender barriers, integrating male-dominated industries and the upper echelons of business. Their pioneering feats landed them in the crosshairs of work-family conflict, the sociologist Pamela Stone noted in her 2007 book, *Opting Out?: Why Women Really Quit Careers and Head Home.* The Hunter College professor of sociology interviewed fifty-four high-achieving women who interrupted their careers to stay home with their children. Many "found themselves marginalized and stigmatized, negatively reinforced for trying to hold on to their careers after becoming mothers," she wrote. The women she spoke with had reached a median age of sixty-one as of 2019, she said in our interview.

GenX executives I met learned from the boomer generation that they can never attain perfect work/life balance—as much as they wish that they could. That's why they assertively embrace work/life sway. The concept captures their view of reality: moms deserve to thrive at home and work. Yet second-wave women also recognize that swaying isn't always the perfect solution to their double load.

Rather than toggle constantly between job and home tasks, they understand the occasional need to establish clear boundaries between the two sides of their jam-packed lives.

Katia Beauchamp, the youthful leader of Birchbox, scrambled to manage her work/family conflicts by setting boundaries after she gave birth to three kids within three years while leading her online beauty start-up. "It's more about burning the candle on both ends," she confessed, covering her face with her hands as she recounted those difficult days.

Though Beauchamp stayed late at Birchbox, she usually arrived home before the trio's bedtime and resumed working there after they fell asleep. Spending only an hour or two with them each workday "was upsetting, for sure," she recalled. "But I also felt like I was very lucky that I cared about my job." She added, "I feel very happy to be a working mom."

Juggling Dinner and Work

Family dinnertime was rarely a happy time for the first cohort of Power Moms such as Penny Herscher. She headed FirstRain, a business analytics company, until 2015. She still regrets missing dinner with her children every weeknight during her first CEO stint years earlier. Her daughter, Melanie, was four years old while her son, Sebastian, was two when she took charge of Simplex Solutions in 1996 at age thirty-six. The California start-up employed a handful of engineers to make software for the design of semiconductors.

As a CEO, "you live under this enormous pressure," Herscher remembered. Sophisticated smartphones didn't exist in the mid-1990s, and her home computer had an agonizingly slow dial-up connection. "To get work done, I had to be in the office [late]."

Herscher's youngsters had finished eating by the time she reached home at 7:30 or 8:00 p.m. "If I could do it over again, I would have tried to organize my life to be home for dinner," she remarked in a tone of regret. "It wouldn't have changed [Simplex's] outcome."

Her employer grew into a profitable business with more than $50 million in revenue. She took the company public in 2001 and sold it the next year. Looking back, she suggested that no work deadline "is ever as important as you think it is."

Some adult daughters of other trailblazing executives described sad scenes of dinners without their high-powered mother. Lynn Gray's decision to resume her job as a real estate executive right after Emily's 1982 birth "defined her for my entire childhood. I have very few memories of being around my mom a lot," her grown daughter told me. "I just didn't feel like she was present in my day-to-day life. It kind of felt like I was a visitor in hers."

Emily's parents divorced when she was seven, and she saw her father only every other weekend. For most of her youth, a sitter prepared her weeknight meals. The girl dined alone at the dining room table in her mother's Manhattan apartment. "I can count on one hand the number of times I ate at the dining room table with my mother—including weekends," she said. "We would go out. My mom is not a very good cook." Years later, however, the young woman came to recognize that her mother is a very good business executive.

I interviewed Emily when she was working for a veterans' service organization. The nonprofit group paid her so little that the nearly thirty-seven-year-old manager had moved back home to save money. Living with her mother in the same Manhattan apartment where she was raised is a real emotional challenge, she admitted. "I have had to address some of those resentments that happened in the past."

Even today, the women still don't dine together on work nights. Emily told me she rarely gets home before her mom goes to bed around 8:00 p.m.

Another daughter named Emily shared an equally poignant saga of tensions about weeknight dinners. Her parents are Wendy Abt, a prominent investment banker who has advised African governments, and Clark Abt, the founder and retired leader of Abt Associates, a research and consulting firm in Cambridge, Massachusetts.

During much of Emily's and her brother's childhoods, their mother was a rising star at Bank of Boston. Wendy Abt came home at least ninety minutes later than her husband's 6:00 p.m. return from Abt Associates. "Every family has their repeated dramas that play out over the years. [Dinnertime] was definitely one of ours," recalled Emily, an independent filmmaker born in 1974.

Clark Abt expressed his irritation with his tardy wife by routinely refusing to feed their hungry kids before she appeared. Wendy Abt believes that his dinnertime delays intensified the pressure on her to leave the office prematurely. "I would say, 'Go ahead and eat,'" she recollected. "He would say, 'No, we'll wait.'"

When she finally showed up, "there would be a fight. My dad would be pissed that she was so late," Emily told me. "This happened over and over again." The repeated dinnertime fights reminded Emily that her mother wasn't around as much as she wanted.

Like Herscher, Wendy Abt acknowledges that she didn't handle family dinner conflicts well. She occasionally promised to come home sooner than she did, for example. But "I couldn't just drop everything," she explained. "I was very distracted by work and very much a workaholic." She sees her daughter as striking a better balance between work and family—and not merely because of her choice of professions. She "can kind of hone [it] better than I could," she added.

Emily agrees, noting that she never misses dinner with her two school-age daughters unless she's out of town making movies. A profession like hers allows for more flexibility than do corporate management positions.

Certain contemporary executive moms express less anxiety than boom-generation ones did when their job disrupts evenings with their children. Alexis DiResta, a former executive of Estée Lauder Companies, is an excellent example. In her final role at the New York–based manufacturer of cosmetics, she oversaw worldwide marketing for a line of men's skin care products. Once she got home, she often conducted two-hour evening calls with colleagues in Asia.

DiResta and her husband, a toy designer, have two young children named Violet and Xavier whom they liked to bathe and put to bed together on weekday evenings.

But when an Asia conference call loomed, "I would come home, literally say 'Hello,' and then go disappear," the thirty-eight-year-old executive remembered, speaking rapidly as we ate Korean vegetarian food in a Manhattan restaurant. At first, she dreaded that her time with her offspring was so abbreviated.

DiResta soon concluded that it was ridiculous to feel guilty about her weeknight work needs, especially since Violet and Xavier seemed perfectly content while their father fed them dinner in the nearby kitchen. "It wasn't as though the kids were desperately trying to get my attention and I was ignoring them," she observed. "I was just creating a problem that didn't exist."

DiResta left Estée Lauder in 2018. She next advised Glossier, a direct-to-consumer beauty business in New York, about product development and marketing. She relished the way part-time consulting gave her complete control over her work hours.

In fall 2019, she halted talks with Glossier about a permanent role in order to lead a new division for Away, an online luggage retailer. "I will have a lot of control over my schedule," DiResta predicted during her first week with the fast-growing start-up, which was valued at $1.4 billion that year. "I let the team know ahead of time that I'd need to work from home on Halloween" so she could attend Violet's Halloween parade and take her trick-or-treating.

Guilt Trips over Trips

The daughter of a powerful first-wave executive badly craved a hug the day she started menstruating. The hug didn't happen. Her mom was visiting Japan for work.

I heard numerous wrenching tales like that from the inaugural cohort of executive mothers whose frequent business trips had aided their ascent into senior management. It was true for Jana Schreuder, the former chief operating officer of Northern Trust. Her husband retired at age fifty in order to care for newborn Allison. The term "stay-at-home dad" didn't enter the popular lexicon until the late twentieth century.

By the time their daughter turned two in 1998, Schreuder was on the road a lot. She figured her regular absences for work didn't bother Allison "as long as she was with her dad."

Schreuder figured wrong. That same year, she flew back a day early from a two-week Singapore trip—her longest ever absence from her daughter. She would surprise her family by returning unannounced and spending the rest of that Friday at home.

Schreuder got her own surprise upon entering their coach house in Lake Bluff, a Chicago suburb: Allison was coloring pictures at the kitchen table while the girl's father stood beside a counter. "I walked in and threw out my arms, like expecting her to run to me," Schreuder recalled. Allison glanced at her mother without moving an inch. "Oh, look, Daddy! Jana's here," she said, then resumed coloring.

Being rejected by Allison devastated the ordinarily well-composed banker. "It was like somebody threw a knife into my chest and twisted it," she said. "I have the feeling now," she went on, reliving her long-ago anxiety by placing her hands on both sides of her forehead. "I thought my life was over."

Once she stopped crying, she realized that Allison felt abandoned because she had no inkling whether her mother might ever come home. The executive started to prepare the toddler for her business trips. Before departing for London a week later, she pulled an atlas from the bookshelf and showed her the location of England on a map.

"Where's your mom?" Allison's grandmother asked the youngster during that London visit.

"Oh, Mommy's in the book on the shelf," the child answered calmly. At least, Schreuder noted wryly, Allison "kind of had that sense that I was coming back and she knew where I was."

The executive recounts the bittersweet episode during conversations with younger moms about making their work/family equation work. "Don't assume that your young child should not be involved in your work life," she advises. Allison "couldn't decide that I wasn't going to travel," she said. "But she could make her needs known."

The pressure to travel for business persists for the latest crop of executive mothers as well. In certain cases, however, they exhibit greater sensitivity to their child's separation anxiety than Schreuder's peers did. Consider Annie Granatstein. She launched an in-house creative studio for the *Washington Post* in 2015 and was directing the agency from Manhattan when we spoke. Her forty staffers created branded content for *Post* advertisers, including articles, video, and video reality segments.

Granatstein's job took her out of town 50 percent of the time because the studio was expanding rapidly. "There's just more to do [and] more sales calls to go on," she said during our session in her windowless office. Her curly red hair made her look younger than forty-three. "I don't think I fathomed that it would be this much travel," she continued, banging her fists together.

Trained as a lawyer and married to a motion graphics designer, Granatstein gave birth to Lily in 2012. They live in Park Slope, a fashionable Brooklyn neighborhood that's popular with young families. The weekend before we met, Granatstein had taken her first grader and two other girls to a playground following a sleepover. Lily had hidden under the jungle gym and begun bawling for no obvious reason.

"Finally, she said, 'You've been traveling. You haven't been around, and I didn't get to see you because I had the sleepover,'" Granatstein recollected. "'And now you're acting like you're my friends' mommy.'"

Granatstein immediately recognized that Lily needed extra TLC. "I had her sit next to me on the bench. We had hugs and kisses," she continued.

"I said, 'I have been traveling more, and I know it is hard. It's really hard on me, too. I miss you, too, and it's good that you tell me these things. You can always talk to me about [your feelings].'" She thinks her daughter now grasps that she should express her emotions rather than bottle them up inside.

In early 2020, Granatstein left the *Washington Post* to become an executive vice president of Edelman, a public relations firm. She traveled far less frequently for work. "It was a bonus."

Power Moms sometimes ease the strain of business trips by making highly personalized items that connect them with their distant children. Jane Stevenson has spent more than thirty years in the executive search industry and won a firm partnership before the births of her daughter, Emily, in 1995 and son, Jonathan, in 1998. Today, she is the vice chair of board and CEO services at Korn Ferry, the world's largest executive search firm.

Stevenson never wanted her heavy work travel to limit her participation in her children's lives, however. "I did whatever I could think of creatively to stay engaged," she explained during our get-together in a thirty-third-floor conference room at Korn Ferry's Manhattan office.

Stevenson's most innovative creation: heartfelt love songs that she composed for her offspring, with each receiving a separate tune and lyrics. She sang one to each child at bedtime every night of every business trip. "Emily, you're my special girl," she would sing over the phone before crooning to Jonathan, "You are my precious love."

Emily, now an associate manager at InterContinental Hotels Group, remembers crying pretty much every time her mother left for a work journey. Nevertheless, hearing her special song comforted her. "It was another way to connect with her when she was gone," she said. Stevenson performed the nighttime ritual during trips until her progeny reached sixth grade.

DiResta took a similar approach. Ahead of her first Asia trip in July 2016, the cosmetics industry executive wrote her daughter six letters, one for each day that she would be gone. DiResta thought it would be fun for Violet to open a missive every morning.

Each letter contained detailed guidance for her nearly six-year-old daughter about that day's activities, such as a gymnastics class. One letter reminded the girl to wear the plastic lei stored in her dresser for her camp's Hawaii Day celebration.

Numerous Power Moms are married to Power Dads. Career couples from both generations have tried to minimize friction over business travel—with mixed results. Their efforts reflect the widespread larger dilemma of figuring out how spouses can advance their careers without derailing their marriage. In 2018, both parents worked among 63 percent of married couples with children under eighteen, the U.S. Bureau of Labor Statistics reported. That proportion is virtually unchanged from 1999.

Jerri DeVard, an executive vice president of the retailer Office Depot when we chatted, is a first-wave Power Mom who has long been part of a dual-income household. The African American marketing maven was employed by Pillsbury Company, a big food maker in Minneapolis, and married to Greg Smith, a human resources manager, when their daughter, Brooke, arrived in 1989. Their son, Alexander, arrived about three years later.

Once they became parents, DeVard and Smith vowed never to take overnight work trips at the same time—partly because a son had been stillborn before they had Brooke. "Our children were just a gift. And maybe if we hadn't lost our first child, we wouldn't have been that adamant," the sixty-year-old DeVard told me during our meeting at the bar of a private club in downtown Manhattan. "We wanted to be there [a lot] because . . . we both had working-parent guilt."

DeVard and Smith coordinated their travel by marking their plans on a calendar attached to their refrigerator. That's how they knew when both needed to leave town for several nights when their youngsters were under five.

"He felt that his trip was just as important as mine, and I felt that mine was as important," DeVard said. They wrangled over who could afford to cancel the travel. DeVard decided to seek permission to skip her Pillsbury meeting because her husband couldn't miss his out-of-town session with an important job candidate. "I was not as critical to that trip as Greg was to his trip."

Winning her boss's permission, DeVard called her husband to announce that she wouldn't take her trip. "I've done this for the team," she declared. "Next time, it's going to be on you." The first-wave mothers I interviewed were more willing to make career compromises than were their contemporary counterparts. That may explain why marital spats over business trips continue to erupt among younger Power Moms.

A hectic travel schedule and an ill baby ignited a nasty confrontation between one GenXer and her husband. The financial services industry executive Nancy Bong was thirty-five when she married Jimmy Ruebenacker, a manager for an operator of gas and electricity networks. She bore their sons, Max and Luke, in 2014 and 2018, respectively.

Hired by OppenheimerFunds in 2015, the new managing director flew 75,000 miles during her first nine months with the big money management firm. She said the crazy travel pace caused her to gain twenty-three pounds and almost crash from exhaustion.

In January 2019, Luke developed a fever while Bong was attending a four-day sales meeting in Atlanta. Ruebenacker left his office to pick him up from their day care center.

"My husband got no work done because he's at home with the baby for two whole days," Bong recalled. That Thursday evening, she heard Luke screaming as she walked into their Brooklyn apartment. Her husband was holding the baby in one arm while tapping on his work laptop with the other hand.

Ruebenacker was clearly fed up with caring for their sick infant. "Take him," he told his wife, who had yet to remove her coat.

"I tried to get here as soon as I could," she said.

"I don't care," he responded. "I'm exhausted."

Once Bong and her husband put their offspring to bed, he expressed deep resentment over her frequent business trips. "You can't just keep going away like this," he fumed during their tense encounter at the dining room table. "I don't even think you like our kids."

Stunned, Bong worried whether their marriage would survive. "Things weren't working," she told me. Since that wintry night, she added, "we've been talking about getting an au pair."

The executive soon quit OppenheimerFunds to lead the private bank channel of VanEck, an asset management firm. It was a rewarding switch. VanEck guaranteed her a 20 percent pay raise and promised to double her compensation if she delivered strong results. Four months after our interview, Bong reported that she was traveling less than before. "I would hope that I have learned my lesson from the last time around."

But she and her husband didn't hire an au pair, and she doubts that their new part-time babysitters will solve the problem of their sons falling ill during her business travel. "This [conflict] is still a work in progress," she conceded.

Indeed, she texted her husband as we wrapped up our breakfast interview in a Manhattan coffee shop. Luke had awakened feverish and screaming that morning, and Ruebenacker had stayed home after their sitter hadn't shown up. The baby seems okay, her husband texted back. But "get home as soon as you can."

The couple's child care problems began to ease after Ruebenacker persuaded his boss to let him work from a company office one minute from their apartment. "This effectively saves him a three-hour round-trip commute," Bong remarked.

Career Clashes with Kids

Whose needs come first when an attractive opportunity looms? Those of an ambitious mom? Or those of her teenagers? Boomer executive Lisa Mann grappled with this work/family conflict when her daughters rebelled over relocating for her high-flying management career.

She was the first member of her family to attend college, completing an undergraduate degree in electrical engineering and a Harvard MBA. In 2008, she won her first executive post at a major corporation: she was named a vice president of Kraft Foods in Chicago when her son, Josh, was fifteen and her twins, Arielle and Rachel, were twelve.

Mann flourished in marketing but yearned for a powerful operational spot. So the forty-eight-year-old executive was excited when Kraft CEO Irene Rosenfeld chose her to take charge of its $2 billion U.S. cookie business in 2011. The unit's well-known brands included Oreo. "It's the crown jewels of the company," Rosenfeld told Mann. "We've been disappointed by results. Go change things."

Moving up required moving from Chicago, however. Mann started her new role that spring at Nabisco headquarters in New Jersey. Her husband, Jack, a cable industry veteran who was switching to software programming for cell phones, relocated their family in July. The twins had just finished their freshman year of high school.

Arielle especially resented being uprooted, telling me she hated her mother for having been extremely selfish about her career. "Whenever my mom and I were in the same room, I would cry or yell," said the strong-willed young woman, now a doctoral student in chemistry.

Arielle yelled at her mother for many months—until a showdown at their new home in suburban Montclair. Seated on the floor outside the kitchen, the unhappy teenager renewed her tirade.

Mann turned and looked hard into Arielle's eyes. "Enough, already. I will not take it anymore. I don't deserve this, and I will not be treated this way." She then demanded that her daughter "buck up and define your life and find your own happiness. Cut the shit."

She doled out the same tough medicine when her other twin begged her to request a transfer back to Chicago. "I felt their pain. It did break my heart," Mann said. However, "you have to be resilient."

The executive doesn't view the relocation as selfish because her family also benefited. "Corporate jobs pay well," she observed. "We had college to pay for."

Mann's next job undoubtedly paid her even bigger bucks. In 2016, PepsiCo recruited her to command its $7 billion Global Nutrition Group. The unit had been formed to accelerate the food giant's push into healthier snacks and beverages. Mann left PepsiCo in 2018 and joined recruiters Raines International as chief marketing officer in 2020.

Long-Distance Mothering

Anne Stevens embodies the work/family conflict and related career trade-offs that several first-wave women like her ran into as long-distance mothers.

A nursing school dropout, Stevens was a thirty-year-old mother of two school-age youngsters by the time she completed her degree in mechanical and materials engineering in 1980. She joined the oil giant then called Exxon Corporation as a middle manager. Keen to progress, she accepted a long-distance commute five years later.

Stevens swapped a technical service job in New Jersey for a high-profile marketing position with a major product line in Houston. Her husband, Bill, a food industry process engineer, stayed behind with their daughter, Jenny, and son, Jonny, until he could find fresh employment in Texas.

The couple expected to live apart briefly. But Bill couldn't find work in Houston. Nor did Stevens like her boss. She said he praised her advancement potential while warning that "I really should think about ditching my excess baggage"—meaning her husband and kids.

"My family is important to me," she retorted.

Every other weekend, she returned to their brownstone in Hoboken, New Jersey. One Friday night, her teenage son met her at the door—in tears. "He had a metal splinter in his eye. He didn't tell his father," Stevens remembered. "He wanted to tell his mom."

She rushed Jonny to a hospital emergency room, where staffers removed the splinter from his swollen though undamaged eye. The mishap upset her badly. After almost a year in Houston, she transferred back to New Jersey and her lower-status job.

The unraveled relocation helped her family but hurt her Exxon career. "When you are on a [high-potential] ladder and do something like that, you really come off the ladder," she said. She quit in 1990 to become a business planner for Ford Motor Company. Five years later, Ford put her in charge of an auto plant.

Stevens ultimately became part of an elite sisterhood by heading two publicly held companies: Carpenter Technology Corporation, a developer and producer of specialty alloys, and later the venerable British manufacturer GKN, which she left after its 2018 takeover by Melrose Industries.

A well-trusted nanny enabled Carol Bartz to commute long distance until her daughter, Layne, turned two in 1990. She toiled sixteen-hour days leading a unit of Sun Microsystems from the Mountain View, California, headquarters of the hardware and software maker. She flew home to Dallas every Thursday night and spent the weekend with her child and husband, Bill Marr. He was a tech industry executive who regularly went out of town for work.

Their live-in nanny, an older Bolivian woman, often cared for Layne day and night between Monday and Thursday. "We couldn't do this [travel] if somebody didn't live with us," Bartz pointed out during our discussion in the glass-roofed conservatory filled with large leafy plants at her suburban San Francisco mansion. She and her family have lived in California since her long-distance commute ended.

Bartz said she had never worried about leaving Layne with their "exceptional" nanny. As Layne grew, so did the arc of Bartz's career. She assumed the number one spot at Autodesk in 1992 and led the manufacturer of design software for fourteen years. The internet company Yahoo! recruited her to be CEO in 2009.

Controversy still rages over employed mothers' use of nannies. In 2020, for example, a chief executive officer who is a single mother posted an ad for a nanny/household manager that ignited a raucous debate on social media. She offered to pay $86,000 if the new hire could research vacation options, cook organic meals, and perform a lengthy array of additional duties.

Online commentators attacked the high-powered mother for seeking someone to serve as her stand-in. But others noted that "high-powered men are rarely criticized for outsourcing child care and household duties," according to a Vox piece about the nanny ad. It was yet another example of the gendered double standard that remains deeply rooted in the American psyche.

MIA Nanny or Nanny Forever?

Californians Diane M. Bryant and Heidi Zak will never forget a certain nanny—for different reasons during different eras. Bryant had an impressive career at Intel Corporation, the big semiconductor company. She moved up from electrical engineer to become its top female executive about three decades later in 2016.

One of Bryant's most memorable moments at Intel happened in September 1996, when she was its thirty-four-year-old director of engineering. A private investigator called her San Jose office with terrifying news about Vicki, the woman caring for her infant daughter.

Vicki had cleaned Bryant's house for years before Annika's birth that summer. She had pledged to watch the baby full-time and stop cleaning other people's homes.

"I thought she was a friend," recalled Bryant, peering over her bright blue–framed glasses as we sat on the windy deck of a San Francisco hotel. "That was my first experience of being a working mom and having to find day care."

Bryant hired the detective after she noticed unused baby bottles and few soiled diapers upon her return home. Cell phones and nanny cameras hadn't been invented yet.

After tracking down Vicki on a warm afternoon, the private eye phoned Bryant at Intel. "She's still cleaning houses. But she's leaving Annika . . . in the back seat of the car while she goes in and cleans the house," he said. The baby was lying wide awake within the locked vehicle, its windows rolled up tight.

"Get her out of that woman's hands immediately!" he warned Bryant. Panic stricken, she dashed from work and drove to the San Jose address where the investigator had discovered Annika trapped inside the nanny's car.

The car was gone. Bryant drove home and spent three anxious hours waiting for Vicki. She had plenty of time "to pace, cry, scream, and plan how I was going to kill her when she arrived," she told me. Her husband blocked her from attacking the nanny as she entered their house. She fired Vicki instead.

Bryant suffers nightmares about the horrible outcome that might have happened if she hadn't retained a detective. "Being a working mom had put my baby at serious risk," she said. By the time Annika turned sixteen, she had employed seven nannies.

There's a different reason Heidi Zak will never forget Lilly, the nanny she chose to care for her infant daughter. Sloane made her debut in 2013, shortly before the debut of ThirdLove, an intimate apparel company founded and led by Zak and her husband, Dave Spector, following stints at bigger businesses. The start-up had sold nearly 5 million bras when I sat down with forty-year-old Zak at its headquarters in a gritty San Francisco neighborhood.

Returning home one evening when Sloane was two, the co-CEO witnessed her toddler sobbing about her nanny's imminent exit. "Mommy, don't leave," Sloane begged Lilly.

Zak sobbed hysterically once the caregiver left—even though she had never cried about Sloane before. "Oh, my God, I'm the worst mom," she scolded herself as tears poured down her face. "She is so attached to her nanny that [she is] not wanting her to leave even when I get home."

Her husband later persuaded her to stop viewing Sloane's intense attachment to Lilly as her worst moment of motherhood. "It's not a bad thing [because] she's so loved by her," he said.

Zak no longer freaks out when Sloane and her younger brother occasionally call Lilly "Mom" because other working mothers have assured her that they went through the same ordeal. "My kids have somebody else in their life . . . [who] can be another mom and [whom] they have this amazing bond with," she noted. (Zak became the sole CEO of ThirdLove in April 2020.)

Vanessa Hallett, the youthful auction house executive, has no trouble accepting her nanny as her sons' "extra mother." In fact, she deliberately sought such a candidate three months after she delivered her elder son in 2013.

"Are you willing to be a second mom to my son?" Hallett asked while interviewing a Bhutanese nanny named Sangay in the ground floor gallery of Phillips' New York office. The nanny said she was willing, landed the job, and treats both boys as if she were their second mom.

Hallett never felt threatened by her sons' strong attachment to Sangay because she is confident about her mothering abilities. She also knew that her children would benefit from "having another woman who loved them just as much."

Though the first wave of Power Moms often viewed their nanny as a trustworthy helper, the present generation is more likely to seek a highly experienced professional who will be a critical member of their home team. These women believe that having a great nanny enables them to be great mothers and business leaders. That's why recruiting someone who can serve as their children's extra mom wins approval from their female peers.

Hire a nanny "you feel can be an extension of you," *Working Mother* urged its readers in 2016. Nearly 60 percent of American families now have nannies or caretakers in their homes—and most of the families aren't privileged, the magazine added.

The intergenerational shift involving nannies illustrates the way coping strategies for work/life conflicts have evolved amid the stress of executives' long work hours, frequent business trips, and long-distance commutes. Despite extensive assistance from nannies, Power Moms usually run their households and coordinate their children's activities. My next chapter will shed light on the persistent quandary of how parents can share domestic chores—and how executive mothers handle this common conundrum.

4

Trials and Triumphs of Domestic Labor

Like countless young women today, I wanted an egalitarian marriage without rigid sex roles.

I had grown up in a family where my dad, an electrical engineer, took charge of appliance repairs, snow removal, and lawn mowing. My mom cooked, cleaned, and took care of us four young kids. She belatedly declared herself "liberated" when she stopped picking up my father's dirty underwear that he had thrown on their bedroom floor every night for many years.

Mike and I envisioned married life as an equal partnership at a time when the typical wife employed outside the home worked a "second shift" of domestic labor. We also wanted a less traditional marriage partly because several states then dictated where a wife had to live—even if she was legally separated. We reinforced our feminist commitment to parity by writing a marriage contract. "Household duties shall be shared equally, but not necessarily cheerfully," our 1972 agreement stated.

The unconventional contract mystified my older relatives. My mother couldn't understand why I had included a declaration about keeping my birth name. On the other hand, our grown son and his wife later agreed that "cooking means you don't do dishes"—based on his memory of our contractual promise to share domestic chores.

Mike and I didn't always practice what we preached, however. He cut the grass once we bought our first home. I knew nothing about dangerous tools such as lawn mowers. Nevertheless, I resented his sweaty hour pushing the mower on weekends. He was washing fewer dirty dishes, pointing out that he did outside chores instead.

"I don't like the way we've fallen into traditional male-female work roles since we moved into the house," I complained to Mike. "I want to learn how to use the lawn mower." Inspired by Mike's quick lesson, I mowed the grass for the first time in my life. I felt so exhilarated by my achievement that I repeatedly hummed "The Daring Young Man on the Flying Trapeze."

Our occasional spats over splitting the household chores increased once my husband and I crossed the life-altering threshold of parenthood. We were clueless about how to raise a family as equal partners. We squabbled over who should skip their journalism job in order to stay home with a feverish child, for example.

University of California, Berkeley, sociologist Arlie Hochschild extensively documented women's second shift in her groundbreaking 1989 book about fifty dual-income pairs with offspring under six years old. The "double day" hurt a mother's career, she wrote in *The Second Shift: Working Families and the Revolution at Home*. She blamed men for not sharing in "the raising of their children and the caring of their homes."

Throughout the world, "there is no known society in which women do not do the majority of child care," the gender researcher Francine M. Deutsch said in her 1999 book, *Halving It All: How Equally Shared Parenting Works*. She interviewed 150 two-earner couples with children to chronicle their largely unequal distribution of unpaid labor. She also cited other studies of domestic life in the 1970s and 1980s showing that men with wives working outside the home didn't perform any more duties at home than did men married to full-time homemakers. That created a huge burden for first-wave Power Moms as many became parents during those decades.

The Generational Divide

Numerous first-generation executives I met had spent extra hours on their domestic responsibilities, based on ingrained social expectations of gender behavior. Beth Comstock, who eventually became the first female vice chair of General Electric Company, typifies the women with double duty.

Decades before her 2015 promotion to that powerful post, the twenty-four-year-old Comstock was the pregnant employed wife of a stockbroker. She worked nights several times a week arranging programs for a cable television station in suburban Arlington, Virginia. During her evening meal breaks, "I remember coming home and cooking my husband dinner and then going back to work," she told me over lunch in a dimly lit Manhattan restaurant. "That's just kind of what I thought [wives] did," she said, sweeping away her long brown hair that drooped over one eye.

The young woman kept preparing her husband's dinner and handling their kitchen cleanup following the 1985 birth of their daughter Katie, and Comstock's switch to a daytime publicity position at NBC. She never asked her husband to cook, much less considered posing that obvious question.

There were a few exceptions among the boomer Power Moms. Betsy Holden said she had reached the pinnacle of Kraft Foods because her husband, Arthur, a veteran leader of the biomedical industry, had fully shared the responsibility of raising their two youngsters. "He was a true partner in baths, bedtimes, coaching teams, parent conferences, [and] teaching Sunday school with me," she recollected. On weekends, he did the bulk of the cooking. The executive couple forged such an equal partnership in bringing up their children that they considered writing a book entitled *Please Pass the Roles*.

The division of domestic labor remains a critical issue for two-career parents at every job level. Unfortunately, they encounter more troubles than triumphs on the home front.

Employed parents under forty-five typically believe in the myth of egalitarian relationships but have yet to figure out how to put the myth into practice, suggested Deutsch, an emeritus professor of psychology at Mount Holyoke College, during our interview. Couples who claim to coparent don't really do so equally, she added. "They mean the father is doing something."

Several studies support her argument. On average, mothers employed full-time spend nearly two-thirds more time feeding, bathing, and otherwise caring for their kids under six than do their employed husbands, according to time-use diaries that the U.S. Bureau of Labor Statistics collected between 2013 and 2017.

This lopsided proportion hasn't budged since 2000, the psychologist Darcy Lockman noted in her 2019 book, *All the Rage: Mothers, Fathers, and the Myth of Equal Partnership*. Why don't fathers pick up the slack? She attributes the problem's tenacity to "biology, cultural mandates around maternal devotion, and the ubiquitous prioritization of men's needs and desires relative to women's."

Nor does the balance of parenting responsibility tilt much even in dual-income households where Mom makes more money than Dad. The woman is more likely to care for kids under eighteen every day in 36 percent of such homes. The comparable figure for all households is 50 percent. These findings come from Gallup surveys of 3,062 heterosexual married or cohabitating American adults between June and August 2019.

"Despite some changes over the past two decades, the division of labor in U.S. households remains largely tilted toward traditional stereotypes," the pollster stated in its January 2020 report. "Women are more likely than their husbands to take care of the house and children."

Same-sex parents usually divide up child care and other daily life duties more equally than do straight couples, other studies suggest. However, researchers have found that one gay partner "often has higher earnings, and one a greater share of household chores and child care," the *New York Times* reported in May 2018. "It shows these roles are not just about gender."

That's exactly how Ann Miller, a second-wave Power Mom, and her wife, Désirée Bliss, run their home and rear their two daughters. Miller is a vice president and the corporate secretary of Nike, where she has steadily moved up since joining the sportswear giant in 2007. A well-paid job enables her to provide for her family—even though it "feels like a typical male model," she observed.

Bliss made less money and worked fewer hours during her years as a grant-making specialist for nonprofit groups. She called herself "the flex spouse" because she could rush home to take care of plumbing emergencies. She also has long performed the majority of their domestic chores. Miller usually washes dishes, pays bills, and attends pediatrician appointments with Bliss.

Two years after giving birth to their second daughter in 2012, Bliss became a self-employed consultant. She began working from their Portland, Oregon, home just fifteen hours a week. "Dési wanted to make sure that one of us was always available for the kids," Miller explained. Compared with typical heterosexual couples, they spend more time sharing feelings about their admittedly traditional division of labor, the executive said. "We're pretty good at telling each other what's not working."

Overall, about 87 percent of full-time working moms manage all or most parenting responsibilities, compared with 83 percent of stay-at-home mothers, concluded a fall 2018 survey of 516 American women by Edison Research. (The market research firm did not inquire about sexual orientation.) Nicole Beniamini, a firm vice president and coleader of the study, told me that she strongly identified with its results. "I am doing all the things that my mother did when she stayed home . . . plus working full-time," the thirtysomething mother of two young daughters grumbled. "I am resentful that this is all on me."

At my request, she scrutinized the study data more closely. Even youthful mothers who view their partner as an equal coparent bear a heavy burden, her separate analysis revealed. Fifty-two percent of coparenting moms under forty-five years old with full-time jobs handle the majority of parental duties. That's nine percentage points *higher* than for all mothers polled by Edison Research. Beniamini suspects that younger mothers likely have younger offspring than the study's overall sample.

How soon will this lopsided coparenting picture brighten? I asked. Contemporary children "see their moms traveling for work and their dads doing laundry, and so they will consider that the norm when they themselves become parents," she predicted.

It's already the norm for present-generation Power Moms who split household chores and child rearing equally. Consider Clara Shih, a cofounder of Hearsay Systems, a fast-growing tech start-up, and its chief executive officer until September 2020. "Culturally, millennial men and women have lower expectations for what millennial women will do at home," the thirty-six-year-old mother and

Google alumna insisted during our interview. She and her husband, Daniel, have a son, Blake, who was born in 2015.

"My husband has never thought I would make dinner every night," Shih said. "He has never asked me to iron his shirts. He has never asked me to vacuum or change our son's diapers."

Because she wanted Daniel to do 50 percent of their domestic labor, she didn't dare object when he dressed Blake in mismatched outfits. Otherwise, he might have refused to perform his share of the household chores. "He [was] trying his hardest." Now, Shih boasted, "my husband does more than fifty percent."

Most modern moms must also plan and organize the endless details of their family's daily lives, such as completing school forms, arranging playdates, and coordinating calendars. In effect, working mothers work an unpaid "third shift" serving as CEO of their hectic households.

Social scientists view the third shift and other types of household management as the last obstacle to truly egalitarian marriages. Deutsch identified the important ingredients needed for equal parenting during her recent research with scholars in twenty-two countries, which focused on twenty-five such couples. She emphasized one: fathers who embrace family tasks traditionally carried out by mothers—including mental work such as remembering to sign school permission slips and buy diapers.

The husbands of the second-wave executives I interviewed sometimes accept aspects of the domestic third shift. In 2016, the thirty-one-year-old Lauren Fanning sought extra aid from her spouse, Marc, after she finished her second maternity leave and resumed work as general counsel of Daymon Worldwide, a global retail services company. Raised by an at-home mom, he hadn't previously realized that "all that stuff to run a household is a full-time job," Fanning recalled.

Marc, a corporate controller, promised to take over booking pediatrician appointments, one of the numerous items filling Fanning's to-do list. "What's the kids' doctor's name again?" he inquired sheepishly.

Such paternal ignorance wouldn't surprise other working mothers. They're grateful that their husbands at least help. Yet no working father ever uttered the words, "At least she helps," Lockman pointed out in her book.

When we spoke, Fanning was pursuing an MBA degree while a full-time executive at Academic Partnerships, a business that converts public universities' classroom courses into online learning. And Marc did pick up the slack, she said. "I feel lucky to have a husband who gets it." In February 2020, Fanning joined Freeman Company, a major event management company, as assistant general counsel.

Overwhelmed by Multiple Demands

Husbands of overburdened Power Moms don't always get it, however. The ways in which each wave coped speak volumes about some favorable changes in managing domestic duties—and why completing the gender revolution awaits a meaningful reversal of perceptions that women make the best parents.

Baby boomers such as Aida Sabo often married men whose high-pressure job and long hours left them largely unavailable for family needs. She became a Hewlett-Packard manager in 1997, when her son was six and her daughter was thirteen. She and her husband, Dave, a high-level marketing executive, lived with their progeny and her parents in a San Francisco suburb.

He took international business trips or worked late so often that

Sabo became the primary caretaker of their youngsters and their house. She resented her nonstop role, however.

"My mom, my dad, and me were raising these children," Sabo said during our discussion at a Whole Foods eatery in suburban New York. "I'm taking all his clothes to go get dry cleaned," she went on. "I'd go to Macy's and buy three suits and see which ones would fit on him, which ones wouldn't. I was also helping [my mom] clean the house."

Sabo and Dave battled constantly over his frequent absences. "All he got to see was this angry woman," Sabo conceded, her voice breaking. She grabbed a brown paper napkin and dabbed her tears.

The couple's biggest blowup occurred on a weekend in 1998 when Dave was home and rolling dough with their son in the kitchen. "I got in a big fight with him about his not being there [enough]," Sabo recollected. "I just grabbed the ball of dough and boom, threw it on the floor."

She and Dave soon divorced. Now a vice president of Parexel International Corporation, the drug research firm, Sabo resides with a male partner who enthusiastically splits their housework. "I don't have to go home and clean," she said, grinning.

The unbalanced distribution of household labor continues to strain marriages these days. "Not surprisingly, studies in the last decade in the UK, Sweden and the United States have all found that couples with low levels of male partner participation are more likely to separate than couples in which men do more," Darcy Lockman said in her book.

The opposite is equally true. "In the long run, the couples who do parent equally are really happy," Francine Deutsch told me.

Certain younger executives, such as Laura Chepucavage, repeatedly run the obstacle course of coparenting with their husbands. A managing director at Bank of America, Chepucavage has a highly demanding job that keeps her far from her family thirteen hours a day. She married her college sweetheart, Mike, who later cofounded a maker of duffel bags. They're raising their small children in a Ridgewood, New Jersey, home with six bedrooms and seven bathrooms.

The couple began trying to equalize their balance of domestic labor after Chepucavage repeatedly forgot to get the three kids' flu shots, which their schools mandated. Mike took over grocery shopping, for instance. Despite extensive help from him and their nanny, she continued to feel overwhelmed because she simultaneously ran a business unit and a household.

One weeknight in 2017, "all of these things come to a head because I start to lose my mind and start having mental breakdowns over wine in the kitchen. I start hysterically crying," Chepucavage remembered, reliving her meltdown with Mike in the present tense.

"Oh, my God, I can't do this anymore. I'm dying," she warned her husband during their encounter at the kitchen's all-white island. "How do we make this work? I'm so tired. Our kids are going to be so fucked up."

They agreed to hire an additional babysitter, and Mike began to assist with other mundane tasks. "He wants me to be happy and us to have a thriving family life and me not having . . . any more meltdowns in the kitchen," Chepucavage said. The banker's scrubbed face, purple nail polish, and flannel shirt made her look younger than thirty-seven on the Sunday we had brunch. She gave birth to a fourth child in 2018.

Morgan Dewan, the youthful vice president of content partnerships at Turner Sports, a media business owned by AT&T, developed a formal check-in system with her husband that minimizes their tension over family chores. She and Brendan, a cardiothoracic surgeon, hold quarterly strategic planning sessions sitting next to each other at their kitchen table. The Saturday-morning meetings and cozy seating arrangement reinforce their conviction that "we're in it together," the thirty-five-year-old executive told me.

They explore what's working and what's not in their marriage and division of labor. "We speak openly about potential relationship killers like resentment, which seems to lurk in the background when I'm feeling particularly burdened with the second [or] third shift," Dewan said. "His schedule is so demanding and unpredictable that he can't be counted on as a reliable source of help or responsibility ownership."

The pair also makes major life decisions during their strategic planning sessions. Before the 2016 birth of their son, Luke, the couple reviewed various child care options. They decided that a live-in nanny made the most sense, given her extensive business travel and his rigorous on-call requirements. When we talked, Dewan was expecting their second son. Hudson arrived a month later.

Dirty Clothes Capers

For Power Moms in each peer group, laundry loads are an important litmus test of sharing the home load. "I just finished the laundry," thirty-seven-year-old Stefanie Strack said weeks after she gave up command of Rag & Bone, a global sportswear company. "There it is," she added, directing my gaze toward two full wash baskets in the art-filled Brooklyn apartment where she and her husband, Alan, dwelled with two children under six. Their tenth-floor residence provided a bird's-eye view of the soaring Brooklyn Bridge.

Strack and her husband had always hated doing laundry. "We fought over it for many years," she recollected, leaning over a marble coffee table and pointing her polished big toes toward each other.

"The things he doesn't like to do, it's like pulling teeth to get him to do it." Though she prefers cooking, Strack did the laundry and Alan prepared dinner.

The college soccer player joined Nike upon her graduation from the University of Montana with a degree in international business. The company promoted her to vice president in 2017.

Strack relocated her family from Portland to begin her first CEO job in September 2018. Although her husband was launching his film art business, "he really stepped up to support me and take on a bigger role in the [Brooklyn] home," she said. Alan did 80 percent of their household laundry during her short stint at Rag & Bone.

The spouses were crafting the next chapter of their soiled clothes saga on the frigid winter morning that Strack and I sipped hot drinks near her laundry baskets. Months later, she decided to form a sports advocacy company whose digital platforms would serve young female athletes. "Since we are both trying to build our own businesses, we take a more even split of the [laundry] load," she emailed me.

The uneven division of domestic labor in two-parent American families became magnified amid the huge work and school dislocations caused by the 2020 coronavirus pandemic. Michele Madansky, a research consultant, documented this pattern by canvassing employed moms that spring. More than five hundred of those surveyed have partners, and nearly 78 percent of them reported that they were doing most of the housecleaning.

Kids' Duties

Offspring with regular chores can also shrink a working mother's load. I taught our daughter to wash her clothes at age twelve largely because I wanted to increase Abra's sense of responsibility. Her older brother, Dan, already did his own laundry.

But Abra disliked being a foot soldier for our household, a sentiment that I knew nothing about at the time. "I felt like the reason we had to do all this was because you were too busy," she told me during a conversation decades later in her childhood bedroom. "You needed us to help run the household to support you toward your goal . . . to be the best you could be and the top of your career." She added that it didn't feel like "my emotions were your highest priority."

Making matters worse, having to do her own laundry "added a level of stress and what I felt like 'adult responsibility' to my life when I wanted to still just be a kid," Abra noted. Her bad memories disheartened me. I apologized for not having been available emotionally when she had needed me. "I hope I have more than made up for it since," I said.

Cheryl Bachelder, a first-wave Power Mom who ultimately ran Popeyes Louisiana Kitchen, a fast-food chain, ran into resistance over doing chores from her older daughter, Tracy. The executive assigned household tasks to her and her then youngest daughter, Katy, while she was a vice president of Domino's Pizza in the 1990s.

Bachelder wanted the girls to learn to take care of themselves and their rooms by making their beds, picking up their towels, and performing other minor chores. She listed and monitored their completion on a paper spreadsheet that she left atop the kitchen counter in their Northville, Michigan, home. It contained certain personal reminders, such as "Tracy, brush your teeth at 8:05 p.m." That particular reminder puzzled school chums who visited Tracy one weekday afternoon when she was thirteen.

"Mom, the spreadsheet has to go," the teen complained once Bachelder returned home from work. "This is humiliating, embarrassing, terrible." The executive threw away the dreaded spreadsheet.

She didn't totally abandon her businesslike approach to mothering, however. "We would call it 'boardroom parenting,'" Katy told me.

Bachelder later adopted a third daughter. She was the CEO of Popeyes for a decade until its sale in 2017 and subsequently took charge of Pier 1 Imports on an interim basis until the retailer chose a permanent leader in November 2019.

Kat Cole, a younger Power Mom, assumed significant child care duties during her own childhood. At age nine, she started watching her six-year-old and three-year-old sisters after school because her freshly divorced mother held three jobs. Meanwhile, she filled a father's traditional shoes by mowing the lawn or cleaning the roof on weekends.

By seventeen, she was working part-time as a clothing store saleswoman and a Hooters hostess. She became a Hooters vice president at twenty-six and the president of Cinnabon at thirty-two in 2010. Cinnabon is owned by Focus Brands, a restaurant franchiser where Cole is now chief operating officer and president of North America.

The executive got her latest promotion just before giving birth for the first time in 2017. She thinks her quasi-parental role at a very young age helped spur her meteoric rise into upper management. "That made the muscle of responsibility more developed," she observed.

Food Fights

The presence of a stay-at-home father usually settles household debates about who buys and prepares food. But not always—as Laurie Siegel, a first-wave mother, discovered. She and eight other executives from both cohorts had male partners who stayed home to care for their kids.

The number of American at-home dads is small but increasing. Fathers accounted for 17 percent of all stay-at-home parents in 2016, up from 10 percent in 1989, according to a 2018 analysis of U.S. Census Bureau data by the Pew Research Center. But government figures undercount the practice, advocacy groups contend. At least 1.7 million men served as their children's main caregiver in 2019, the National At-Home Dad Network estimated.

This reversal of traditional parental roles enabled some Power Moms to accelerate their advancement into upper management. It was exactly what Siegel had in mind. Her husband, Joe, quit his professional job at AT&T in order to rear their two school-age girls as her career progress took her to the highest human resources spot at the conglomerate Tyco International.

Joe inaugurated his stay-at-home role in 2000 after Siegel won an influential human resources post at Honeywell International, an industrial company, and relocated their family to Phoenix. "This gave me the chance to be a business partner to a CEO of a business [unit]," the sixty-three-year-old executive recollected during our encounter. "It was a big deal for me."

It was a big deal for Joe, too. Their last nanny had lived with them for seven years in Morristown, New Jersey, and cared for their daughters, who had been born in 1992 and 1994. In Phoenix, no one cooked regularly on weeknights. The family went out to eat, ordered in food, or ate leftovers from the weekend. Joe had not yet adjusted to being a stay-at-home dad.

Two months after their move, Siegel came back from a business trip and opened the refrigerator to fetch milk for one of her girls. The refrigerator contained nothing except condiments. She confronted Joe, highly irritated by his failure to grocery shop during her absence.

"You had all day, and you couldn't fill the refrigerator with basics?"

she asked her husband. "I'm not asking you to cook gourmet meals. But I expected to come home to the things that a decently stocked house should have."

Siegel's exasperation over the scant food supply reflected her deeper worries about their daughters "having the kind of home life they should have," she told me. Her words exuded working-mother guilt.

Indeed, moms feel the greatest pressure to safeguard their youngsters' consumption of food. Americans judge mothers—but not fathers—on whether their family makes healthy food choices, concluded a study of 1,603 U.S. adults published in December 2018. "The social costs for not meeting these ideals are more severe for mothers than for fathers," the study researchers observed. Though they didn't spell out those costs, their findings demonstrate "that people tend to ascribe the responsibility to make consumption choices to mothers, not fathers."

"You have got to invest in this [stay-at-home] role," Siegel chided Joe.

"I get it," he said. He quickly embraced his obligation to shop and fix their family's weeknight meals. Joe continues to cook for his wife—though she no longer works full-time and their adult daughters have left home. "He enjoys it," she said. And "he's good at it."

Sick of Sick Children?

Boomer moms such as Anne Weisberg routinely left their office during the workday to pick up their sick schoolchildren and take them home. Yet Weisberg never asked her husband, a Goldman Sachs investment banker, to perform the task because he would have refused. "He felt like there would have been no permission for him playing that kind of role," recalled Weisberg, the women's initiative director at Paul, Weiss. "He was never available that way." At the same time, she was expected to conform with her era's social expectations that a mother should take charge of an ill child.

The situation has improved slightly for the second wave of executive mothers, but less than I had anticipated. Among couples with parents employed full-time, 75 percent of the mothers stay home from work when their child is too sick to attend school, the Edison Research study showed.

Tatyana Zlotsky typifies how contemporary Power Moms handle this issue with mixed results. She earned a vice presidency at American Express Company two years after the major financial services company hired her—and just months after the 2012 birth of her elder son, Ian. She and her husband, Stan, a fellow Russian immigrant who's a technology industry analyst, also have a second son named Nathan.

The digital marketing specialist was leading a roughly eighty-member team within a multibillion-dollar division when we spoke in a thirty-second-floor corporate conference room overlooking the Hudson River. Not long after Nathan's first birthday in June 2016, the two boys caught viruses every other week for six months, Zlotsky remembered. "That just really took pieces [out] of me."

She and Stan took turns taking an ill child to the doctor. Yet even when he did so, "I ended up coming home a lot of times because I would feel guilty that the kids were sick," she said.

The American Express executive felt equally guilty about missing work so much—despite strong support from her sympathetic male boss. Ahead of a jam-packed day as a vice president, "you wake up at two in the morning with one of the kids screaming, and you realize they have a 102 [degree] fever."

Zlotsky suggested that Stan assume full responsibility for taking their sons to the doctor for illnesses and routine exams. "I was just like 'Look, I'm falling apart here. I am run down, I'm exhausted,'" she said, running her hands through her hair. "He needed to stand up [at work] and say, 'I need more flexibility because my wife has a full-time job and I have two little babies and I need to work from home some days.'"

Stan agreed and obtained his employer's blessing to toil from home when necessary. Looking back, Zlotsky regrets that she waited so long before requesting extra help from her husband. As a working mom, "you don't even like what help looks like because at the same time, you want to be the person that fixes everything."

Solo Night Owl

A working mother's career move can upset well-laid efforts at co-parenting on weeknights. That happened to both me and Lindsay Kaplan, the millennial cofounder of Chief, the network for female leaders.

During the 1980s, Mike and I spent virtually every weekday evening at our suburban Maryland home. We jointly made dinner, bathed our kids, and put them to bed. The equitable arrangement ended when the *Wall Street Journal* elevated me to news editor of its London bureau in 1987.

"He will be the mainly responsible parent as I will be working until 8:30 p.m. every night," I wrote in my diary shortly before we moved abroad. "I am terrified and elated at the same time."

With good reason: my late hours forced Mike into a single-parent role that he had never bargained for. "Initially, I was very resentful," he recalled. "I had no choice." Hired by a news service of Dow Jones & Company, the *Journal*'s parent company, he was greeted eagerly by Dan and Abra every evening at 6:30. Their London nanny had fed them dinner, but they hungered for parental attention. Their hungry dad felt compelled to spend time with them before taking his first bite of food.

Our new arrangement proved to be a disguised blessing. Mike organized geography quizzes, made colored clay bowls, and baked corn muffins with our progeny. "As the kids and I adjusted, we began to find new things we enjoyed doing together," he said. "I began to understand what a great opportunity it was to be involved with them alone on weeknights."

In a similar fashion, Kaplan and her husband, Richard, dedicated themselves to a fair division of domestic labor from the outset of their relationship. But the 2015 birth of Max and the 2019 launch of Chief tested their commitment. Richard was working until 5:00 p.m. as head of product for an art inventory management platform. Kaplan often stayed much later for her start-up in order to attend business dinners and member programs.

"He really steps up and takes on a lot of evening [parenting] shifts," the entrepreneur said. "It weighs on him."

The prior Friday night, Kaplan's frequent evening absences had sparked a quarrel as the Manhattan couple drove to their weekend home in upstate New York. The drive had ended a week during which Richard had taken care of Max for three consecutive nights. He talked about feeling completely worn out before he wondered, "How many nights this [coming] week?"

"Don't you know how hard I work?" Kaplan retorted tartly. "It's hard to do a start-up."

"I want to know how many nights you're going to be away," Richard fired back.

"Who cares?" Kaplan snapped. "You're home every night anyway."

Richard also repeatedly asks his wife to put her evening work events on his calendar in advance, because he's much more organized than his creative wife is. She doesn't always comply, however.

"Even tonight, I have an event at Chief. I'm going to be late," Kaplan admitted during our afternoon get-together there. "Did I put it on his calendar today? No, I totally forgot," she went on, looking sheepish. She vowed to pop it into his calendar thirty minutes before her expected homecoming that evening.

"Add tonight's event to Richard's calendar now," I urged her at 4:30 p.m. "Your marriage will be more joyful. Or at least more planned."

Kaplan grabbed her iPhone and complied with my suggestion. Still, she rarely worries about her marriage. Given the traditional gender identity attached to parenting, "he and I both recognize I am more of a dad in that way," she remarked. "It's why I love him, and it's why we are compatible."

Can both parents be superstars on the job? Or must one always play the role of a hardworking dad, irrespective of gender? In practicing work/life sway, second-wave women frequently forge strong marriages because they and their spouse are invested in their mutual career success. "We believe we can both 'star' at work so long as we communicate, delegate, and enlist extra support from child care [providers]," Kaplan said.

The Not-So-Golden Mother Load

I recognized the harsh reality of working mothers' mental load nowadays when I visited Stacey Tank, then the head of a multibillion-dollar unit of Home Depot. That spring Monday was her second consecutive day of work for the week. The thirty-seven-year-old mother of two boys had spent seven hours at her Home Depot office on Sunday, attacking work and household organizational tasks from her to-do list of roughly two thousand items.

On her fingers, she ticked off the domestic tasks that she had finished there on Sunday: she had planned a tenth birthday party for her son Jackson, ordered his birthday presents, alerted relatives about his gift preferences, and checked up on the family travel arrangements.

I wondered how Tank amasses and completes her incredibly massive to-do list. "It's everything I need to think about for the year," she explained. "I look at everything at least once a week." Nor does she believe that her husband, Trevor, should carry a larger mental load, because he is already a very involved dad.

Such duties constitute what Elizabeth Emens, a Columbia Law School professor, calls "life admin," which she defines as the office work of life. "It is harder to sell parents on the idea that they somehow benefit from doing more of the household admin," she noted in her 2019 book, *Life Admin: How I Learned to Do Less, Do Better, and Live More*. "Thus, the allocation of admin work within relationships is a more bare-bones fairness issue, since spreading it around has no obvious upside for the one who has to accept more of the load."

In households where mothers bring home the bigger paycheck, they're not just highly involved in parental duties; they are also nearly twice as likely to make sure that all family responsibilities are taken care of as are breadwinner fathers. So found a study of 2,082 employed Americans with at least one child under eighteen. The 2017 research was commissioned by Bright Horizons, the big provider of child care services.

Women's mental burden requires them "to be not just parents and caretakers, but also unofficial keepers of where the entire family needs to be and when, and perpetual guardians against anything falling through the cracks," the Bright Horizons report stated.

This invisible, unpaid work is essentially an additional mother load. "That's because in our culture, 'mom' has been deemed the she-fault"—the default parent who manages the kids and the household, wrote Eve Rodsky, a philanthropic adviser and attorney, in her 2019 book, *Fair Play: A Game-Changing Solution for When You Have Too Much to Do (and More Life to Live)*.

With many millions of U.S. families stuck at home during the 2020 pandemic, Rodsky informally polled more than a hundred women about who was managing the mental load of household tasks during the unprecedented health crisis. "Women are taking on the conception and planning for everything," she reported in a *Harper's Bazaar* piece.

Genevieve Roth, the founder and president of Invisible Hand, the social impact strategy and events agency, depends on a personal assistant to lighten her household chores and mental lists. She typically employs musical theater students, paying them $20 an hour to work ten hours a week at her Manhattan apartment.

The assistant simplifies life for Roth and her husband, Jordan, in little-noticed ways, such as by researching classes for their young daughter, returning unwanted purchases, and booking a refrigerator repairman. When the family lost hot water and electricity the day before we conferred, their part-time helper dealt with the electrician and "managed that whole process," Roth told me.

The aide also eliminates her friction with Jordan over, say, who will replace an empty toilet paper roll by making sure their home stays stocked with important supplies. So when he wonders whether they really need an assistant, Roth replies, "How many times in the last two and a half years have you [bought] toilet paper? Zero."

But even with a personal assistant, the entrepreneur is so busy growing her small business that mundane tasks still fall into the cracks. Among those tasks: writing personalized thank-you notes.

Her aide writes the notes for her to sign and send. More than a year after Roth's baby shower in spring 2018, she had not yet mailed thank-you notes for several gifts because she needed to track down the givers' addresses. "It's just one of those projects that has gotten lost in the tornado of life," she said.

A whirlwind of domestic demands buffeted Power Moms from both waves. Unlike most members of the prior generation, however, GenXers such as Roth swear by the myth of spousal egalitarianism for household and parenting tasks. I was encouraged to hear about some innovative approaches by her generation. Among the most notable: couples' reaffirmation of their commitment to careers and family through regularly scheduled check-in sessions or substantive informal chats when needed.

Achieving real spousal parity would lessen the pay and promotion gaps between the genders. But for now, it remains a work in progress. Too many younger dads hesitate to request the workplace accommodations required for them to carry their fair share of home duties. And younger moms still carry a burdensome mental load because they accept the popular presumption that the mother should be the primary parent.

Further complicating their domestic dilemmas, Power Moms are major multitaskers. Multitasking is especially tough for the current crop because their job demands and digital devices often keep them wedded to work 24/7. I will look at how they must be "always on" in the next chapter.

5

Being Always On
Doesn't Always Work

It's late at night, and I'm home after another arduous day at the *Wall Street Journal* in London.

But I can't go to bed yet. As second in command of this important *Journal* bureau, I'm the final point of deadline contact for our New York editors every work night. Suddenly the phone rings loudly in our apartment's living room. I grab the receiver before the harsh jangle wakes my two sleeping children.

"Hey, is it like midnight there?" a *Journal* copy desk guy in New York inquires.

"Yep. Same time it was when you called last night," I reply wearily.

The nocturnal London scene happened repeatedly until the *Journal* transferred me to New York in 1990. I never again held an on-call role. Equally important, I refused to toil on Saturdays. I preserved my day of rest even after the *Journal* gave me a nifty email device known as a BlackBerry. My gadget remained turned off between Friday night and Sunday morning.

Most first-wave Power Moms I met could stop working once they returned home without fear of career repercussions. Regrettably, the opposite is true today. Technological advances have fostered an "always on" work culture. We're essentially tethered to our mobile devices 24/7. It's the downside of being able to work remotely at odd hours—an arrangement that gives employed mothers greater flexibility to sway.

"Always on" has become the default setting for most professionals because ubiquitous smartphones, slim computers, and innovative apps expand "the workday's boundaries until it seamlessly blurs with the rest of civilian life," wrote Matthew Kitchen, the *Journal's* Gear & Gadgets editor, in late 2018. More than four in ten U.S. adults check their work email every few hours outside of normal work hours, according to a 2019 survey of 1,002 individuals by Adobe Systems.

Young adults sense the greatest compulsion to do so, a different study showed. About 62 percent of 1,772 such people feel pressure to always be accessible via email, Slack, or other forms of work communication. Nearly the same proportion are pressured to work longer or overtime hours. The results come from a 2019 poll about workplace burnout by Yellowbrick, a mental health center in Evanston, Illinois, a suburb of Chicago.

That same year, the World Health Organization revamped its description of burnout, stating that the syndrome reduces professional efficacy. The agency blamed burnout on "chronic workplace stress that has not been successfully managed."

Other investigators link burnout to the constant checking of email, texts, and social media accounts. Northern Illinois University researchers coined the term "telepressure" to describe the urge to quickly answer emails, texts, and voice mails whether or not you're in the office.

Larissa K. Barber and Alecia M. Santuzzi, psychology faculty members at Northern Illinois University, published a study about telepressure in 2015. The results reflected data they had collected from 303 individuals about the frequency of their responses to email on weekdays, weekends, vacations, and sick days. Those with the most workplace telepressure were more likely to miss work for health reasons and experience poor sleep quality.

Managers and members of so-called greedy professions such as consulting, finance, and law face the greatest demands to serve their clients and colleagues day and night. But inescapable job demands especially penalize women with children.

Individuals working more than fifty hours a week earn about 4.5 percent more an hour than similarly qualified employees working thirty-five to forty-nine hours. This reverses the pay patterns seen before 2000, when long-hour workers made less money per hour, according to research led by Kim Weeden, a sociology professor at Cornell University.

A *Wall Street Journal* article describing her research blamed the pay gap reversal on employers that award the highest-paid positions to individuals capable of working continuously for long blocks of time. Mothers are less likely to toil fifty-plus hours a week. "This helps widen a gender gap in wages between working mothers and everyone else," the 2019 article pointed out.

Pillow Talk with Your Smartphone

Genevieve Aronson, an experienced public relations executive, knows all too well why you must be "always on" to succeed on the job these days. She's the North American vice president of communications at Nielsen Holdings, a TV ratings company. Her daughter, Luella, was born in 2012.

During much of her fifteen-year PR career, she was "always sleeping with my phone in my hand," the thirty-eight-year-old executive recalled during our chat at a Nielsen office in downtown Manhattan.

Being always on "is innately tied in with what I do," she added. "I am that point of contact for journalists who are on a deadline."

Sleeping with her smartphone took on higher importance for Aronson at her previous employer, a New York public relations agency. Her female boss frequently emailed her in the middle of the night, then made snide comments when she didn't reply right away.

Aronson began answering those nocturnal emails fast. The young woman's open-ended availability benefited her career. "You build up this reputation that 'she'll respond immediately. She has the answers. She's working all night long,'" Aronson remarked. She quit the PR agency to join Nielsen as a middle manager and was promoted to vice president about two years later. The job was her first executive role.

Aronson still keeps her phone turned on in her bedroom at night, even though her Nielsen boss never emails her in the wee hours. She currently goes one step further to stay connected: she deliberately awakens at 2:00 or 3:00 a.m. Tuesday through Thursday—mainly because she wants to get an uninterrupted head start on work. She inaugurated the schedule following her 2017 promotion to VP.

"I'm so ambitious," the Asian-American executive explained. "I want to try to get everything done, and the only way that I think that I can do it is to just squeeze out as much as I can out of the twenty-four hours."

On the day we talked, Aronson had arisen at 2:45 a.m.—less than three hours after she had finished caring for her sick daughter and fallen asleep in her suburban New York home. She had caught up on email and completed other job tasks until 5:00 a.m. without disturbing her sleeping child and husband.

She hoped to go to bed by 9:00 p.m. that night, she confided to me. Otherwise, she said half seriously, "I'm going to be like . . . Ms. Cranky Pants."

Always On While Out of Town

Many executive mothers never unplug during business trips because they want to stay in touch with their family, their job, or both. Vanessa Hallett is typical. She travels extensively for Phillips, the auction house where she runs the worldwide photographs collection.

While out of town, "I always have my phone on, since that is my connection to my husband and children," she said. "I may be physically far away, but I am very accessible at all times to keep their lives consistent."

For instance, Hallett makes sure that she's always available for anything that her family needs, whether scheduling playdates or ordering badly needed groceries. She uses online grocery delivery services such as FreshDirect.

During one business trip to Shanghai, her ringing smartphone unexpectedly woke her around 6:00 a.m. The doorman in her Manhattan apartment building was on the line. He announced that her FreshDirect groceries had arrived. Should the delivery messenger take the food items to her apartment?

"Yep, send them up," Hallett replied. She had ordered her family's groceries while in Shanghai because "I know exactly what everyone wants to eat."

It's also hard to break the bonds of being always on during work breaks. A serious client crisis forced Mary Baglivo, a boomer Power Mom, to toil a lot during her family's vacation on the small Caribbean island of Nevis.

The 2005 crisis erupted four months after the forty-seven-year-old had taken charge of the New York office of Saatchi & Saatchi, a global advertising agency that's owned by Publicis Groupe. On Valentine's Day that year, fourteen key staffers assigned to its General

Mills account quit Saatchi en masse. Baglivo flew to Minneapolis the next day to reassure General Mills officials at company headquarters.

The big producer of packaged foods represented the second largest account of Saatchi's New York office, generating nearly $30 million in revenue. Saatchi or a predecessor agency had handled its brands for eighty years. The departed employees soon joined a rival agency amid rumors that they hoped to poach the General Mills account.

Baglivo was still scrambling to retain that lucrative business plus hire replacement staff when she accompanied her husband and their two youngsters on their spring break trip to the Caribbean. In Nevis, "I'm on my phone all the time," she remembered. "The client needed to know that I was available constantly."

But the local cell service was so lousy that the advertising executive had to crawl under a Nevis restaurant table multiple times to get a connection. She was trying to reach Steve Sanger, the CEO of General Mills, and members of her Saatchi team. Even when she wasn't making business calls, the account crisis weighed heavily on her. She also agreed to cut short her holiday and fly back to the United States if the upheaval at Saatchi worsened.

Yet such extreme devotion to her job didn't faze her because she routinely worked during about 25 percent of her vacations. She retained the General Mills account and subsequently ran the Americas for Saatchi until she left the agency in 2013. She presently serves on the boards of three public companies.

Staying in frequent touch with the office when you're out of the office has become far more common today. Nearly six in ten employed U.S. professionals check in with their bosses or coworkers at least once a day during vacation, concluded a 2019 LinkedIn survey of more than one thousand people.

Some second-wave executive mothers stayed highly connected to their jobs during work breaks until they figured out a strategy to limit being always on. "We're all learning about what this new technology is doing and where the lines are," observed Julie Smolyansky, the CEO of Lifeway Foods, a maker of a cultured dairy product called kefir. "'Everything can wait' is what I've learned."

The swift-talking, highly driven boss took command of Lifeway in 2002 at age twenty-seven. At the time, she was the youngest female leader of a publicly held U.S. company. Her parents had launched the Chicago business after emigrating from the former Soviet Union when she was a baby.

Smolyansky choked up while recounting her mother's extremely long work hours. As a child, "I do remember missing her so much," the forty-three-year-old executive told me over breakfast at a Manhattan hotel. She and her domestic partner, an artist manager named Jason Burdeen, have daughters who were born in 2008 and 2010.

Smolyansky, a lifelong athlete, had completed thirteen marathons by the time we met. She enjoys working out, but she doesn't enjoy being cut off from Lifeway. "I've found myself walking for twelve miles while I do all my [work] conference calls," she said.

Her hands-on style also used to mean that Smolyansky pushed Lifeway employees whenever a crucial deadline loomed and never disconnected from her company when she took a vacation. An "aha" moment changed her style. During her 2015 summer vacation in Long Island's posh Southampton, she decided to attend a forty-five-minute weekday session at SoulCycle.

The popular fitness chain bans participants' phones from its exercise studios. "I was like 'How can I be forty-five minutes without my phone? I can't look at it for forty-five minutes?'" she recollected as she anxiously played with her long, dark hair. "I was very angry that I couldn't take my phone in."

Yet nothing important occurred at Lifeway while she worked out that summer day. Nor has she missed any important work calls during her frequent SoulCycle sessions since then. That's because she empowered her lieutenants to perform more tasks independently and to own some decisions. "I'm not there to micromanage the minutiae of everything," she pointed out. "The things that I used to do were silly."

Kids Versus Multitasking Moms

Technology not only lets you multitask, it "demands that you do those things," suggested Shelley J. Correll, the gender researcher. You're supposed to be always on for work—and always there for your kids. "That's where the guilt comes from," she continued.

Some children of the current cohort of Power Moms resent seeing them almost always powered on. That happened to Meaghan Schmidt, the AlixPartners managing director. Her elder son, Ryan, was six years old when he began begging his mother to shut down her iPhone during work conference calls within his earshot at home. He disliked her taking time away from him.

As a result, Schmidt said, "I have made a more mindful effort, particularly now that I've had my third kid, to be more present while I'm home." She and her husband, Andrew, a financial executive at a real estate asset management firm, negotiated an unusual pact: when they're home on weekends, they check their smartphones only from behind a closed door.

The couple hides the devices in the walk-in kitchen pantry of their suburban New Jersey residence. Concealing job distractions from their offspring makes Schmidt feel better about herself.

But how does hiding in the pantry solve the persistent problem that you're always on for work? I asked her. After all, I said, you're not going to want to tear yourself away from the kids in order to heed AlixPartners demands that arise during your gadget checks.

Schmidt agreed that the odd arrangement doesn't solve everything. After all, she usually sneaks inside to pore over office email at least ten times on Saturdays and at least ten times again on Sundays. Her email messages sometimes require her to make work calls right away.

The AlixPartners executive and her husband are sticking with the weekend pantry caper until their children figure out why they disappear so suddenly. "The water cooler happens to be located in there," Schmidt explained. Walking out with a cup of water in her hand maintains the secret work hideaway—and the fiction that she isn't working.

Meanwhile, Schmidt keeps her iPhone on all night beside her bed because foreign clients of the global consultancy sometimes summon her help before dawn. Improved technology "is a double-edged sword," she pointed out. "It's easier for you. But at the same time, there's no excuse not to answer your phone."

Genevieve Aronson, the Nielsen leader, modified her always-on habits following a rebuke from her four-year-old daughter a few years ago. She was using her phone to answer work email one weekend as Luella sat nearby in their living room, quietly playing with a dollhouse.

"Mommy, you pay attention to your phone just as much as me," the youngster fretted. Luella's surprise comment filled Aronson with sadness and guilt. "I need to change," she scolded herself. She stopped keeping her phone within reach when she and her daughter interact at home. Thanks to those efforts, she said, Luella no longer feels "like she's splitting time with my phone."

Yet she never completely divorces herself from being always

reachable for Nielsen. She announces to Luella, "Oh, I have to go to the bathroom," then checks work email while seated on the toilet.

Certain first-wave Power Moms grappled with the same issue of jealous progeny long before smartphones arrived. Consider Diane M. Bryant, the former Intel executive. She was a rising star at the semiconductor company, accepting bigger and bigger jobs throughout the childhoods of her daughter, Annika, and her adopted son, Vitaly.

Upon her return from Intel each evening, she kept worrying about critical work projects and colleagues' requests. "Even when you're home, you're not home," she remembered, reliving the scene in the present tense. "I'm still stressed. I'm still thinking about work. I'm still thinking about that meeting tomorrow morning, that presentation at noon. And that stress fills the air [at home]."

Her mother's decision to be so mentally focused on work after coming home distressed Annika. "You're physically sitting there and my daughter's trying to talk to me and tell me about her hardships at school," she went on. "[But] I'm drifting."

Annika viewed such distracted behavior as "a direct insult that she's not important," Bryant said. "She'd just get very angry at me and scream, 'You're not listening to me!'" before storming down the hall and slamming her bedroom door.

Bryant regrets that she was always on inside her head after she came home from Intel. "It's heartbreaking," she admitted. "If I could go back and change one thing, I would ensure that when I was present, I was present."

She spent the last five of her thirty-two years at Intel running a business group whose revenue reached $19 billion during 2017. She next became the chief operating officer of Google Cloud, a division of Alphabet. In early 2020, she was hired as chairman and chief executive officer of NovaSignal. The medical robotics company, which

Bryant expected would go public soon, already had U.S. government approval for a device that enables paramedics in the field to diagnose severe strokes.

Turning Off the Always-On Switch

More sweeping steps by businesses and individuals could free today's working parents from being glued to their smartphones nonstop. Countless employers inadvertently create an environment in which everyone feels compelled to stay constantly connected—such as by routinely dispatching email after hours.

But Boston Consulting Group proved that a company can overturn its ingrained culture of being always on. Leslie Perlow, a leadership professor at Harvard Business School, helped the global management consultancy reconsider how its teams of consultants work by making time off predictable and required. Starting in 2007, she spent a year studying BCG and realized that nearly all of its consulting teams seemed mired in the 24/7 mystique.

Debbie Lovich, a BCG senior partner, knew that mystique all too well. At the time, the mother of four kids under twelve years of age typically worked more than sixty hours a week. "I had zero control over my life," she said. "I was burning it at both ends." Fellow overachievers at BCG felt overburdened by work, too.

One new consultant on Lovich's team told her that he kept his BlackBerry under his pillow so he wouldn't miss late-night emails from the leader of his prior BCG team. Yet "no one told this guy to sleep with his BlackBerry," Lovich observed. She assured him that she would not email him in the middle of the night.

Perlow designed an experimental alternative for BCG consultants: participants had to take one scheduled night off every week after 6:00 p.m. and not check or answer their email or other messages. The idea was "to explore whether ambitious management consultants could disconnect from work—and reconnect with their personal lives," she wrote in *Sleeping With Your Smartphone: How to Break the 24/7 Habit and Change the Way You Work.* Her 2012 book chronicled the BCG odyssey.

Perlow's pioneering approach improved BCG's staff satisfaction, efficiency, and business results. "The cycle of 24/7 responsiveness can be broken if people collectively challenge the mind-set," she wrote in a 2009 *Harvard Business Review* article about the initial results of the BCG experiment.

The company finished rolling out its initiative to every office worldwide by 2014. BCG operates in more than fifty countries. Today, the highly structured effort includes a collectively agreed time-off goal for each team member.

"This program is all about better work and better life outside work," Lovich told me. "It's not like we've turned into a nine-to-five culture." She went on, "We do intense work. We also know that people need to . . . have time with their families."

The upshot? "Our new norm is sometimes always on—when required," she added.

A few other U.S. businesses also have acted to reduce work creep outside their regular hours. Bandwidth, a telecom company, prohibits staffers from dealing with work during their vacations. The blackout policy even covers its CEO, the *Wall Street Journal* reported in 2019.

Stefanie Strack, the youthful entrepreneur who briefly led Rag & Bone, the sportswear manufacturer, epitomizes how extensive reordering of individual priorities can also have a broad workplace impact. A leader's decision "to manage your always-on behavior is going to set the tone for your whole division," she noted.

Strack was a hardworking middle manager for Nike when she became pregnant with her first child. "I'd get home. I'd get something to eat. I'd turn the computer right back on and then just keep working," she recollected. "There wasn't a lot of separation [from Nike]."

But once Siena arrived in 2013, Strack stopped taking work home or sending weekend emails to colleagues because she wanted to devote a lot of attention to her daughter. If Nike associates reached out to her at home, Strack started pausing before she reacted.

"Do I really need to respond tonight? Or could this wait until the morning?" she asked herself. The disciplined reversal of her always-on mind-set "was one of the best things I did."

Strack bolstered her retreat from being always available for Nike following the 2015 birth of her son, Parker. She bought a second smartphone, inspired by the example set by many fellow executives older than her. Several also had kids. Those Nike leaders' experience helped her realize "that work is one facet of my life."

Strack left her work device at home during weekend outings with the kids or dates with her husband. Disconnecting completely from Nike freed her to focus more on her family. The extra separation between work and home "has just been a game changer for me," she commented. "I just wish I'd done it earlier."

Improved technology paradoxically liberates and limits second-wave women to a far greater degree than their predecessors could have ever imagined. Their freedom to toil remotely anytime is offset by an always-on culture that tethers younger executives to their jobs 24/7. Luckily, they often work for businesses with numerous other females in upper management who could join forces to curb work creep after hours.

Building a strong work team can further relieve the pressure to be always on. "Focus on the people you surround yourself with,"

Strack suggested. "Don't be afraid to hire people who are smarter than you." Otherwise, she continued, "you won't have the time and space for your partner [and] kids."

Parents with every type of job face the challenge of making work decisions that make sense for their family. Managing the challenge wisely is all that matters. What if you prefer to integrate your children's lives more fully into your work life? In the next chapter, you'll learn how both generations of Power Moms grappled with this issue. Several arranged their work habits in smart ways that profoundly affected their families and their careers.

6

Making Room for Careers and Kids

I was working hard at the office and home before I delivered my second child in January 1983. Too hard.

Keen to spend extra time with my family, I sought a four-day schedule following my maternity leave from the Washington bureau of the *Wall Street Journal*. A reduced workweek is highly unusual, I noted in my proposal. But by satisfying an important personal need, the arrangement "would permit me to channel even higher energy levels into my *Journal* assignments."

Management rejected my request. Luckily, I finally got my wish in fall 1983, after Norm Pearlstine became the *Journal*'s managing editor and Al Hunt its Washington bureau chief. Both bosses greatly valued working women. Hunt and his wife, Judy Woodruff, a White House correspondent for NBC News, had a toddler son.

Pearlstine gave me Fridays off without cutting my pay or benefits because I was one of the *Journal*'s most seasoned female reporters. He also said I could work normal hours for the rest of the week and keep covering my beat, which was organized labor. Pearlstine and Hunt believed I would be just as productive on a four-day schedule.

"An incredible deal," I exulted in my diary that day. Abra was eight months old, and Dan had recently turned four. My Fridays at home turned into such a precious time for our kids and me that Abra nicknamed them "Mommy Day."

But I chose to conceal my incredible deal from my Washington coworkers. Like many baby boom–generation moms, I kept quiet to protect my reputation for being laser focused on my career. The other employees in the *Journal* bureau remained clueless about my special arrangement until a local journalism review broke the news a few years later with an article about me and other star journalists.

The revelation of my four-day week bothered some men in the bureau. "If I get pregnant, can I take Fridays off, too?" one male reporter needled me.

The best work arrangements enable mothers to simultaneously accelerate their careers and build deeper ties with their children. There is no universal solution, however. Amid the gradual ascension of businesswomen into upper management, each generation of Power Moms featured in this book tackled this dilemma differently.

Baby-boomer women I interviewed yearned to be considered one of the guys, rather than risk being pigeonholed as an employed parent with divided loyalties. "You couldn't embrace the fact you were a mom publicly in the workplace," observed Meredith Bodgas, the editor of *Working Mother* magazine. You could get mommy tracked, "taking you out of the running for plum assignments and promotions because of a perceived desire to put your children first."

Challis Lowe encountered that misogynistic realm decades ago. We first met in 1977, when I profiled her for the *Journal*'s front page because Lowe was the first black female officer at Continental Bank in Chicago. The thirty-one-year-old middle manager had entered the business arena after two years as an elementary school substitute teacher.

Lowe, a mother of two, ran into extensive sexism in the business world. She never put up photos of her young daughters at her

Continental office because male colleagues thought that "a woman with small children should be at home with those children," she remembered years later. In turn, she wanted the leaders of the bank to see her as lacking "any encumbrances that would keep me from doing my job as well as my male peers."

For the same reason, she never took her girls to her office or Continental family events during the initial phase of her management career. She was the mom they rarely saw, rather than the mom with an important job.

Lowe now regrets that she excluded her youngsters from her work life. "They lost connecting to that . . . big part of me," the soft-spoken executive told me in a wistful voice. "There was a big disconnect for them."

Her daughter agreed. "I didn't really know what she was doing [for Continental]," recalled Candice Lowe-Swift, an associate professor of anthropology at Vassar College. Lowe ultimately became the highest human resources officer for three big businesses: Beneficial Corporation, Ryder System, and Dollar General Corporation.

By contrast, most current executive mothers view parenthood as an integral piece of their professional lives because they feel confident about the combination's chances of success. It's a key way those women practice work/life sway and why they pursue alternative work habits. "Things have changed for the better because the prior generation of women bravely fought against that negative perception of working mothers," Bodgas pointed out.

The day we chatted, the magazine editor was sitting in an open office in midtown Manhattan surrounded by staffers from *Field & Stream*, *Popular Science*, and other periodicals owned by Bonnier Corporation, the publisher of *Working Mother*. A photo of her two young sons hugging each other appears every time that she opens the home page on her laptop. Their joyful image proudly signals that "they are part of the workplace," Bodgas said. "Working mothers today are proud to have their kids' photos on their desks."

Younger Power Moms also tend to win support for their parenting commitment from highly empathetic associates. Not so for Marissa Mayer, however. In 2012, the brand-new CEO of Yahoo! ignited an outcry after she transformed an empty alcove next to her office into a nursery for her newborn son, Macallister. The thirty-seven-year-old leader paid to soundproof the roughly eighty-square-foot space at the company's headquarters in Sunnyvale, California.

Mayer's private nursery sparked discontent within the foundering internet icon because it was unique. Other employees couldn't bring their infants and caregivers to work. Yahoo! was struggling with high staff turnover and declines in ad revenue.

Board members had selected the longtime Google executive to run Yahoo! shortly ahead of her fall due date. Mayer was known for having helped design the highly popular search engine at Google, where she would have taken off six months for her well-paid maternity leave. At Yahoo!, she resumed command within two weeks of Macallister's arrival—a decision that also stirred criticism of the new CEO.

"Yahoo! was a sinking ship. I had to pull this thing off the bottom of the ocean," Mayer recalled during our chat at Lumi Labs, a tech start-up in Palo Alto, California. She cofounded the enterprise after her 2017 departure from Yahoo! "There was no way that Yahoo! could have let me take the [CEO] job, work for eight weeks, and then be gone for six months."

The executive spoke in a raspy, rapid-fire voice as she hunched over her desk to nibble from a bowlful of blueberries. She occupied a small Lumi Labs office on the other side of the wall from where she sat when she became Google employee number twenty at that start-up in 1999.

Before giving birth, Mayer informed her fellow Yahoo! directors that she would bring her firstborn plus a nanny to headquarters until the baby turned six months old. "'Look, I'm going to invert my maternity leave,'" she told the board.

"I was sad to miss out on the more classic maternity leave," Mayer explained to me. "But it was wonderful to have my son there," she went on. "I was able to see him throughout the day."

Mayer still resents being criticized for taking Macallister to Yahoo!, especially since she drafted plans to expand workers' parental leave before she set up her office nursery. She unveiled the improved paid benefit—sixteen weeks for mothers and eight weeks for fathers—once her inverted maternity leave ended in spring 2013.

The Yahoo! chief came under fire again for staying home less than a month following her second pregnancy. Her twin girls, born in December 2015, spent the full workweek at their mother's office for four months.

"There's just entirely too much judgment . . . about how quickly you go back to work or whether you go back to work at all—[and] how you do your leave," she complained bitterly. She ardently believes that every working woman should deal with the incredibly personal experience of motherhood in whatever way works best for her. But her earnest sentiments might sound tone deaf to less affluent working women who aren't privileged enough to make parenthood work perfectly.

Win-Win Frameworks

Employed mothers enjoy treasured moments with their kids if they feel free to leave work and attend their school band recitals or Little

League games. Yet midday office escapes often proved difficult for first-wave Power Moms. They often toiled in testosterone-rich environments with few female bosses to emulate.

That's what Lynn Gray experienced during the 1990s while an executive of Lehman Brothers Holdings, the big investment bank. She had grown up playing field hockey, basketball, softball, and tennis. The former student athlete was thrilled when her daughter, Emily, turned into a great volleyball player during middle school. Gray desperately wanted to watch her only child play.

But Lehman men and women played by different rules. When a guy on its trading floor alerted his male coworkers that he was leaving to watch his kid's soccer game, the men replied, "'Attaboy! You are a great dad!'" Gray recollected. "If I told my cronies that I was going to see Emily play volleyball, they would say, 'God, she's not serious about her job.'"

Gray solved the problem through deception. "I would say, 'I've got to go to the doctor. I'll be back tomorrow.'" She gave the same false excuse every time she walked out of Lehman to attend all ten of Emily's seventh-grade games. The man she worked for and the men she worked with suspected that she suffered from a serious illness.

In hindsight, other boomer executives wish they hadn't internalized their era's pervasive attitudes about acceptable work habits for moms. Consider Michele Buck, the CEO of the Hershey Company. The candy maker's famous brands include Reese's peanut butter cups and chocolate Kisses.

Buck comes from a modest background. Her mother was raised on a farm without indoor plumbing. Her father was the first member of his family to finish high school. As an adult, he completed a master's degree at night.

"Growing up in that environment shaped my work ethic," Buck said. For her first job at age ten, she delivered newspapers. She excelled during her protracted management career in the food industry, achieving her first executive position at age thirty-six.

Buck was a relatively new senior vice president at Hershey and nearly forty-five years old when she bore her third child in 2006. Eleven years later, she took the helm of Hershey. She occupies a large corner office within its original factory building in bucolic Hershey, Pennsylvania. A faint aroma of chocolate fills the air.

Buck keeps photos of her son and two daughters on her desk shelf and nearby bookcase. They ranged in age from twelve to twenty on the spring afternoon we munched on Caesar salads. During their early childhoods, Buck figured she could make only limited trade-offs between her job and her youngsters' school activities before work associates would conclude that she was too focused on the mom side of her life.

Such self-imposed restrictions ultimately distressed her. You feel as though "you can't do what's important in your kids' lives," she said, raising her hands for emphasis.

Looking back, "I could have given myself a lot more flexibility to leave [the office], to do things that were important . . . like the kids' Halloween parade at the preschool," Buck noted. "You just draw the line on certain things that you probably didn't have to."

GenX executive mothers are more likely to demand such flexibility because their ranks have grown and they can draw inspiration from pacesetters such as Laurie Ann Goldman, another boomer Power Mom. Goldman decided to deliberately stop drawing such artificial lines. Her management roles at the Coca-Cola Company while raising kids persuaded her to pursue formal protection for their needs from her next employer.

"I want to put it [out] to the universe that I want a leadership job *and* the ability to have a family," she told herself during a stroll in the park with her infant third son after she left her Coca-Cola global licensing position in 2000. She subsequently obtained the highest job at Spanx, a producer of women's apparel that's best known for its lower-body shaper. Goldman was the fifth employee of the Atlanta start-up, which its founder, Sara Blakely, housed in a rented bungalow.

The new Spanx CEO negotiated an employment contract that recognized the importance of her three boys under eight years old. "The Company acknowledges that you have obligations to your family and community that will cause you at times to be away from the office during normal working hours," her contract stated.

She insisted on the written pledge because "this was my core value and . . . how I wanted to live my life," the fifty-six-year-old executive said during our interview. That contractual provision "would give me permission to do what I needed to do."

Indeed, she went on, she gave herself permission to do what her sons needed because she had psychologically freed herself from working-mother guilt. She was determined to focus equally hard on growing Spanx. "And if I do that," she recalled musing, "nobody cares how much time I spend at [the boys'] sporting events."

Spanx boomed during Goldman's twelve-year tenure. The tiny firm grew into a global enterprise and reached an estimated market value of $1 billion by fall 2013. She quit in early 2014.

Her next CEO stint didn't last very long. Goldman was in charge of New Avon for only eight months. The North American cosmetics business had previously split from Avon Products. She exited in August 2019 amid New Avon's pending sale to LG Household & Health Care, a Korean consumer goods company. "I would definitely want to be a third-time CEO," Goldman said afterward. "I'm well suited to the role and not looking to slow down."

Some second-wave executive moms such as Melanie Steinbach design a broader formal framework for their child-focused work habits. While chief talent officer of McDonald's, she wrote a user manual about herself. She said she hoped the manual would educate the fifty-seven members of her worldwide team about what it takes to work for her—such as by spelling out her high priorities for her two daughters.

"My family is really important to me," she declared in the first of her manual's seven chapters. "I love my work, but I love my family more. This shows up in many ways. I try hard to respond to my family when they need me during the day."

In her user manual, the McDonald's officer also assured her lieutenants that they won't ever have to justify leaving work early for a family event. "I am very understanding about family commitments," she wrote. She handed out her guidebook to every team newcomer and encouraged her team members to prepare their own manuals. In a sense, the user manual represents the workplace equivalent of my marriage contract. Both describe preferred behavior and norms for key interactions.

Career Gains with Reduced Hours

My reduced hours at the *Journal* didn't reduce my output. The quality and quantity of my Washington stories stayed excellent, according to my supervisor. I stopped working a four-day week once the *Journal* elevated me to news editor of its London bureau in 1987.

But Abra was unhappy that I no longer stayed home every Friday. "What happened to the Mommy Days that were school days?" she implored, tugging at my heartstrings.

Like me, several other boomer Power Moms initially found themselves rebuffed over their efforts to work less and parent more. They're exemplified by Nina McIntyre, who is chief marketing officer of ETQ, a software technology company. The tech industry veteran delivered her eldest daughter in 1988, when she was a senior product manager for a division of Eastman Kodak Company. Kodak had introduced photography to the masses at the dawn of the twentieth century.

McIntyre asked for a four-day schedule once her three-month maternity leave ended. "A weekday at home was really precious and worth finding a way to make happen," she said. The new mom figured that her boss, the unit's new vice president of marketing, would let her take Fridays off because she was a working mother, too.

McIntyre figured wrong. The older woman reacted to the four-day proposal by describing how she had worked and attended Harvard Business School full-time after giving birth years earlier.

"She then smiled and said, 'No, you may not go part-time,'" according to McIntyre. "She just didn't believe in part-time . . . because she didn't need it. So why would anyone else?"

The first-time mother resigned weeks later, wooed away by a part-time arrangement at Lotus Development Corporation, a software maker. Her hiring manager was a former Kodak colleague who matched her full-time pay of about $40,000 for a three-day schedule at Lotus.

McIntyre expected that her career advancement would pause while she worked fewer hours. Instead, her work received recognition. Her outstanding performance during three years of shortened schedules opened doors to higher-level spots with regular hours.

She was the full-time supervisor of seventeen staffers when her younger daughter arrived in 1994. Upon McIntyre's return from that maternity leave, Lotus elevated her to general manager. She assumed command of a software development team for the first time, overseeing eighty-three people.

"I was surprised to be given such a big job," she remarked. Other employers noticed her progress. Invention Machine Corporation, a small software provider, recruited her to be its chief operating officer in 1997. She helped the business raise $10 million before moving on. She held marketing management posts at seven more companies—interspersed with part-time consulting gigs—before ETQ hired her in 2018.

"Very few of the companies I have worked in over the last twenty years make it easy for managers to work part-time," she said. Nevertheless, she advises younger women to imitate her example of intermittent part-time employment. After all, she continued, "you don't always have to be on this full-time, intense trajectory."

Work from Home Takes Work

The spread of telecommuting illustrates the dramatic transformation of work habits between the prior and present generations of Power Moms. Businesses eager to attract top talent increasingly tout the perk, aided by better tools for completing job tasks anywhere.

About 4.7 million employees work from home at least half the time, concluded a 2019 analysis of recent U.S. government data by Workplace Analytics, a research-based consultancy. Regular work at home "has grown by 159 percent since 2005, more than eleven times faster than the rest of the workforce," the report stated. (Its figures exclude the self-employed.)

An even more significant finding emerged from a different 2019 study about telecommuters and other individuals toiling outside conventional office space. Senior leaders accounted for the highest proportion of full-time remote employees among 1,202 people canvassed by Owl Labs, a provider of immersive videoconferencing technology. As the coronavirus spread in early 2020, U.S. employers asked many staffers to work from home for an extended period.

Sheltering in place shuttered schools and child care facilities across the land, turning parents into ersatz teachers. The timing proved terrible for Stefanie Strack, the former Rag & Bone and Nike executive. She had been spending weekdays at a coworking space as she prepared to formally launch VIS Holdings, her start-up for female athletes.

Strack moved her fledgling enterprise to her Brooklyn apartment so that she and Alan, the owner of a film art start-up, could jointly educate and care for their housebound youngsters. "Our lives got completely thrown up in the air," she recalled. "We [were] not going to be able to work on our businesses very much."

Strack and her husband alternated three-hour stints helping Siena, a first grader, and Parker, a pre-K student, with schoolwork. The couple gave up after eight weeks. They temporarily relocated to her hometown of Anchorage, Alaska, where her parents still live. Her kids would stay with them a few days a week throughout the summer, freeing her and Alan to work for their firms fifteen hours a day, Strack said.

The giant telecommuting experiment might outlast the pandemic and trigger a tectonic cultural shift in gender role expectations, experts predict. Many businesses adopted work-from-home options on a large scale for the first time, four academic economists noted in an April 2020 analysis of the pandemic's impact on gender equality and remarked, "It is likely that some of these changes [will] persist, leading to more workplace flexibility in the future."

Employed mothers in these households will also benefit as fathers shoulder additional responsibilities for home-schooling and child care, the analysis went on. "While women carry a higher burden during the crisis, it is still highly likely that we will observe a sizable [positive] impact of this forced experiment on social norms, and ultimately on gender equality." The nonprofit National Bureau of Economic Research published the paper.

Other second-wave executives such as Alison Rand were already performing high-powered jobs from home because nearly everyone at their employer also works remotely. When we spoke, the mother of two daughters was leading design operations for a high-tech company from her Brooklyn residence. Rand's next business meeting that day would occur at a coworking space. Her scruffy, faded jeans and long, wavy hair made her look younger than her forty-four years.

Rand was then a first-time executive at Automattic, the owner of a popular publishing platform sold by WordPress.com that powers many websites. Automattic has always been almost entirely remote, with 1,148 staffers spread across seventy-two countries by 2019. She oversaw about sixty employees in the company's far-flung design organization.

Rand, who began her career as a web developer for IBM, joined Automattic in March 2018. Her elder daughter, Luna, was nearly sixteen, and Ever was not yet three years old. She eagerly anticipated spending more time with her family by working full-time from home. With Ever in particular, she added, "I wanted to really . . . be as present as possible."

Rand partly fulfilled her goal by picking up Ever from school once a week. "We go to the park. We go get ice cream. We get slices of pizza," she said. "She just loves that I'm there at 3:30. It makes her happy."

On the other hand, the downsides of living and working in the same space made Rand unhappy. The boundary lines between her home and job blurred. And, she noted, "I do the lion's share of just managing the house." She's married to Scott Schneider, a public relations agency executive with a long work commute—the burdensome slog that Rand previously had.

"Now if the heat's not working or a wire's not working or we need this or that [fixed], I'm home," she said. The arrival of the plumber or the cable repair guy disrupted Rand's workday. She finally stopped scheduling home repair appointments between 9:00 a.m. and 6:00 p.m. on weekdays.

Her husband also suggested that she schedule those visits before or after her nine-hour work window. "We are trying to draw some very hard and fast lines," she explained. "Working from home for a company that's almost entirely remote has been an adjustment."

In August 2019, Rand became a senior director of InVision, a high-tech company whose eight hundred–plus staffers toil remotely. Working from home finally works really well for her because she has overcome the growing pains. "I don't have to spend a lot of time commuting and can easily access all of the facets of my career from my home office," she said.

An interruptive toddler soured Sarah Hofstetter, another contemporary Power Mom, on telecommuting, however. She had a five-year-old daughter named Abigail and a three-year-old son named Sam in 2004, when she launched a marketing communications business from their suburban Long Island home. She chose entrepreneurship after six frustrating years at net2phone, a major player in the internet phone market.

"It was a male-dominated organization, heavily chauvinistic," she said. "I had reached the glass ceiling there probably a few years prior. I was killing myself, and I wasn't enjoying it."

She ran her home-based enterprise from an office on its second floor. But "I took on more clients than I had hours in a day," she told me, fiddling nervously with a long silver necklace that nearly reached her waist. "I was exhausted."

Her toddler son sometimes sneaked upstairs without his babysitter noticing. He did so one day while Hofstetter was on the phone with an important client. He banged hard on her locked office door. "You don't love me!" he screamed at his mother inside. Hofstetter muted her end of the business call. Her son kept repeating his loud accusation.

"Sam, shut the hell up!" Hofstetter thought to herself. Then she started to cry. "I didn't have any food to just shove in his mouth and make him quiet," and you can't reason with a three-year-old, she told me. "There was nothing I could do."

Except find different office space—fast. Very soon after Sam's tirade, "I called one of my clients, and I said, 'Can I use one of your desks? Because I need the physical separation.'" Looking back, she noted, "working from home was not good for me at all."

Hofstetter abandoned entrepreneurship after sixteen months. She joined 360i, a digital ad and media agency, where she created and built its social media practice. The agency promoted her to CEO in 2013. She was still the chairwoman of 360i when Comscore, a troubled media measurement company, chose her as its president in fall 2018. We chatted weeks later in a windowless conference room in Comscore's Manhattan office.

Certain companies now seek to keep their rising stars by installing them in remote offices near their homes. This family-friendly arrangement has retained Morgan Dewan. The ambitious young woman joined the Turner Sports unit of Time Warner as its director of social media in 2013 and worked at the unit's Atlanta headquarters.

Dewan requested a remote setup in 2015 because she was moving to Denver, where her husband would commence a postresidency surgical fellowship. The couple didn't have any offspring yet.

"I know this is unconventional [for Turner], but I love my job . . .

I would really like to stay," she recalled telling her boss. Turner granted Dewan's request and arranged office space a mile from her Denver house. She said she had toiled hard, traveling a lot and staying available for her associates at all hours. She hoped to disprove a high-level colleague who had warned her, "You'll never get promoted remotely."

She did disprove that downbeat prediction. Turner elevated thirty-two-year-old Dewan to a vice presidency in spring 2016, six months before she delivered her elder son, Luke. For several weeks following her maternity leave, she drove home from her remote office once or twice a day in order to breastfeed her baby.

Dewan again relocated in 2018, when her husband joined his father's medical practice in Austin, Texas. Turner again rented a remote office for Dewan not far from her home. In her opinion, driving a short distance is a better way to start your workday than "taking an office call while you're doing a load of whites [at home]."

Yet the Turner business card Dewan handed me lists Atlanta as her work address. "Listing a 'remote' address could signal to new connections that my work is somehow devalued because I work remotely," she said. "That plays into the insecurity I have about being one of [Turner's] few remote employees." AT&T is the latest owner of Time Warner.

Junior on the Job

Marissa Mayer isn't the only mother taking her new baby to the office these days. More than two hundred U.S. employers in thirty different industries operate babies-at-work programs, estimated Carla Moquin, the president of the Parenting in the Workplace Institute. The nonprofit advocacy and resource group has kept track of this practice since 2005. "The concept has really taken off in recent years," she said.

Most employers with babies-at-work programs are small businesses, government agencies, and nonprofit organizations. They generally let new moms or dads bring their newborns to work for up to six months. Participating parents save thousands of dollars that they would have spent on infant child care, Moquin observed. Borshoff, a small advertising and PR agency in Indianapolis, inaugurated its program in 2000.

The woman-owned company had seen thirteen mothers bring eighteen infants to work as of fall 2019. But "we still can't get that [new] dad to bring the baby in," reported Karen Alter, the head of Borshoff.

Participants accept a modest pay cut, reflecting the time they spend with their infant at the agency. Borshoff provides a private office if a new parent normally works in an open area. Babies "graduate" when they reach six months of age.

The program has boosted employee retention, morale, and creative playfulness throughout the forty-five-person agency. "Our bring-your-baby-to-work program does wonders for the parent. It also does wonders for everybody else," observed Jennifer Berry, a Borshoff partner since 2015.

Recruited as a graphic designer in 1999, she was its first staffer to bring a newborn to the office. She won two promotions before her son turned one in February 2001. Her daughter, born later that year, also accompanied her to Borshoff. Berry moved up to senior art director in 2002. "My productivity skyrocketed when both of my kids were here," she said.

Some younger executive mothers grappled with more complicated challenges than Mayer or Berry in bringing their new baby to work. That was true for Katia Beauchamp. The leader of Birchbox gave birth to her fourth child in September 2018. She returned to the online beauty business ten weeks later, accompanied by newborn West. The company cofounder initially enjoyed taking her tiny daughter to its Manhattan headquarters, where Beauchamp sits at a tiny desk in a large, open room.

"She peeps and then I nurse her, and she's asleep again," she told me, recalling the scene in the present tense. "She's just a very chill baby."

However, West soon contracted a life-threatening respiratory virus that often afflicts newborns. Beauchamp rushed her to a hospital by ambulance. The infant remained hospitalized during the same December week that the CEO launched a partnership between Birchbox and Walgreens Boots Alliance. The drugstore chain began selling Birchbox products at six stores in several major cities and expanded to eleven during the summer of 2019.

"Going back and forth between the hospital and my big kids and work was extremely stressful," Beauchamp said. "It was the craziest week." Once West recovered, the traumatized new mom no longer took her to Birchbox every day.

Up, Up, and Away with Kids

Inhi Cho Suh, the youthful IBM executive, devised a junior-on-the-job tactic that cured her business-travel blues. Her sons, Jacob, born in 2007, and Noah, born in 2011, accompany her on 25 percent of her frequent work trips. She takes along at least one of her parents, who are retired small-business owners, to supervise them. She scrutinizes the boys' school calendar a year in advance and books their travel with her during scheduled school breaks.

"I'm on the road at least five months [a year]," she explained. "If they do four to six trips a year, I get a month back with them of time," she went on. "It gives us as a family a different way of living [because] I'm actually away from them no more than three to four months of the year."

Suh cooked up the idea in January 2010 following her return from a nine-day IBM journey to three Asian cities. It was her longest separation ever from seventeen-month-old Jacob. As she walked into their home in Spartanburg, South Carolina, the toddler greeted her with a huge grin—and then ran away before she could hug him. "He was mad I was gone so long," she recollected.

"That was the 'aha' moment," she said. She realized that she didn't have to choose between her career and her personal life. She could practice work/life sway by having Jacob join her on a significant portion of work trips.

A handful of U.S. companies recently began to subsidize child-focused business travel by paying for staffers to take their babies and nannies along during an infant's first year. Among them is Kohlberg Kravis Roberts & Co., a private equity firm where extensive travel and long hours are the norm.

I doubt that flying nannies will ever become the norm. But I anticipate the spread of less sweeping steps, such as the approach taken by first-wave Power Moms like Lynn Gray to involve their offspring in their work world. She was an executive at La Salle Partners, a real estate advisory and property management company, during a portion of her daughter's childhood. Her marriage ended when Emily was seven.

As a result, she sometimes took the school-age youngster to her evening negotiations over real estate deals at a major Manhattan law firm. One such lengthy session involved the possible relocation of the New York commodities exchanges to New Jersey. The talks dragged on for hours that night in 1990.

Yet rather than leave eight-year-old Emily and her Game Boy videogame console outside the meeting room, Gray sat her down at a round conference table alongside the male partners of the law firm. "They just were amazed at how well behaved she was," Gray recalled. "I said, 'She's used to being in law firms. She's been doing this for years.'"

More important, Emily got a close-up look at how her executive mother excelled on the job. Such sessions left a strong impression on the growing girl. "The amount of confidence she had as a Power Mom . . . was incredibly impressive," Emily told me. "I never saw her doubt herself at work."

Emily now works alongside a lot of guys at a veterans' service organization, where she isn't afraid to speak her mind—even though her male colleagues don't always agree with her. "The reason I can do that is because of her," Emily pointed out, alluding to her mother.

Despite their best efforts, many first-wave Power Moms found it difficult to devise family-friendly work habits because their bosses often weren't sympathetic about the need to balance work and children. More executive mothers today carry out strong game plans for blending career and family needs. Their solutions include more flexible workweeks, telecommuting, workplace user manuals that acknowledge the importance of parenting, and taking a child along for occasional business meetings or trips. As a result, prior stereotypes about employed parents are starting to fade.

Another unexpected dividend: tighter ties between Power Moms and their daughters, who often view their mothers as influential role models and valuable career coaches. These connections haven't always worked out as well as the executives had hoped, though. I'll share some of their mixed experiences in the coming chapter.

7

My Mother, My Coach

One spring evening, our daughter joins my husband and me for dinner at a noisy Lebanese restaurant in Washington, DC. She excitedly describes her expected offer for a new job at a state government agency out of town.

"Make sure to push for a bigger salary than they want to pay," I suggest to Abra. "If you don't ask, you don't get."

I smugly believe that I know what I'm talking about. After all, I'm the career columnist for the *Wall Street Journal*, where I've worked for decades. I have provided countless uncommon solutions for common career dilemmas since I inaugurated my *Journal* column in 1993.

Yet my sage advice fails to impress Abra, a thirty-five-year-old organizational consultant. "Mom, how many job offers have you negotiated in the past ten years?" she replies with far greater sagacity. She has held more jobs than I ever will. And she helps design multimillion-dollar projects for consulting clients of her current employer.

"You're the expert," I concede grudgingly. Leaning over, I give her a big hug.

Working mothers want all of their children to lead happy and fulfilled lives. Nevertheless, they often exert extra effort so their daughters will ably navigate the male-dominated world of work. Second-wave feminists during the late twentieth century inspired mothers "to not only rethink their own position in society but also prepare their daughters to be new sorts of women," Amy Westervelt noted in her book *Forget "Having It All": How America Messed Up Motherhood—and How to Fix It.*

That's why many first-generation Power Moms became informal career advisers for their grown daughters. They gave invaluable pointers about landing great jobs, battling gender bias, and moving up the corporate ladder. High-achieving mothers also served as strategic door openers and sounding boards.

Nor did every boomer boss wait until her female progeny hit adulthood to start managing their careers. One advertising executive required her daughter to write a résumé and sign up for LinkedIn before the high school sophomore applied for a summer camp job.

The grown children of hyperinvolved parents can experience detrimental effects, however. Though they tend to succeed at finding good jobs, research shows that they're less self-reliant and more likely to suffer from anxiety or depression, the *New York Times* reported in 2019.

As a daughter matures and tries to forge an independent identity, her well-rooted ties with Mom typically turn rocky. How similar she will be and how different she may want to be from her mother "are questions that shape, day to day, both the broad and immediate themes of her life," wrote Terri Apter, a family dynamics researcher, in *You Don't Really Know Me: Why Mothers and Daughters Fight and How Both Can Win.* A daughter "wants her mother to respect her growth and maturity and independence, but not yet to let go."

A mother wearing the guise of de facto career guide should assist her offspring in avoiding workplace mistakes, former Wall Street executive Pamela F. Lenehan told me. Yet "you don't want to drive the car for them," cautioned Lenehan, the author of *My Mother, My Mentor: What Grown Children of Working Mothers Want You to Know.* The book describes her research and tells stories about adult children of working mothers.

Like Abra, some of the twenty-five grown daughters I interviewed resisted job tips from their Power Mom—despite her extensive knowledge about how to succeed in business. On the other hand, numerous daughters view their pacesetter mother as their unique workplace weapon *precisely* because she succeeded in business.

Those young women include Emma Nosofsky, an executive search professional at recruiters Russell Reynolds Associates. She's a daughter of Laurie Siegel, the former top human resources officer at the conglomerate Tyco International. Siegel now holds seats on corporate boards of directors.

"My mom is my built-in career coach," the nearly twenty-five-year-old Nosofsky boasted. "She is the most important person in my life . . . [and] the first person I call about work things."

In summer 2018, Nosofsky decided to quit an arts industry position that she disliked. She said she spoke with her mother every day during her months of job hunting. Siegel urged her younger daughter to consider the executive recruitment industry. She introduced Nosofsky to a friend at Spencer Stuart, a rival of Russell Reynolds. That contact educated the young woman about why executive recruiting might make sense for her. Siegel also assisted her with job interview preparations.

"There are a lot of young women my age who don't feel like they have role models like [her]," Nosofsky pointed out. Russell Reynolds hired her in fall 2018.

For certain contemporary female executives I interviewed, their mom is a significant role model even if she never reached upper management or stayed home for years. Genevieve Roth's mother inspired the ex–*Glamour* executive to create Invisible Hand, a social impact strategy and events agency that focuses on serving women.

"Women's empowerment is the nerve center of everything I do . . . because I watched my mother blossom intellectually later in life," Roth explained. She grew up in Alaska, where her mother taught school and her father was a banker. "My dad made the financial decisions in the family. His job was the job that mattered," she said.

Roth belatedly recognized the instability of a social structure that expects a man to be the family breadwinner. Her father and two uncles died in a plane crash when she was twelve years old. Her mother, then in her midforties, obtained a second master's degree and switched professions to guidance counseling. "For the first time," Roth continued, "[she] got a job she really liked."

She feels passionate about realizing her ambitious goal of improving humanity in far more independent ways than her mother foresaw. "Those were not questions [that] my mom's generation was taught to ask," she pointed out.

Mom as a Young Girl's Idol

From childhood, several daughters of powerful executives envisioned themselves as powerful executives, too. Take Charlotte Diamond, for example.

Her mother is Alexandra Lebenthal, the executive who took the helm of her family's municipal bond firm the year before she bore Diamond in 1996. Around age four, the youngster created a fictitious jewelry repair business that she called Diamonds Diamonds Diamonds. She appointed herself chief executive officer of its imaginary employees, Mr. Greek and Little Joe. And she devised a motto for her pretend enterprise: "We fix diamonds so you can have them back."

Lebenthal was thrilled that the youngster aspired to emulate her business success—so thrilled that in 2002, she took her six-year-old daughter to a conference in Manhattan hosted by the Committee of 200. The C200 is an invitation-only organization of female business leaders around the globe.

At the conference, Lebenthal and Diamond walked into a hotel ballroom crowded with influential women. The first grader wore bows in her hair and a gray wool dress with a faux lambskin collar. "I don't have any memory of feeling out of place [there]," she told me. "My parents have always treated us [children] like adults."

Conference staffers handed the girl a personalized name tag. "Charlotte Diamond, CEO of Diamonds Diamonds Diamonds," it read. Lebenthal treasured that name tag for years.

Mindful of her mom's professional accomplishments, Diamond continues to set her career sights high. "I always knew you could be a woman and be the most important person in the room," she said.

"Do you aim to run a real business by age thirty-one like your mother did?" I asked Diamond, who would soon turn twenty-three.

"I don't know what company I will be president and CEO of, but why shouldn't I do that?" she asked. Months later, she moved up to assistant market editor from jewelry market assistant for *Vogue*.

Malena Higuera, a second-wave Power Mom, also decided during early girlhood that she wanted to imitate her mother. Ironically, the way she expressed her wish transformed both of their career paths.

Higuera now works for L'Oréal, a cosmetics giant that she joined in 2006. She runs Dermablend Professional, a global skin care brand, from a gleaming white Manhattan office that is packed with product samples and promotional posters. She proudly showed me a large photo of her young sons, Sébastien and Luca.

Higuera's parents are natives of Cuba who immigrated to the United States years before her birth in 1979. Her mother, a chemical engineer, was one of the first female graduates of Stevens Institute of Technology, an engineering school in Hoboken, New Jersey. She stopped working after Higuera arrived.

One day when Higuera was about five years old, she noticed her mom washing dishes in the kitchen of their suburban New Jersey home. The chore looked like fun. "Oh, I want to be like you when I grow up and clean the house," the girl said.

Higuera's comment persuaded her mother to no longer stay home. The cosmetics maker Revlon hired her weeks later. "She wanted me to see what it would be like . . . for her to work," Higuera said.

Her mom's success at reentering the workforce while raising two children after her subsequent divorce shaped Higuera's upbeat attitude about becoming an employed parent herself. The Latina executive realized that mothering and working aren't mutually exclusive decisions. "It isn't one or the other," she remarked.

Yet juvenile perceptions about the role of working women haven't entirely caught up with twenty-first-century realities. Her elder son expressed surprise when he heard his parents talking about his father's female boss one weekday morning in summer 2018.

"Well, how can she be a boss?" the school-age boy demanded. "She's a girl."

"My husband stepped in and said, 'Well, Sébastien, your mom is a big boss,'" Higuera recollected. "'Anyone, no matter what, can be a boss.'"

At the same time, Higuera educated their son about her pride in being a boss and her critical role at work. He needed "to understand that I am making a difference."

Moms' Rocky Ties with Rebellious Teens

Strains almost always arise to a greater degree between mothers and their adolescent girls than between mothers and their teenage sons. A daughter senses "an urge to exaggerate her differences from her mother," the Apter book states. ". . . Sometimes she fights her mother to clarify her difference to herself, and sometimes her mother experiences this as rejection."

Such tensions may worsen when Mom is a powerful business leader who casts a long shadow over her daughter. That was true for Alison Harvey during her adolescence. Her mother, Cathie Black, was then the president of Hearst Magazines, a major publisher of popular publications such as *Cosmopolitan*, *Seventeen*, and *Esquire*.

Black came to Hearst after stints as the publisher of *New York* magazine and the president and publisher of *USA Today*. She helped grow *USA Today* into the nation's largest-circulation daily paper. Black and her husband had adopted their newborn daughter in 1991.

Harvey loved writing short stories and poetry during girlhood. But at times, having a big-business boss for a mother intimidated her. "She always was in the spotlight," Black's daughter told me. "I wanted a spotlight of my own."

Further complicating matters, Harvey said, she had suffered from anxiety and a panic disorder during high school. Nor could she easily embrace her mother's philosophy that you should "stop worrying about what other people are thinking and go do what you want."

When Harvey was fifteen years old, Black arranged a monthlong internship at *Seventeen* magazine and helped her assemble a professional look for her first day of work. "As we were completing my outfit, I spotted a pair of black flats with rhinestones . . . in her closet," Harvey remembered. "My mom watched me squish my feet into them. [She] gently warned that they looked small and I would end up miserable if I wore them all day."

Harvey insisted that her mother's flats fit just fine. "I already knew what would and wouldn't work in life." She spent numerous hours that day taking pictures at five different Manhattan locations for potential *Seventeen* photo shoots. She returned home with blistered and bloody, swollen feet.

"You poor baby!" Black exclaimed upon seeing her injured daughter, flats in hand. Rushing over to comfort her, the Hearst executive kept mum about her warning that morning. The too-tight shoes fiasco demonstrated that "she was still there to help me when I chose to not take her advice," Harvey commented.

The adolescent intern worked forty floors below her mom's skyscraper office alongside fellow interns in their twenties. Her supervisor gave her excessively easy assignments, reflecting "an overactive awareness of who my mother was," Harvey noted. Nor did she like writing quizzes about celebrities for *Seventeen*.

With Black in charge of Hearst Magazines, "I wasn't able to fully experience what it was really like to work there," Harvey went on. "I took a step back and decided I didn't want to be in publishing." Black insists that she never pressured her daughter to become a high-powered publishing executive like her.

As high school graduation loomed, Harvey again felt overshadowed by her mom. Her Connecticut boarding school chose Black to be its commencement speaker. The teenager feared that the appearance of her illustrious mother might steal from her limelight—especially since she hoped to win a school award for one of her short stories. "Can I just have this one day [for me]?" she fretted to herself.

Fortunately, the school bestowed the writing award on Harvey at a ceremony held the day before her graduation. "I had my [lime-light] moments," she said. "They definitely weren't stolen."

As an adult, Harvey considers her mother a good friend who is devoted to what's best for her. Following false starts at launching a career, she aims to pursue her passion for creative writing via a master's degree.

The adolescent daughter of another boomer Power Mom got a maternal tongue-lashing over her preferred college major. You first read about Arielle Mann in the chapter about work/family conflicts. She was the angry teenage twin who opposed being uprooted to accommodate the promotion of her mother, Lisa.

Lisa Mann earned an undergraduate degree in electrical engineering and a Harvard MBA. She moved her husband and three kids from Chicago to New Jersey in 2011 so she could take charge of Kraft Foods' $2 billion U.S. cookie business.

Equally bullheaded, Mann and Arielle next locked horns during the latter's first year at Tufts University, Mann's alma mater. "I am definitely going to be a science major, and it likely will be chemistry," she announced to her mother at a Middle Eastern restaurant in Manhattan. She had just finished her first set of final exams, excelling in science. But the Tufts freshman was clueless about the type of chemistry career she should choose.

"What the fuck are you doing?" Mann asked angrily. "You should consider chemical engineering." In her opinion, chemical engineering offered a stronger business orientation and wider professional options than an academic area such as chemistry.

Mann's outburst didn't fluster Arielle. She knew that her mother uttered "What the fuck" to challenge the twin girls only when she expected that a pending personal decision would derail them. She tried to placate her mom by describing how a chemistry major would put her into the forefront of science.

Mann doesn't give up easily, however. She had encouraged her daughters to pick college majors that would bring them good jobs and financial independence. Eluding dependence on a man "was always a big thing of mine," she said.

The executive switched gears, proposing that Arielle instead become a physician. Mann pointed out that Arielle could have a great career and raise children by working part-time. She even promised to pay for her daughter's simultaneous completion of doctoral and medical degrees.

Arielle stubbornly resisted that proposal as well because she dislikes biology. "I had to minor-league rebel against my mother," the twenty-three-year-old recollected during our interview.

In Mann's opinion, Arielle won their college major argument because she explained her logic well. "I was always planning my career, and I made pivots and moved," noted the executive, who subsequently commanded a bigger PepsiCo unit than the cookie business. "I wanted to know that [my children] were thinking ahead and not just thinking like kids, that there was some sort of [career] planning."

Arielle was ultimately admitted to a doctoral program in organic chemistry at New York University. She intends to engage in corporate research and development. So she's headed for the business world—and the fulfillment of her mom's hopes.

Mothers Who Open Doors in Different Ways

Once a daughter approaches or reaches adulthood, her employed mother often suggests a range of strategies to boost her foothold in business. "The business skills, experience, and networks [such] mothers can offer their children have tremendous value," Pamela

Lenehan observed in her book. ". . . The grown children have a deeper appreciation of their multi-talented working mothers. Many become working mothers themselves."

Martha Olson, a first-wave Power Mom, worked hard for years to ensure that her daughter, Megan Keane, would flourish in adulthood—largely because she had borne her only child following four failed pregnancies. "This little miracle . . . needs to have lots of choices because she earned it," she recalled thinking.

She was a senior leader of Warnaco Group, an apparel company, when she decided that her artistic high schooler needed to begin making professional connections. She introduced Keane to the niece of an acquaintance employed by Christie's, an art auction company.

The teenager resented her mother's networking effort. "I felt like my mom was trying to do this [outreach] for me," she explained. "Instead of letting me discover what I was interested in organically, she was pushing me down her own agenda and timeline." Keane definitely did not appreciate "what my mother was trying to do for me."

She grudgingly met the Christie's staffer for coffee and toured the company's Manhattan office. The get-together helped steer Keane away from becoming an artist by exposing her to other career tracks in the arts. "I [came] away liking the idea of working with art at a well-known institution," she said, and that altered perspective affected her pursuit of future internships.

Olson played a similar hands-on role during Keane's exploration of colleges. The executive prepared detailed spreadsheets to compare the pluses and minuses of more than fifteen campuses that the family toured. But her daughter didn't care to know the results of her mom's spreadsheet analysis.

"I was visiting the schools and going with my gut about them,"

Keane observed. She selected Colgate University, relying on an instinctual feeling that she would be content there. Which she was. The art history major interned at two major art museums while attending Colgate and graduated magna cum laude.

The day we spoke, Olson's twenty-five-year-old daughter was a client strategist for iCrossing, an ad agency owned by Hearst Corporation, a media conglomerate. An uncle had opened the door for her via a friend who headed the iCrossing department she joined in 2016.

Keane now appreciates the importance of good connections because "your network is actually a reflection of your hard work and experience." In July 2019, she became a senior strategist for Dentsu Aegis Network, an advertising group owned by Dentsu Group in Japan.

A former iCrossing executive employed by Dentsu alerted her about that opportunity. The ex-colleague "thought I would be a good fit for the job," Keane said. "I am definitely walking through the doors opened by professional connections."

The working mother of a present-generation executive named Dana Spinola played a key part in shaping her postcollege career. Spinola is the first member of her immediate family to go to college. She later launched fab'rik, a chain of women's clothing boutiques. The Atlanta-based company grew to thirty-nine outlets by November 2019.

Her parents wed as teenagers. Long-haired hippies with artistic ambitions, "they built themselves," Spinola said. Their three kids "grew up with no money but felt so rich." Her mom sewed clothes for her and didn't commence full-time employment as an interior decorator until Spinola was in college.

She inspired her eldest child to dream big, Spinola recalled. "She would always say, 'If it's worth doing, it's worth overdoing,'" the lanky forty-four-year-old founder remembered. "She just didn't believe in the word 'no.' It was all possible."

Spinola and I chatted at fab'rik's headquarters, a converted warehouse with black garage doors and an oversized "INSPIRATION" sign on a wall outside her glassed-in office. In kindergarten, she was asked what she wanted to be when she grew up. "The best," she replied.

By her late twenties, Spinola was a rising star at the consulting arm of Deloitte, a major accounting firm that even paid for her dry cleaning. She yearned to leave Deloitte and open a clothing boutique. She figured that owning a small business would better facilitate her dream of future motherhood than being a management consultant who flew to three cities every week for work.

Though she lacked a business plan, she expected her mother to embrace her entrepreneurial vision enthusiastically. She phoned her with the big news in 2001 while seated on the floor of her Atlanta apartment, surrounded by scattered papers.

"I'm going to quit corporate America and start a store," she announced excitedly.

"Well, sweetie, how are you going to do that?" her mom asked skeptically. "What's your plan?" She cautioned Spinola about the perils of abandoning a salaried position for an occupation with no financial security. "It's going to be the hardest decision you've ever made."

Her dour reaction deeply disappointed Spinola. In recounting their tense conversation, the fab'rik executive crossed her arms and clenched her teeth. "God, I love this woman and hate her," she recalled thinking. "She's not going to let me off the hook. She would never let me leap into something that didn't have the [planning] work behind it."

The aspiring entrepreneur promised to draft a formal business plan. Spinola said she pitched her boutique idea to about fourteen banks. All fourteen rejected her. She finally landed a $70,000 line of credit from a friend of her dad.

In 2002, Spinola opened her first fab'rik store in downtown Atlanta. Combining entrepreneurship with parenthood worked out. "Fab'rik was my first baby," she quipped. She has given birth to three sons and adopted one daughter since 2006, the year that she began fab'rik franchises.

Coping with Tough Job Quandaries

Everyone's career success requires deft handling of difficult colleagues—and difficult assignments. A few first-wave Power Moms armed their grown daughters with tested tactics to deal with these common work quandaries.

Melanie Kusin did so based on her frequent encounters with gender bias during a protracted career in the executive search business. The vice chair of the executive-recruiting company Korn Ferry told her daughter, Avery Rowe, that she hadn't been taken seriously as a woman unless she overprepared for every search assignment pitch.

Kusin and another female recruiter once pitched four older male executives about finding a new CEO for a retailer, an industry in which both women had established a track record. Yet the men called the recruiters "gals" and dismissed Kusin midway through her presentation.

The Korn Ferry executive encouraged Rowe to stand her ground in such uncomfortable work situations. Her daughter entered the labor force savvy about sexism, and "nobody was going to get her," Kusin said.

A senior male executive of a business where Rowe worked for a period after her 2011 college graduation mistakenly assumed that a younger man was in charge of the small team she led. He also angrily criticized numerical data that she presented at a meeting. "It was clearly gender bias," Rowe noted.

His weekly tirades persisted. Distressed, Rowe sought advice from her mother almost every day. "She would give me different tips about how to [coolly] communicate with people who were getting really heated." In addition, Kusin said, her twentysomething daughter should find someone to witness the male executive's mistreatment.

Rowe sought support from a high-level woman who oversaw her program but didn't attend every update meeting. At her request, the program director attended a session where the male executive renewed his attack.

"He starts yelling at me," Rowe recollected. "He is pointing his finger in my face, saying 'You are going to fail! And thousands of people are going to get fired as a result of it!'"

Heeding her mother's counsel, Rowe refused to be cowed by the enraged executive. "You can't speak to me that way," she told him and walked out of the meeting room.

The program director summoned her to her office. Rowe worried that she might be fired. Instead, the director expressed pride in Rowe and wondered how she hadn't lost her cool. "It was because of my mom," Rowe responded. The senior woman vowed to ban the man from participating in the program's current or future projects.

Ellen Kullman is a perfect example of a boomer Power Mom whose exposure to tough work assignments benefited her grown daughter, Maggie. The experience prepared Kullman to coach her about the same issue years later.

Educated as a mechanical engineer, she joined DuPont as a

marketing manager in 1988. She became its first female vice president at age thirty-nine in 1995. Her success in a highly risky DuPont role outside her comfort zone—via her creation of a safety consulting unit—paved the path for her 2009 ascension to its corner office. Unless you push yourself outside your comfort zone, she told me, "you're never going to know your true capability, and you're not going to make as much progress." She acted out her point by shaking both fists over the long dining table in her family's sprawling redbrick home in Wilmington, Delaware.

She was the first female CEO of DuPont, known for Kevlar body armor and Teflon nonstick pan coating. She ran the major chemical manufacturer until October 2015. Four years later, she took the top job at Carbon, a 3D printing start-up with about five hundred employees. She had served on its board since 2016.

Kullman's second CEO gig was another risky move for her. Only two female heads of Fortune 500 companies have repeated the feat at another business, *Fortune* reported on the day of Carbon's announcement in late November 2019.

Maggie, the eldest of Kullman's three children, was exposed to the workplace at a very young age. She was just three weeks old in 1990 when Kullman interrupted her maternity leave to conduct an unexpected meeting with her DuPont team at the family's home. Team members seated around the kitchen table took turns holding the newborn.

Maggie graduated in 2012 from Tufts University, her mother's alma mater. General Electric Company, where Kullman had worked before DuPont, hired Maggie for its communications leadership development program. She completed brief rotational assignments in locales such as GE's midtown Manhattan office and Connecticut corporate headquarters.

As the two-year program ended, Maggie needed to arrange a permanent GE post. She considered opportunities such as an internal communications spot covering about a thousand workers at two sizable manufacturing facilities and a slightly smaller warehouse in Fort Worth, Texas. Men made up almost the entire workforce at the plants, which produced locomotives and mining equipment.

The problem? She had never lived far from a big city or toiled in a factory. "Working with hourly employees in a manufacturing plant wasn't exactly my comfort zone," she said.

Maggie and her mother debated the Texas job over dinner at a Manhattan restaurant. Kullman suggested that her daughter accept the position because a challenging job "is going to help you see all the different aspects of the business and how they interact."

Maggie told me that she finally took the risky job partly because she knew her mom had thrived outside her comfort zone through her creation of the DuPont safety consulting division. However, the job proved harder than expected for a young woman accustomed to wearing a dress and heels in fancy offices occupied by GE's big brass.

In Texas, Maggie wore steel-toed boots, a hard hat, Dickies work jeans, and a GE shirt embroidered with her name. The tarantulas she occasionally saw in her Fort Worth plant frightened her. "It probably was my toughest job and definitely the steepest learning curve," she said.

Yet she also became well acquainted with many blue-collar guys and their concerns. A good manager understands all aspects of a business, Maggie stressed, echoing her mother's words. The knowledge will be "very helpful no matter what I do in the future."

Maggie left GE in 2017 to return to school and received her MBA degree in mid-2019. When the new year dawned, she took a new job as a marketing program manager for Clari, a software start-up in

Sunnyvale, California. The company produces a machine learning system that enables businesses to forecast and manage their sales and marketing.

Big Helpings of Help for Promotions

Other high-powered women from the trailblazer generation taught their ambitious daughters tactics for moving ahead. Among them is Hope Neiman, the chief marketing officer of Tillster, a digital commerce company for the restaurant industry that is headquartered in Los Angeles. She has devoted decades to advancing in marketing management. By the late 1990s, she had a daughter named Alex Sarkowsky and was running marketing for a unit of Walt Disney Company.

The executive and her only child maintain very close bonds. "She has 24/7 access to me and can ask me things over and over," Neiman's twenty-six-year-old daughter observed. "At the end of the day, it has been advice I needed."

Sarkowsky majored in anthropology at Wesleyan University, her mother's alma mater, because Neiman recommended that major. Following her daughter's 2014 graduation, Neiman pushed her to seek a business career—with a focus on developing and managing products.

"She's very fearless when it comes to doing things that nobody has done before, and that's why I knew product was a great place for her," the Tillster marketing chief observed. "She said 'no' until she finally was willing to give it a chance." Sarkowsky said she had finally agreed because her mother is a very persistent person.

The new college grad joined the Bouqs Company, an online floral vendor, as an email intern. She gradually moved up to the job of associate marketing manager. When a product manager left in 2017, she knew she should raise her hand for the opening.

But she had no inkling how to sell herself to Bouqs higher-ups because she lacked "the right lingo to come across as believable." So she turned to her mom to plot a game plan for winning the coveted promotion.

Over a weekend, mother and daughter brainstormed at the kitchen table of the family's second home in Mammoth Lakes, California. "Be sure and tell them what you are bringing [to this job]," Neiman proposed. She also crafted talking points for her daughter to bring up during her pitch meeting. Sarkowsky took notes and later reviewed those talking points by phone with her mom.

Citing her inexperience, Bouqs promoted her only to associate product manager. Sarkowsky's next supervisor unsuccessfully pressed to get her the product manager title. She didn't mind. "The important thing [was] that product is now on my résumé," she pointed out. "I could go anywhere."

As she did. In 2018, she noticed an online listing for a product manager's job at Fair, a car-leasing start-up in Santa Monica, California. Candidates needed two years' experience, however. She asked her mother whether she should apply.

"Absolutely. You make the case for yourself," Neiman recommended. "You have to ask for the things that you want in life, and this is one of them."

Neiman then greased the wheels for Sarkowsky. Fair had recently recruited a Tillster executive as its vice president of product. Neiman introduced her daughter to the vice president and coached her about standing out during the job interview.

Thanks to the connection with her mother, the Fair vice president "didn't feel the need to do any reference checks before giving me the job," Sarkowsky said. Fair promoted her to senior product manager fifteen months after her debut.

Sarkowsky knows why she has moved up so fast during her brief career: "I have [Mom] as a secret weapon."

I was pleasantly surprised that not only powerful executives served as a secret weapon. Certain mothers who had never held high-level jobs gave their daughters valuable advice about right and wrong job decisions.

I was equally impressed that first-wave executives boosted their daughters' careers despite the vastly altered work landscape. Their insights as informal coaches, door openers, and sounding boards could assist any working woman. Among them:

- Create and nurture broad professional networks.
- Dive deep and learn everything you can about a new position, industry, or locale before making such a risky move.
- Fight gender bias by enlisting senior female leaders as internal allies.
- Take the long view in planning your career—and always dream big.

Power Moms from both waves who guided their daughters well reached upper management because they excelled at guiding their staffers, too. How do better bosses make better mothers? And vice versa? The next chapter offers answers.

8

Better Mom, Better Boss

Motherhood transforms many women into better leaders.

The same proved true for me—eventually. Being blunt, pushy, and impatient made me shine as a *Wall Street Journal* reporter. But I had to learn that being a good journalist wasn't enough to make me a good boss.

I learned that painful lesson while I supervised a young *Journal* reporter named Kris Maher during the early 2000s. We worked in the open newsroom of our New York bureau. One afternoon, I chewed him out publicly over weak spots in a *Journal* piece of his that I had edited.

My boss soon marched over to my desk. She chewed me out publicly for treating Maher harshly. I fled the newsroom in tears. Years later, Maher told me how my harsh tone had convinced him that he needed thicker skin. His next statement overcame my fears that my blunt impatience had made me a bad parent, too. "You were a good mentor," he said. My assistance had enabled a novice like him to learn journalism on the job. On the day he joined our *Journal* team in 1999, he recalled, I had handed him a list of my best sources on the management issues beat. "It was a totally unexpected act of generosity," he said.

A number of *Journal* colleagues subsequently expressed their gratitude for my mentoring them over the years. Guiding Dan and Abra throughout their childhoods had taught me how to be an effective mentor. I led by example, setting a high standard for what I hoped my offspring and fellow journalists could become.

Power Moms from both generations reported to me that they had become better bosses by raising families. Tapping skills honed as time-starved parents, they set priorities well, multitasked, and delegated effectively. They also managed with empathy. It's a quality greatly valued by companies because they must operate in an increasingly complex and diverse global economy.

"The number one thing you learn instinctively about being a parent is empathy," observed Sarah Hofstetter, a former president of Comscore, the media measurement firm. Putting yourself into somebody else's shoes is very different when it involves your child, the current-generation executive continued. "I feel my kid's stomachache. It's totally visceral."

Hofstetter reacts the same way on the job. She gets very intensely involved in the personal problems of her employees. That was how she handled a lieutenant's family difficulty in 2012, when she presided over 360i, the digital ad and media agency.

Fearful of appearing uncommitted to her job, the staffer concealed her sick daughter's hospitalization from practically everyone at work. After hearing about the ill child from the agency's human resources department, Hofstetter arranged to visit a distant client with the employee. Their ninety-minute drive created a window for Hofstetter to conduct a heartfelt chat.

"I was able to both empathize with her as well as be vulnerable," she recollected. She described her own struggles over whether to divulge her work/life conflicts involving her two children and noted that 360i men and women regularly confronted the same kind of situation.

The staffer finally admitted that she felt bad about not devoting more time to her ailing daughter. "What kind of a successful professional are you going to be when your brain is on something else?" Hofstetter demanded. "Just take the time." The woman did. Hofstetter left Comscore in April 2019. A year later, she became president of Profitero, an e-commerce technology start-up.

An empathetic management style enabled certain first-wave executive mothers to serve as highly visible boosters and role models for their employer's working parents.

In 2005, Avon Products CEO Andrea Jung encountered a fellow executive mom while they were walking into a senior management team meeting at the cosmetics giant. Her colleague said she might have to duck out for a call because her son was being rushed to the hospital following a fall from a school swing. As the working mother of two school-age youngsters, Jung felt she must "take that guilt-making decision off her shoulders."

She ordered the anxious executive to leave the meeting immediately. "You have an emergency," Jung declared in front of her predominantly male team. "This is a priority. Avon will live."

She believes that her announcement signaled that "we really are going to walk the talk [about] being 'the company for women,'" she noted in our interview. Jung presently leads Grameen America, a microfinance nonprofit organization that helps turn poor U.S. women into entrepreneurs.

Similarly, Hershey CEO Michele Buck now broadly communicates her mantra that "it's not about where you are when you're doing the work," she said. "It's about getting the work done." Buck lets Hershey employees arrive late or leave early to care for their youngsters' needs, for instance.

Her increased commitment to flexibility reflects the years she spent rearing three offspring. "Having lived it, it's very top of mind," she emphasized. "This is how you have to support your employees in this day and age."

"When we are better at home, we are better at work," concurred Malena Higuera, the youthful L'Oréal executive. She never misses an event that her two sons will remember she missed—"and I won't remember why." At work, she assigns her highest priority to actions that are "changing lives and thus creating market share."

Executive Amy Henderson explored how parenthood accelerates effectiveness on the job after she delivered her third child several years ago. She worried about maintaining her performance as the chief innovation officer for a national initiative to train youths to be computer coders.

Henderson interviewed 223 moms and dads who were seen as excelling at home and work. Her investigation gave birth to Tend-Lab. The consultancy, which she cofounded in 2015, provides employers with smart strategies to aid working parents, such as the formation or expansion of in-house parenting groups.

During workshops for TendLab clients, Henderson describes the results of her interviews with parents. The vast majority of both genders think that "parenthood enhances their capacity to perform in their careers," she reported to me. About 80 percent of the interviewed mothers and fathers are present or past executives.

Henderson also dug up scientific evidence that parenthood neurologically motivates us to develop the skills required for work success. Through TendLab, "we are trying to transform our cultural perception of parenthood's [negative] impact on career performance," she said.

Large-scale research has uncovered strong indications that motherhood positively affects leadership performance. In a 2018 survey, 89 percent of working Americans agreed that working moms bring out the best in employees. About 84 percent backed the notion that businesses will be more successful with mothers in their leadership ranks.

Conducted for Bright Horizons, the major child care provider, the poll covered 2,143 adults. Respondents were nearly evenly split between parents and nonparents. "Working moms are the best equipped to bring twenty-first century leadership skills to the workplace," the survey concluded.

A high proportion of younger mothers and fathers believe that parenthood makes them better leaders, another study revealed. About 55 percent of parents under thirty-five "strongly agree" that's true—compared with 28 percent of ones over forty-five, a 2019 survey of 1,003 individuals with and without children stated. The poll was organized by Berlin Cameron, a unit of WPP Group, and two cosponsors. The integrated creative agency offers such services as advertising, branding, and design.

This generational difference "suggests a potential shift in societal views," the survey noted. Another positive finding: staffers without children think their "mom bosses" are better at team bonding.

Overall, female bosses inspire greater job satisfaction among the rank-and-file workforce than do male bosses, according to a 2019 study of almost sixty thousand employees in forty-three countries. Workers expressed higher confidence in businesses where women make up more than half of managers than at male-led ones, especially in areas such as corporate mission, products, and strategies. Peakon, a developer of human resources analytics software, carried out the global study.

The problem, of course, is the paucity of enterprises worldwide in which women dominate management. More than half of 21,980 businesses in ninety-one countries have no female senior executives, a 2016 analysis found. I was equally disturbed by the lack of researchers who systematically count the noses of manager moms around the world. What gets measured gets noticed and, perhaps, fixed.

Listen Well, Lead Well

The best bosses lead well by listening well—even though they may not always agree. Alison Rand improved her professional listening skills through occasionally tense interactions with her adolescent daughter. On the morning we met, the forty-four-year-old novice executive described the complex challenges of managing about sixty design staffers for Automattic, the high-tech company.

Her team largely consisted of individuals younger than herself. She said that most of them complained and felt very entitled. Those team members demanded that Rand fix their work problems. "Give me a better project," they pleaded. "Or promote me."

Though she tried hard to understand their viewpoint, the Automattic executive decided to resist the requests. "You need to be able to start to see a solution yourself," Rand informed her employees. She exhibited strong listening skills that she had developed while mothering sixteen-year-old Luna. "I've learned that she often just needs me to listen well without the intent of providing a solution."

Rand played the part of good listener when Luna sought permission to drop her advanced-placement Spanish class in fall 2018. "I hate the teacher, and I'm failing," Luna said tearfully.

But Rand yearned for her elder daughter to speak Spanish fluently. "It's the only little bit of our heritage that we have left," the Latina executive explained during our interview.

She informed Luna that she wouldn't advocate on her behalf at school until she regularly finished her Spanish homework and attended Spanish tutoring sessions. Rand also talked about the teen's chance to develop resilience from her painful failures. "Failing is part of the process, and it sucks," she pointed out to Luna. "You dust yourself off, and you try again."

The teenager stuck with her advanced Spanish class—primarily because her mother and teacher assured her that "her perseverance is what would ultimately shine," Rand told me a year later. "The teacher ended up writing a college recommendation for [Luna] based mostly on her resilience and growth in the face of adversity."

Anne Stevens gleaned a different insight into effective listening on the job from her teenage daughter, Jennifer. The brash, fearless executive has driven race cars and flown in a two-seater fighter jet. She is the former CEO of two publicly held manufacturers, Carpenter Technology Corporation and GKN.

"The most honest feedback I have ever gotten in my entire life is from my daughter," she said. "Jen made me a better boss." She vividly recalled one such episode from the 1980s, when she had been midway through her decade at Exxon and her daughter had been a high school junior

Jennifer hoped to attend Brown University, a highly selective school. However, she didn't study much because "I wanted to have fun and be with my friends," she conceded to me. She occasionally brought home a C on her report card.

"You never are going to get into Brown with grades like this," Stevens warned her one day as she climbed the spiral staircase to the master bedroom of their suburban New Jersey home.

Jennifer approached her mother from behind. "Your expectations of me are not what my expectations are!" she yelled.

Her outburst halted Stevens's ascent. "You are absolutely right," she declared, looking hard at Jennifer. Her daughter was willing to accept the consequences of her lax attitude toward academic studies—and Stevens ultimately accepted her decision.

"It was a whole lesson [that] my expectations and my standards are different than a lot of other people," she said. "As a boss, you better align your expectations with your subordinates'." The clash with Jennifer served as a wake-up call for the hard-driving Exxon manager. She needed to fix an identical disconnect between her expectations and her staffers' expectations.

She said that some subordinates had been shocked when she had given them negative annual performance reviews, as they had assumed that they had performed well during the previous year.

Rather than waiting to do year-end evaluations, Stevens began holding in-depth conversations with her team members throughout the year in order to review their objectives and provide feedback. She learned to listen closely for "what was holding someone's performance back." Individual performance and overall teamwork improved, she said. And "I never had the disconnect again."

Bringing Managerial Moxie Home

Most of the female executives I met while assembling this book already knew how to manage subordinates well by the time their offspring arrived. Being a better boss made several of them better parents.

Challis Lowe typifies such Power Moms. The first black female officer at Continental Bank decades ago ultimately won the top HR spot at three major corporations.

Lowe joined the Chicago bank in 1971. Candice, her younger daughter, was three years old, and Daphne was five. "I was trained how to be a good boss," she observed. "Nobody ever taught me how to be a good mom."

She assumed supervisory duties two years after her first management development training in 1973. The training created an epiphany about smart supervising: you can steer employees, but you can't force them to do what they don't want to do.

So the bank officer laid out expectations for her direct reports without telling them how to complete their duties. "Not only can you do work your way, you have to do it your way," she told them.

Lowe attempted to apply the same managerial approach to mothering her daughters—with mixed results. She knew that "you can't make them become what you think they should be."

The veteran businesswoman figured that her really smart girls would make outstanding businesswomen. "I tried . . . to make them into mini me's," she admitted.

She changed her perspective after she and Candice commuted together during the college student's summer internship at Continental. Lowe finally realized "that I didn't want her to be me," she said, nervously placing her left hand on her throat. "I wanted her to be a successful version of her."

She and Candice soon began to interact differently. Lowe was both supportive and skeptical when her daughter decided to become a cultural anthropologist. Because the profession required a doctoral degree, "I just wasn't sure she would stay committed for the [required] time," Lowe said.

Candice is now a Vassar College associate professor, a quasi-administrative role in which she deals with the same issues that her mother dealt with as a business executive. Daphne is a real estate investor who tapped her financial acumen to accumulate residential properties in three U.S. cities.

"Despite their attempts to roll away," Lowe quipped, "the apples rolled back fairly close to the tree."

Teaching Daughters to Be Good Bosses

Contemporary executive moms such as Rand came up with tactics for handling their progeny that enabled them to handle demanding millennial employees. In turn, some boomer Power Moms taught their grown daughters wise ways to be effective bosses.

They include Melanie Healey, the first woman to run the North American arm of Procter & Gamble Company. The biggest consumer products company in the world hired her as a brand manager in her native Brazil in 1990. She took unpopular stances while she rose through management. She successfully pushed to revamp the look of P&G's feminine care products—and, for the first time, launch a tampon designed with consumers in mind.

Healey embraces uncomfortable situations. "I am a person who my entire life has gotten out of my comfort zone. It is part of who I am," she stated.

Her adult daughter, Jackie, said she embraces her mother's philosophy because Healey taught her "to be really strong and independent—and how to not take shit." She was only twenty-two years old in August 2017 when she took charge of about fifty people at Amazon.com. Her employees picked shoes for shipping from the internet giant's fulfillment centers in Shepherdsville, Kentucky.

Most of the workers were much older than their youthful boss, and persuading them to follow her orders "was a little nerve-racking at first," she remembered. "I am very hard on myself. I always want to be the best." She explained how "part of that comes from . . . Mom being such a big influence on my life."

Healey suggested that her daughter lead by example and exert extra efforts to assist her subordinates. Jackie earned the respect of her hourly employees by pulling heavy pallets of merchandise across the Kentucky facility—just as they did. "There is no job that is beneath me, and Amazonians can see that and know they can . . . count on me to help them," she remarked. "This has been a big key to my success at Amazon."

When we spoke, Jackie was an area manager in charge of a single department. She later moved up to the position of operations manager. She took responsibility for an entire shift, larger projects, and developing team members to move to higher-level jobs.

Jane Parker, an advertising industry executive, offered equally knowledgeable tips about bossing early in the marketing career of Samantha "Sam" Gladis, her only child. Parker is the longtime global CEO of InterbrandHealth, a unit of Omnicom Group. She was working for a rival ad giant the day her twentysomething daughter, a novice supervisor, called with an urgent plea for help.

Gladis needed to confront a female subordinate about her poor performance. "I had never had a conversation like that," she recollected. Disrupting someone's career "was going to be hard for both me and the person."

Gladis described her dilemma to her mother from a busy street corner in Manhattan. "I was coming from a meeting, going back to the office, and had gotten an email [saying] 'This has to be handled today,'" she told her mom.

"Be honest," Parker recommended to her daughter. Set clear expectations about corrective steps. But "don't be mean," she added.

During their phone conversation, the pair used Parker's proposed talking points to informally role-play the imminent encounter. The younger woman wanted to make sure that she delivered her bad news sensitively. "I'd lay out a piece of critical feedback that I wanted to relay, and we'd talk through a strategy for doing so with empathy, constructive guidance, and authority," she told me.

Parker easily acted out the feedback scenario. "I've always really applied myself to [giving] good feedback for people that work for me. It's just something that matters to me," she explained when I ate lunch with her and her daughter at a hotel coffee shop in mid-town Manhattan. Perched at either end of a narrow table, they repeatedly exchanged affectionate glances.

Parker remains a larger-than-life figure in her daughter's life. "The professional guidance and mentorship component of our relationship was the catalyst to becoming as close as we are," Gladis said. "Whenever something big happens in our life, I want her there."

At the time, the thirty-five-year-old marketer was the executive director of a Hearst unit. Thanks to the work experience acquired since her midtwenties, she observed, "I'm more willing to fail and . . . put myself at risk because I value that [experience]."

Gladis no longer phones her mother frequently with queries about the best supervisory techniques. She has incorporated Jane's work wisdom into a mental construct that she dubs WWJD. "What would Jane do?" she asks herself. Or alternatively, "What would Sam do?"

How often do you feel grateful toward the woman at the opposite end of this table? I asked Gladis, with a nod toward Parker.

"Every minute of every day," she answered emphatically. "I would not be where I am without her. Period."

"Thank you," Parker murmured as her light blond bangs fell over her beaming eyes.

Just a few months later, Gladis advanced to vice president of ad product marketing for Hearst Magazines.

Executive Push for Working Parents

Moms in powerful business positions carry enough clout to better the lives of other working parents, too. While running the retailer Charming Shoppes, Dorrit J. Bern established a child care center for its headquarters staffers. She even employed a nurse in case any of the youngsters there got sick.

During her command of Autodesk, the maker of design software, Carol Bartz insisted that all employees volunteer at their children's school one day a month. (Nonparents could engage in other types of community service.)

No wonder that half of Americans would prefer to work for a company led by a woman, according to a 2017 survey of 2,066 adults by the Harris Poll. About 78 percent of those canvassed said that a female-led business is more likely to provide access to child care.

Second-wave executive mothers today often adopt highly innovative practices, such as generous paternity leave, breast milk shipment, and management training to ease new parents' resumption of work. Jennifer Hyman, the CEO of Rent the Runway, embodies this contemporary cohort.

Yet even Hyman didn't equalize family-friendly benefits for salaried and hourly workers until 2018—eight years after she cofounded the clothing rental company. "Our warehouse, customer service and store employees now have the same bereavement, parental leave, family sick leave and sabbatical packages that corporate employees have," Hyman reported in an opinion piece for the *New York Times*.

As a fairly new mother, she wrote, "I have a deeper understanding . . . about the ways [that] missing safety nets contribute to unemployment and limit social mobility." Business leaders should fulfill "their moral duty to society to treat every worker equally."

Hyman elaborated about her policy shift during our interview in her Manhattan office. At that time, every Rent the Runway staffer could receive three months of paid parental leave. I wondered why she had waited so long to equalize the benefits. "When I started Rent the Runway, I was twenty-seven years old, and I just followed suit to what other companies did," she replied.

The entrepreneur watched hundreds of different life circumstances unfold as Rent the Runway grew to 1,500 employees. Unmarried team members got engaged, got married, and had kids, the thirty-eight-year-old said, tapping her fingertips hard on her white desk. "My own life has gone through that same transition."

The day we chatted, Hyman was pregnant for the second time. She was already so overburdened by parenting and running a start-up that she sometimes bought extra underwear and socks instead of washing dirty items. I sensed that mothering two kids under three years old would further widen her commitment to aiding Rent the Runway parents.

Hyman agreed. "I've always wanted to build an organization that exemplifies what the workplace of the future will be."

An associate poked her head inside the CEO's office near the end of our session, and Hyman told her she would leave soon for her next appointment. Moments later, the tall executive strode down the hall to Room 602. "In use" the door sign read.

"Sorry to be late," she told a crowd crammed inside a small conference room. Female colleagues and colorful balloons surrounded a radiant vice president. They were celebrating the imminent birth of her second child.

First-wave executive mothers such as Alexandra Lebenthal sometimes discovered that fostering a family-friendly workplace isn't a simple task. She took the helm of her family's municipal bond firm in 1995. The thirty-one-year-old mother of a toddler son bore a daughter the following year.

Lebenthal's limited exposure to business leadership and motherhood left her ill equipped for the office outcry that erupted over her

adoption of a flexible schedule during the late 1990s. She let sales-
women with kids arrive at 8:00 a.m. and leave work by 3:00 p.m.

Resentful male salesmen demanded to know why working moms
deserved special treatment. Their criticism "still makes me mad to
this day," Lebenthal told me. The women "were actually doing better
than they had been when they were working full-time," she pointed
out. "Who cared when they left?"

Obviously, the men cared. Lebenthal bowed to their complaints
by killing the flexible arrangement after six months. "I just didn't
have the confidence or the experience to be able to deal with [the
attacks]," she said.

Then a saleswoman who had taken advantage of the reduced
schedule quit and filed an arbitration claim challenging Lebenthal's
abandonment of the perquisite. The departed staffer accused the
young CEO of unfairly discriminating against women.

Though her firm won the arbitration case, Lebenthal recognized
that she should stop believing that "I can do it all on my own," she
recollected, waving her arms back and forth. She retained the executive coach Dee Soder for advice on how to be a stronger leader.

Dr. Soder raised her awareness that staffers had questioned her
leadership because of her age and gender. Lebenthal revived the
flexible schedule, welcoming male participation. And "I became
very conscious of decisions I might make that were driven from
who I was," she said. "[Like] the need to be perfect."

On the home front, Lebenthal's high expectations heightened the
pressures facing her elder daughter, Charlotte Diamond. The teen
developed anorexia at the end of her junior year of high school. She
felt "like she had to be perfect and [found] a way to be in control
through her eating," Lebenthal said.

Diamond concurred that her need "to feel in control of my sur-
roundings [was] a huge root of my eating disorder." At the same

time, she had sought to be the perfect adolescent by always smil-
ing and completing her homework before her parents arrived home
from work. "I needed to be the constant when everything else was
in flux," she told me. "That did not do much to help me out in the
end."

Lebenthal's husband took care of their daughter during her anorexia treatment because the executive had just completed a stint
with a real estate investment trust. "He would go with me to all of
my doctors' and therapy appointments, make and pack my meals
with a menu and little note of encouragement, eat with me, talk me
through any issues, and just give me love," Diamond remembered.
"I was really lucky that he was home when all of this was going on."
Because her mother was working, she added, "she was unable to be
as present."

No one can ever be a perfect parent. But my interviews and review
of research debunked the myths that employed parents must be
less committed to their jobs than nonparents. Instead, female executives I met from both waves excelled at setting priorities, multitasking, and delegating effectively once they became time-pressed
mothers.

Leading effectively at work before tackling parenthood could
help you raise a family effectively later. You will already know how
to guide people and set high standards. More important, you will
already be a highly empathetic listener.

9

Power over Pain

In early 2014, Abra called us with bad news: she finally knew why she had been suffering from constant chest pain for the past two years.

Our thirty-one-year-old daughter had found it so hard to speak or even breathe that she had taken unpaid medical leave from a job she loved, managing multimillion-dollar projects for international consulting clients of her employer. Pain had made it difficult for her to meet the demands of her job.

Doctors had concluded that Abra suffered from Ehlers-Danlos syndrome, an incurable genetic condition without effective treatment options. The connective tissue disorder is related to the defective production of collagen, which holds the body together. The version of EDS she inherited from me created highly mobile joints that can painfully slip out of place or dislocate.

Abra sobbed uncontrollably throughout our hour-long call, frustrated and weary from living with nonstop severe pain. She asked how Mike and I had coped with situations where we had lost all hope. I lacked an answer. I had never lost all hope or feared losing my job.

"She is close to doing both right now," I lamented in my diary.

"There is nothing I can do to make her feel better except sob as loud as she did tonight."

Yet not only did Abra return to work part-time, she eventually regained her full-time schedule and won a managerial promotion. Physical therapy alleviates her pain for brief periods. I continue to be amazed by how she copes with the depressing daily debilitation of EDS.

"How do you get up every day knowing that you will have to deal with this again?" I bluntly asked her several years later during an evening stroll near her residence in Washington.

"You decide to end your life or to live with it," she responded. "Which are you going to do?" Standing on a busy sidewalk, I burst into tears of gratitude that she had chosen life.

Abra's stark comparison of her options shocked me. I suddenly recognized that I had failed to provide her with sufficient emotional support in her darkest hours. Trained as a journalist, I prefer digging up facts over grappling with raw feelings. I desperately wanted a rational remedy for our daughter's irrational affliction.

Sooner or later, we all encounter a significant health problem—whether the malady strikes you, your spouse, your parent, or your progeny. Numerous Power Moms exhibited tremendous resilience following a major medical crisis, even if their afflicted family member died. Trials by illness often became inspirational turning points in their lives. These women changed their views of themselves, their professional trajectories, and their need for work/life sway. By swaying, you accept life's ebbs and flows so you can fully focus on work at key moments—and easily move to focus on your family at other moments.

Their management background better equipped some executive mothers to power over pain. That was the case for Stacey Tank, the executive who nearly died twice from a blood pressure condition during her 2009 and 2014 pregnancies.

Then Trevor, her physically fit husband, had a massive stroke while working out at their Atlanta home one Saturday in October 2017. He fell ill days before his thirty-ninth birthday and shortly after Tank moved up to an operational vice presidency.

She had arrived at the home improvement chain in 2015 after stints with units of Heineken and General Electric, where she had helped manage corporate crises. The stressful events included a beer bottle recall and a nuclear power plant meltdown. Tank grasped the importance of "putting one foot in front of the other [and] dealing with one thing at a time," she said. "You have to prioritize fiercely, constantly."

On the day of Trevor's stroke, Tank drove him and their young sons to an Atlanta hospital. "I've never seen anyone that sick in my life. It was awful," she remembered, furrowing her dark eyebrows.

The Home Depot executive never lost her cool during the four days and nights she stayed beside Trevor in the hospital. She rolled his gurney down the hall for tests, relieved his nausea with cold towels, and took copious notes about his injured brain. In addition, she acted as his highly organized advocate with doctors and nurses.

"I was working like a businessperson would work a [business] problem," she explained.

Trevor had to relearn the critical skills of eating, talking, and speaking, but he did so very quickly. The digital technology specialist returned to the cable and entertainment giant Comcast Corporation just six weeks after his stroke. "He has some lingering effects, but nothing that takes away from his work or family life," Tank reported.

The frightening episode intensified her work/life sway by blurring the lines between work and family life. "You don't have a work self and a home self," she pointed out.

Her husband's stroke also strengthened her belief in bringing "your humanity to work and [enabling] that for your people," the thirty-seven-year-old vice president told me. Small gestures on the job "can really lift someone else up and help them be supported in a moment where it really matters to them."

During Tank's visit to a Home Depot branch office in 2019, for instance, an hourly employee pulled her aside to divulge that she was battling metastatic breast cancer. "I know your mom had breast cancer and you have the mutation," the woman added. "I just want you to know that I'm fighting."

Tank and her mother have a mutation on a BRCA gene, which highly raises an individual's risk of getting hereditary breast or ovarian cancer. Her mom was then battling both diseases. The Home Depot executive had spoken openly about those highly personal problems with many of her colleagues.

Tank embraced her ailing associate. She views the encounter as a special part of that business trip. A hug appears to have "nothing to do with work. But it has everything to do with work because our people are our company," she argued. "We're a family-oriented culture." If employees or their family members have health issues, their care takes priority and "we'll cover the work."

The Fatal Illness of a Parent

The 2012 death of her sixty-four-year-old father was a watershed event for Danielle Scalzo, an ambitious young lawyer at Willkie Farr & Gallagher. The venerable law firm, founded in 1888, was once home to a future U.S. Supreme Court justice and two New York governors.

"I lost my dad very suddenly to a heart attack," Scalzo recollected sadly. As the finance chief of a small company, "he spent his whole life working." We chatted while seated at a pale blond oval table in a Willkie Farr conference room. Our forty-fifth-floor venue provided a panoramic view of midtown Manhattan.

Scalzo and her husband were not yet parents when her father died. "I was very focused on my career," she said. "I was working all the time. I was staying at the office until three in the morning because I could." She worked weekends, too, because she believed she should—and "there was always something to do."

She had commenced her legal career at Willkie Farr in 2006, aspiring to be a partner someday. But the demise of her father before he could retire starkly reminded Scalzo that work can consume too much time. "You kind of have this existential crisis of 'What am I doing with my life?'" She wondered whether she should drop her pursuit of a partnership.

Rather than abandon her career goal, she vowed to seek an equilibrium between her job and her personal life. "If I could find a way to do [the work] with some balance, then maybe it was something that I could do longer term," she pointed out. "The way that I was doing it before was not sustainable for the rest of my life."

She acquired some balance by revamping her work habits. She stopped checking every draft document four times. She delegated more administrative duties to others. And she concentrated her time and energy on what mattered most to her clients.

In 2013, she gave birth for the first time. "The combination of my dad dying and my daughter being born were really . . . the biggest catalysts in that change [of perspective] for me," she went on.

Willkie Farr picked the thirty-four-year-old associate for a partnership during her second maternity leave in 2015. Scalzo's mother died of uterine cancer the next year. She delivered her younger son in 2018. She ended her latest maternity leave weeks before our sky-scraper session.

With three small children, the corporate law specialist is work-ing on her improved version of work/life sway. "You're not on a daily basis going to achieve any sort of balance," she remarked.

But you can sway. Staying at the office past her kids' bedtime to-night won't upset her because "tomorrow I'll sneak out early and read them a book before bed," she told me that March day. "You kind of lose the guilt."

Allard Dembe, a retired Ohio State University public health pro-fessor, offered another good reason why thirtysomething execu-tive mothers should curb their workaholic tendencies: "You may be forsaking your [future] health." He found a connection between women driving themselves hard early in their careers and develop-ing chronic diseases in their fifties and sixties.

Dembe documented this link as the lead investigator on a study, published in 2016, that analyzed thirty-two years of the job histo-ries of 7,492 Americans. He and his coauthor, Xiaoxi Yao, explored the impact of prolonged heavy work schedules on the occurrence of eight major illnesses years later. Women, who made up about 51 percent of their sample, were more likely to later develop serious illnesses than were men.

Female employees regularly toiling more than sixty hours a week were more than three times as likely to eventually develop heart dis-ease, cancer, arthritis, or diabetes—and twice as likely to develop chronic lung disease or asthma—than those on a conventional forty-hour schedule. Even women averaging between forty-one and fifty hours a week substantially increased their long-term chances of developing a serious disease.

The threefold increased risk among women with workdays ex-ceeding twelve hours "was a very unexpected finding," Dembe said during our interview. "I was flabbergasted." Until recently, occupational health researchers had never analyzed data by gender, he continued. "They didn't view it as an important question."

The implications are huge. Many working women have never understood the necessity of avoiding various health risks because male-dominated science didn't bother to track their health. Medical research into serious lung and heart diseases includes few women or omits tallying results by gender, other investigators have reported.

A Seriously Ill Infant

It's tough enough to be a first-time working mother; dealing with a seriously ill newborn seriously complicates life—as Nancy Bong found. Her older son, Max, was born in December 2014, days after she interviewed at OppenheimerFunds for her first executive spot. At the time, the thirty-six-year-old manager was working for Neuberger Berman Group, a rival money management firm.

Bong endured more than twenty-four hours of unsuccessful labor. Nine-pound Max arrived via an emergency cesarean section. Four days later, she and her husband were ready to take him home. But "the baby won't stop crying. He's inconsolable," she said, recalling the nightmarish moments in the present tense. A nurse caught him having a seizure.

Max was bleeding in his brain due to a skull fracture. No one knew whether his delivery or a hospital mishap had caused his head injury. "That's probably one of the scariest things you could ever think of," Bong said.

The newborn stayed in an intensive care unit for six nights. Hopeful that his fractured skull would heal on its own, physicians postponed surgery.

Their wait-and-see attitude thrust the sleep-deprived new parents into a state of constant fear about Max. "We never knew if he was crying because he was in pain or because he was a baby," Bong said. And "we didn't know if we would have a special needs child going forward."

She received an offer to be a managing director of OppenheimerFunds during the fourth week of her twelve-week maternity leave from Neuberger Berman. "It was a great promotion," she went on. "I couldn't believe that this was happening to me."

Yet the new mother felt too tired and stressed out from Max to press OppenheimerFunds for a generous pay package. "I don't recommend negotiating your offer while you're sleep deprived," she commented. She began her executive position in March 2015.

Max's skull fracture healed without surgery. But because he started talking late, he needed speech therapy the summer before his second birthday. "Even now, he's not as articulate as some of his friends at school," Bong told me. "We'll always continue to monitor him."

A very sick child "definitely puts everything into perspective," she noted. She left OppenheimerFunds in 2019 to join VanEck, the asset management firm. When problems arise at the office, she remembers that such setbacks are nothing compared to what she endured after Max fractured his skull.

Midcareer Health Crises

A startling health scare midway through their managerial ascents served as a wake-up call for certain older Power Moms. Among them is Pernille Spiers-Lopez, the global chief human resource officer of

IKEA Group between 2009 and 2011. She had previously been in charge of North America for the furniture giant.

In 1990, IKEA hired the native of Denmark to be a U.S. sales manager on the West Coast. By the late 1990s, she was managing an IKEA store in Pittsburgh. That was when she was promoted to managing human resources for North America.

She and her husband, a middle school principal, were then the parents of a boy and girl under six years old. Rather than uproot her family from Pittsburgh, Spiers-Lopez commuted back and forth every week between her home and her Philadelphia office. Her demanding new assignment also required extensive business travel. "I kept adding to my plate" without setting priorities, she confessed. "I call it 'the years of living in the pressure cooker.'"

Compounding those pressures, Spiers-Lopez was pushing male IKEA executives to place more women in key leadership roles. But she felt as though she was making little headway. Around 1999, she conducted a lengthy meeting about creating a diversity agenda for the company. She ignored the numbness in her arm throughout her daylong session in Philadelphia.

"I don't feel well," she told the IKEA colleague she was driving back to their hotel that evening. Sensing that she was going to black out, she pulled off the freeway. She feared she had had a heart attack.

An ambulance rushed her to a hospital. En route, "I remember looking at my feet and the blinking red light while I was laying [sic] there and saying 'Is this success?'"

An emergency room doctor concluded that she had had an anxiety attack. "This is what stress does to you over a long period of time," the physician stated sternly.

Looking back, Spiers-Lopez views the harsh warning as the best gift anyone ever bestowed on her. The anxiety attack made the forty-year-old executive realize that she could no longer keep running on all cylinders. Months of thoughtful introspection and keeping a journal enabled her to acknowledge her vincibility.

At the same time, drafting a personal mission statement and a list of her core values empowered her to resist certain requests. "That [word] 'should' is what gets you into trouble," she observed.

When IKEA elevated her to its North American presidency in 2001, she refused to let the powerful post consume her completely. "Nothing fazed me like the way it had earlier," she continued. Her husband obtained a job as a high school principal near Philadelphia, and the family relocated there.

Laurie Siegel, another first-wave executive, reset her priorities after a difficult bout of double pneumonia. "I'm sure [the illness] was a direct result of doing too much," she recollected. Like Spiers-Lopez, she confronted her health crisis during a long-distance commute.

Siegel's husband, Joe, and their two school-age daughters didn't immediately follow her in early 2000, when Honeywell International gave her an influential human resources role for a Phoenix unit of the industrial company. She anticipated that her weekly commute between Morristown, New Jersey, and Phoenix would not last long. Her husband intended to move their family once the girls finished their school year four months later.

However, "it was the worst four months in my entire career," she said. "I was in a new role. So I was really trying to prove myself."

She worked twelve-hour days because "I had nothing else going on." The forty-four-year-old HR leader usually felt run down and too exhausted to cook. For solo dinners in her rental apartment, "I would pull up a fork at the refrigerator and eat whatever Chinese food was left."

During her flight from New Jersey to Arizona early one Monday morning, she started vomiting. "I was kind of delirious," she recalled. She was taken away in an ambulance shortly after her plane landed.

It turned out that she had severe double pneumonia, which required her to spend five days in the intensive care unit of a Phoenix hospital. It was the first time she had ever been hospitalized for an illness. Doctors grounded her for another two weeks and made her wear an oxygen mask when she finally flew home to her family.

Once Siegel recovered, she reexamined her roles as a busy executive and mom. She recognized that she was operating within a fragile ecosystem. "I had to be more thoughtful about how I spent my energy." She became less willing to take nonvital international work trips. She also got more involved in arranging memorable vacations for her family.

Siegel's illness proved a crucial turning point for her husband as well. Following their Phoenix move, Joe quit AT&T in order to rear their daughters. He had overseen risk management in the telecom company's leasing business.

"Someone needs to be home and . . . be there for our kids to make sure that our lives are prioritized right," he told his wife. "It's not going to be you, because you're clearly on a [senior management] path that I'm not on." Siegel eventually became the chief human resources officer of Tyco International.

Significant Sickness Strikes the CEO

The timing is almost always bad when an executive mom at the apex of a business develops a serious malady. Carol Bartz learned that she had breast cancer on her first day as the first female CEO of Autodesk.

Bartz underwent surgery on both breasts a month later and soon resumed her leadership of Autodesk. She increased its revenue and share price during her fourteen years in its corner office. She stepped down in 2006 and later became the CEO of Yahoo!

It was a similar story of awful timing for Katia Beauchamp, the cofounder and CEO of Birchbox, the online beauty business. While expecting her fourth child in late 2018, the thirty-five-year-old executive developed a dangerous pregnancy complication. She said she had agreed to be hospitalized because she had faced "a very high risk of bleeding to death."

Beauchamp led Birchbox from her hospital bed during the final hundred days of her pregnancy, surrounded by desk photos of her one-year-old son and four-year-old twin boys. Her husband, Greg, became their de facto single parent, assisted by their nanny and visiting grandparents. "He actually had to deal with the fact that they were getting less parenting," she observed. "That was hard." Greg, who owns a commercial and film production company, managed the daily child care while "taking care of all of the fundamentals like groceries, kids' supplies, [and] activities for fun."

His extensive parental duties during Beauchamp's lengthy hospitalization solidified her positive attitude about their coparenting. "It isn't about this strict definition of 'Well, you cook and I do dishes,'" she noted. "It's much more about thinking [of the] big picture: What can we each bring that makes our life work and makes it wonderful?"

Though Beauchamp hated being isolated from her family, "I actually worked from the hospital very well," she said during our interview. In a *Fortune* article about CEOs bearing babies, she recollected how she had initially felt nervous "to be that vulnerable, but I got comfortable with it." Staffers conferred with Beauchamp in her

Manhattan hospital room, and she did video chats with Birchbox board members, the 2019 piece stated.

She even negotiated her company's important partnership deal with Walgreens Boots Alliance during her lengthy stay. She closed the deal from her hospital bed on the day she unexpectedly went into labor.

The drugstore chain inaugurated sales of Birchbox products in several major cities that December—the same week Beauchamp's newborn daughter was in the hospital fighting a life-threatening respiratory virus. The baby fully recovered.

In another case of ill-timed executive illness, Penny Herscher prevailed despite a trio of strokes. The boomer mother began her first CEO stint in 1996 at Simplex Solutions, a California start-up that made software for designing semiconductors. Her daughter, Melanie, was four, and her son, Sebastian, was two.

Herscher suffered her first stroke in 2000 at the age of forty while preparing to take Simplex public. The stroke slurred her speech and left her bedridden for six weeks. Her chief financial officer had to complete a pending acquisition without her.

The CEO recovered sufficiently to take Simplex public in 2001. "I was [still] pushing very, very hard, working at all hours," she admitted the first time we met in 2015. "Too much alcohol and Diet Coke and not enough working out."

The following year, she sold Simplex to Cadence Design Systems, a software company. She suffered two more serious strokes in 2003, when she was the general manager of a Cadence division. She lost the normal use of her eye muscles, and she couldn't read for a year.

She intended to resume working again. But "the stress was too high," she said. "I didn't understand the price of being that driven at that time." Herscher quit Cadence, took trips abroad, and reconsidered her reckless approach to life. "You have to get over the idea that you are immortal," she explained. With the second round of strokes, "I definitely got a whack on the side of the head [from God]."

The tech industry veteran decided to care for herself better. It took a life-threatening illness to force her to take the care issue seriously, she conceded. She stuck with her healthier lifestyle after assuming the top job at FirstRain, a business analytics company, in 2004.

She ate well, swam long distances, and made sure that she slept enough every night. She commanded FirstRain until 2015 and its board of directors until 2017. These days, she urges her grown offspring to embrace a healthy lifestyle. Her message? "Don't live on Diet Cokes and Advils when you are working very hard."

Melanie grasped that lesson long ago after growing up with an overworked mother overcome by a stroke. It was frightening "to think your mom is going to die every day after her strokes," she said during our interview. "I never want to be [someone] who's ignorant of what's important—whether it's my health or my family."

Distress over an Offspring's Pain Puzzle

Like Penny Herscher, Denise Ramos is a hard-driving executive. Yet her successful management career left her ill prepared to cope with her son's years of persistent, undiagnosed pain. In 2016, doctors figured out that her twenty-eight-year-old son has EDS—the same disabling genetic disorder that besets Abra.

"My son's situation was very emotional and very complex," Ramos remembered. "My job was [always] very complex. You only have so much capacity to absorb so much."

After completing her MBA degree, Ramos joined Atlantic Richfield Company as a financial analyst in 1979. She leveraged her type A personality and financial acumen to move up the executive ladder at the global energy company and other big businesses.

Her relentless ambition bore fruit in 2011, when she took the helm of ITT, a manufacturing conglomerate. The new chief executive officer arose at 2:00 every morning and viewed her lofty position as a 24/7 obligation. "You have no time to think or do anything else."

Her son's pain problems commenced during high school. At the time, Ramos was a financial executive for Yum! Brands, the owner of KFC and other fast-food chains. She and her husband, a stay-at-home dad, lived with their son and daughter in Louisville, Kentucky.

Clueless about the cause of his discomfort, the teen "started self-medicating," Ramos said. "It takes quite a bit of opioids just to manage pain." His high school suspended him for erratic behavior and drug abuse, according to Ramos. He ended up migrating from school to school and struggled academically.

"He could not get his pain down to a manageable level," Ramos told me. "It was a very tough time for all of us."

During her son's junior year, Ramos became a chief financial officer for the first time—and a long-distance commuter. She was recruited by Furniture Brands International, a major manufacturer headquartered in St. Louis.

The executive insisted that her husband deal with their teen's troubles. "I was so focused on my job and my career. I just shut that part of my life out," she told me, her voice breaking with emotion. "I feel like I should have been there for my son," she went on. "My husband did his best. . . . [But] it was my accountability also as a parent."

Ramos regrets blocking off her son when he needed her greatly. "I made a choice. I would make a different choice today," she said. Her desire for closer ties with him influenced her decision to retire from ITT's number one job in 2019 at age sixty-two.

These days, "I have very real and honest conversations with my son, [who] is grateful I am there for him," she continued. "We are so close. He shares everything. It is a totally different relationship."

When we spoke, the former ITT leader had just retained an expert to find him the best pain medication specialist in New York. She knows that her son must grapple with EDS for the rest of his days.

Mothering a Chronically Ill Adult

I'm still figuring out how to effectively mother a chronically ill adult. For example, I didn't fully grasp that EDS had destroyed Abra's dreams of a global career until we chatted for this book.

She graduated from the University of Chicago with a degree in international studies and worked in Malawi for seven months before getting an MBA degree from Brandeis University. Her next employer dispatched organizational consultants like her on temporary gigs in countries all over the world.

The EDS diagnosis was especially upsetting because "I had to literally give up how I think of myself. What I want for myself long term," Abra revealed during our dinner at a noisy Italian restaurant in a Minneapolis suburb.

"I really wanted to have a global career overseas [and] live in developing countries," she informed me. "I had to give that up because there isn't good medical care in those places, and my health isn't stable enough to be able to work those kinds of jobs."

Abra lost far more than her preferred career path. "I lost friends," she said wistfully. "I lost my personality [by] not being able to be as out there in the world as I want to be."

Yet somehow my strong-willed daughter did progress from intense anger over her painful condition to a Zen-like acceptance of her altered self. "Culturally, we invest so much in people's value for what they do," she explained. "You have to realize that you're still worth something—even if you can't do the things that you had envisioned for yourself."

In 2015, she attended a conference of the Ehlers-Danlos Society, a group committed to improving the lives of those affected by her disorder. She will never forget a comment posted on a message whiteboard there. "Remember, you are a human being," a conference participant had scribbled. "Not a human doing."

Living with a chronic health condition has taught Abra that it's okay to seek help. Expressing a request "allows me to be more authentic," she noted. "I have more practice admitting that I'm vulnerable."

I asked my daughter how I and other working mothers could better assist their adult offspring who have chronic health conditions.

"Going through the stages of grief is actually relevant" because your grown child will never get better, she replied. In my case, "you have to drop your expectations so that your daughter can live the life that is real for her—and not the life that you thought you wanted for her."

Abra also expressed gratitude for my increased understanding of her EDS-related needs. Nevertheless, she wishes that I had been more empathetic at the outset of her painful journey. "Saying 'Wow, this sounds really hard. This sounds really frustrating. What can I do to help?' is probably an orientation that's more helpful ultimately," she said.

Truly wrenching moments occur when we or a loved one suffers a serious health crisis. The executives I interviewed sought ways to turn their trials by illness into pivotal moments. Some drew on their professional crisis management experience to deal with such setbacks. Their life lessons might help every working mother to cope better.

One critical lesson: Give high priority to keeping yourself healthy, both physically and mentally. Consider whether you work too much and vacation too little. Bring more of your authentic self to work. Review your coparenting arrangements to make sure that they're equitable before a health crisis strikes.

Another important point is that browbeating ourselves over inadequate parenting in such an awful situation—as I did—isn't a good idea. I now recognize that working-mother guilt can be a corrosive, counterproductive sentiment. Savvy Power Moms have figured out ways to ditch those feelings. The next chapter describes their ten best tactics.

10

Ditch Working-Mother Guilt

My *Wall Street Journal* essay about combining motherhood and a career triggered a tsunami of hostility from both men and women.

The *Journal* published a full page of scathing letters to the editor the day after I stopped breastfeeding seven-month-old Dan—a move that happened sooner than I would have preferred. One letter writer said my son was better off that I worked because I was obviously an unfit mother. A bulging folder atop my desk held another forty letters that the *Journal* considered too nasty to print.

Sick to my stomach and even sicker at heart, I left the Washington office early that afternoon. During my morose walk home from the bus stop, I rang the doorbell of a nearby friend, Susan Wildstrom. The mother of two boys enjoyed teaching high school mathematics part-time.

Seated in a living room armchair, I tearfully described readers' venomous reactions to my first-person essay on the *Journal*'s editorial page. Their comments had rattled me so much that I might abandon my career, I confided to my friend.

"But do you enjoy working?" she asked.

"Of course," I replied. "I wouldn't be happy staying home full-time."

"Then fuck 'em," she said.

My friend was right. I would be a better mother for Dan because I worked outside our suburban Maryland home. I intensified my commitment to making working motherhood work. I never again doubted my decision—despite occasional recurrences of angst. In effect, I ditched the broader guilt trip imposed on me by the narrow-minded norms of the 1980s.

Working-mother guilt persists in American society today because gender role expectations haven't evolved enough. Such guilt has troubled Power Moms from both generations. Yet most have sought to reject it as a debilitating waste of energy.

Melanie Healey, the first female group president of North America for Procter & Gamble, repeatedly encourages younger mothers to drop their guilt. "There is so much you are doing by being a working mom in terms of role modeling . . . and still being around [your kids] when it matters most," she suggests. Rather than fretting over your family's late weeknight dinners, turn that apparent negative into a positive by reminding yourself that "at least you're eating together."

For instance, she always ate breakfast and dinner with her children and read them bedtime stories when she wasn't away on a business trip. "Building in wonderful quality time when you are together . . . helps ditch the guilt," she told me.

Fellow boomer Andrea Jung, the first female CEO of Avon Products, ditched her guilt partly through strict self-discipline. She decided to no longer worry whether she chose wisely between her two youngsters' athletic events and her business meetings.

Hired by the cosmetics company as a product manager in 1994, Jung was a single mother throughout her twelve years at its helm. Accepting her difficult choices about work and family meant that "one day Avon wins, and one day the children win," she commented during our interview. "The one thing that helped me for the lion's share of my career was [saying] 'I am not even going to think about what I am not at,'" she continued. "And live in the moment."

But living in the moment isn't always easy. Nor is it a surefire antidote for guilt—as GenX executive mothers such as Kathy O'Sullivan can attest. She's an audit partner in the real estate practice of Ernst & Young, the U.S. affiliate of the big accounting and consulting firm. She gave birth to triplet boys at age thirty-three in June 2013, weeks after she learned that she had been tapped for a partnership. Her daughter arrived four years later.

"When I am with [my kids], I strive to be completely present for them," O'Sullivan told me. "That's how I ditch the guilt."

Motivated by that credo, she took all four children along when she purchased Thanksgiving groceries right before the 2018 holiday. She and her attorney husband were expecting thirty-three guests at their family's Thanksgiving feast. He was making beds and tidying their attached home in Queens during her Stop & Shop trek that Saturday.

Their kids "were just happy to be with me," O'Sullivan remembered. Her happiness over being with them quickly evaporated, however. She failed to notice that her boys were grabbing their favorite food items and tossing them into her grocery cart.

"I ended up with three bags of Oreos," she said ruefully. "Why didn't I just leave them home with my husband? It would have been much easier." She believes that taking her quartet of youngsters grocery shopping for Thanksgiving reflected her underlying guilt over not spending enough time with them.

Employed fathers don't experience the same sentiments, according to Eve Rodsky's book, *Fair Play: A Game-Changing Solution for When You Have Too Much to Do (and More Life to Live)*. "Recent research exploring mother's guilt found that working mothers feel far guiltier than working fathers, especially around the idea of missing out on moments when they 'should be there,'" she wrote.

Other Power Moms from the current cadre are highly outspoken about the futility of guilt, however. "This whole concept of working mothers' guilt is more like a social contrivance," insisted Bonny Lee, the vice president of corporate finance at SiriusXM Radio, the satellite radio company. Her daughter, Francesca, was ten years old and her son, Jude, was eight when we met in December 2018. A Frank Sinatra song blared loudly in the lobby of the midtown Manhattan skyscraper where Lee works.

"I personally don't feel guilty about working. And I don't even feel particularly guilty about sometimes preferring work over spending time with the children," the forty-three-year-old executive said. "I place a lot of value on how I define myself by my professional success." It's so important that "I don't care if you think that's shallow," she continued.

A number of executive moms interviewed for this book described how ditching working-mother guilt had positively affected both their careers and their kids. Here are their ten best life hacks for allaying guilt.

Number 1: Find and Keep A Great Child Care Provider

Nothing is more essential to an employed mother's professional success than reliable, high-quality child care. Some prior-generation executives, such as lawyer Anne Weisberg, gained that peace of mind by keeping the same nanny/housekeeper for decades. Otherwise, "I would not be where I am today," the Paul, Weiss executive declared. "You have to see the [child care] help you get as an investment in your career."

A nanny's protracted tenure also boosted the career trajectory of Mindy Grossman, the two-time commander of a public company. She selected Lesbia Raez to care for her only child when Elysabeth, nicknamed "Lizzy," was eighteen months old.

Grossman fondly regarded Raez as her secret weapon. The nanny's tight bond with Lizzy "gave me great comfort," she said. "We were all family, making things work."

In 2000, the executive wouldn't accept an attractive offer from Nike to run its global apparel business until she knew that her planned long-distance commute from New York would suit Raez. The sneaker giant is headquartered near Portland, Oregon.

Grossman discussed the Nike offer with her nanny and her husband, Neil. Raez would need to arrive before he departed for work and stay overnight with ten-year-old Lizzy during his business trips. After the nanny agreed to the schedule, Grossman began overseeing the big Nike unit.

She was its sole woman in senior management. She flew east to see her family for about half of her Nike tenure. In Grossman's absence, Raez went the extra mile for Neil and Lizzy. She commenced work at 6:00 a.m. and occasionally stayed at their Manhattan apartment until 9:00 p.m.—or later.

During Grossman's six-year stewardship, Nike's global apparel business grew to a $4 billion operation. She next became the chief executive officer of HSN, a retailer known for its home shopping network. She and fellow executives took HSN public in August 2008. She earned accolades for restoring profitability and transforming the shopping service into a digital company. In 2017, she took charge of WW International, a diet-and-wellness business that was previously called Weight Watchers International.

Grossman retained her valued nanny for twenty years. Once Lizzy entered college, Raez "ended up taking care of the dog and the house," the CEO recalled during our session at the Manhattan headquarters of WW International. More than two dozen family photos crowd the narrow desk in her office, leaving scant space for her to work.

Raez attended Lizzy's wedding and baby showers. "We talk on every holiday. She's come to visit," Grossman reported. "We still all are very close."

A longtime nanny named Paulette helped assuage the guilt of boomer mom Laurie Siegel by compiling a comprehensive description of her daughters' activities every day for seven years. "It was a way for me to understand some of the [key] details of my kids' lives," the former HR executive said. "I could talk to the kids about things that had happened [throughout] their day," such as why they fought with each other or how they had performed during swim class.

During our get-together, Siegel gingerly handed me a worn black-and-white composition notebook filled with Paulette's daily log about the girls. Julia and Emma "were both pretty grumpy on the way home from ballet," one handwritten entry read. On a different page, Paulette disclosed that Emma "has been unhappy today. She has thrown fits for really no reason."

Now that both daughters are grown, Siegel has thrown away their juvenile drawings and letters from camp. But she refuses to throw away their nanny's log. "It's such a record of my children's childhood," she said.

Certain time-starved contemporary mothers depend on two caregivers. They can often afford the extra expense because they landed a well-paid position at a relatively young age. Laura Chepucavage, the Bank of America executive, recruited a second nanny after the 2018 birth of her fourth child.

Her full-time nanny works from 7:30 a.m. until 6:00 p.m., assisted by a part-time one who works three weekdays from 2:30 p.m.

to 7:30 p.m. Chepucavage typically reaches her suburban New Jersey home around 6:30 p.m. Now, she said, "I can go up and get changed and have like two minutes just to gather myself" before she and the second nanny bathe her kids.

Of course, few employed parents earn enough money to have multiple providers of child care. But less pricey alternatives exist, such as a shared nanny or time trades with stay-at-home moms. Betsy Holden, the former co-CEO of Kraft Foods, sometimes enlisted aid from such neighborhood mothers for her son and daughter. In turn, she invited their kids to her suburban Chicago home on Friday nights and served them new foods from the Kraft test kitchens.

You should create your own group of "alloparents," said Amy Westervelt in her book *Forget "Having It All": How America Messed Up Motherhood—and How to Fix It*. She defines alloparenting as various adults in a community sharing responsibility for its children with biological parents. She proposed "forming a tight-knit group of other parents in your community, people with whom you would comfortably swap parenting duties."

Number 2: Give Children a Voice in Your Work Life

As a rising star at P&G, Melanie Healey traveled a lot while her son and daughter were growing up. Yet "they never put the guilt trip on me," she recollected.

A key reason: Healey made Nick and Jackie feel important by explaining her rationale for every work trip. She started doing so once Nick turned five years old and Jackie was three. After they reached school age, the executive alerted them ahead of time of her expected travel-related absence from, say, one of their lacrosse games.

"But I want you to know I am thinking of you. I am rooting for you," she assured each child. "When I am back, I will be here for your [next] game." She also encouraged her kids to select the most important events that they wanted her to attend throughout their school year.

She elaborated on her approach during our interview for this book. Teaching children to participate in their working parents' decision-making process "sets things up for a more positive, all-around experience," she observed.

Dana Spinola, a second-wave Power Mom, goes much further by involving her three sons in an unconventional way. The founder of fab'rik, the Atlanta-based chain of clothing boutiques, she organized a personal "board of directors"—and installed the boys alongside its adult members. This "wise council" reminds her to stick to her work and family goals.

Spinola credits her sons with curbing her tendency to focus too hard on fab'rik when she's with them. "They're wiser than anyone," she said. "They don't really ever say, 'I need your time,' unless they need it." Roughly once a week, one of her boys expresses that need by invoking his right to a family movie night in their home.

On such evenings, "there will be nothing else done [for work]," Spinola explained. Multitasking, computers, and cell phones are banned because "we are all watching the movie."

Number 3: Arrange Workday Getaways with Your Kids

Like Spinola, Mary Hamilton significantly expanded a remedy for guilt that the prior generation of executive moms merely flirted with. Boomers rarely skipped work in order to spend a day with their offspring.

Hamilton, a managing director at Accenture, the global management consultancy, inaugurated a regular Mama Day during her workweek for each of her three sons in September 2018. Theo had just turned four years old, and her twins, William and Marcus, were toddlers.

She uses three days of vacation every quarter for the outings, taking a different boy to San Francisco–area museums and parks every day. "What I'm trying to do is create some independent memories for each of them," she observed.

She initially hoped to arrange her special excursions once a month, but that proved to be too ambitious. "In the long run," she continued, "we'll be able to create many great special memories— probably even more so if the special days are a bit more scarce."

Mama Days are usually magical moments for her sons. After Theo saw scuba divers at the California Academy of Sciences, "he was obsessed with scuba divers for months," Hamilton recalled. Her twins have enjoyed visiting locales ranging from a tall bell tower to a children's creativity museum with a carousel nearby.

Number 4: Enlist Extensive Help from Extended Family

Certain women from both generations avoided working-mother guilt because their own mothers helped bring up their children. They're typified by Margaret Keane, the CEO of Synchrony, the big issuer of credit cards.

She was a Citibank middle manager when she bore Brian in 1989. Upon resuming work, she dropped off her son at her mother's home every weekday morning. The latter lived just blocks away from Keane's residence in Lynbrook, a New York suburb. Keane's husband, Jerry, a building doorman for a Manhattan apartment building, picked up Brian after work.

Keane's mother moved in with them when their daughter, Kaity, born in 1992, was two years old. She stayed for the next twenty-two years. She prepared home-cooked meals, and "my kids ate dinner the same time every night—whether I was there or not," the Synchrony CEO said. "Six o'clock on the dot. [But] I probably was never there." She blames her long commute.

"My mother was a huge personality, larger than life," she reminisced fondly. "She knew how to do everything." When her eighty-nine-year-old mom died in 2017, Keane was by her side.

Number 5: Carve Out Time for Yourself

Anjali Sud toils long days as the leader of Vimeo, which is owned by IAC, a media holding company. Vimeo tools assist filmmakers, small businesses, and other video creators to produce and distribute online content. She manages a team of more than six hundred people.

The former investment banker was only thirty-three years old when IAC announced her promotion to Vimeo CEO in mid-2017. The appointment made her the youngest head of any IAC unit. In 2018, Vimeo generated nearly $160 million in revenue.

On weekday evenings and weekends, Sud devotes a lot of time to her son. Saavan was born in November 2018. On Sundays, however, she devotes at least two hours to herself.

"I need . . . time for just me," she said during our session in her second-floor Manhattan office soon after her maternity leave ended. She sat near an oversized whiteboard, casually dressed in tight black jeans and a bulky blue sweater.

Her husband, Matt, a full-time investor, likes bonding alone with their son during Sud's Sunday "me time." She typically dons her

AirPods to "just walk around the city by myself," she said, locking both hands around her left knee. "I'll go get a coffee. I run errands. I read a celebrity magazine." Occasionally, she also arranges Sunday brunch with friends.

"I'm very proactively and explicitly trying to rejuvenate every week," she pointed out. "I genuinely feel zero guilt for taking this time."

As a result, she loves her intensely demanding job even more than she did before she became a mom. "Taking time for myself has not only helped me be more effective as a CEO," she went on, because "it has helped me be a more relaxed, happy, and fulfilled mother."

Finding guilt-free time for yourself is a common parental challenge. Parents are more likely than nonparents to admit feeling guilty when they take time for various types of self-care. About 36 percent of U.S. parents compared with 26 percent of individuals without progeny acknowledged feeling such guilt in a 2019 survey of 1,070 adults conducted for Birchbox, the online beauty business.

Many present-generation Power Moms with little kids recognize that taking time for themselves can lessen their guilt feelings by making them better executives and parents. Some found time to stay fit by installing sophisticated home equipment such as a Peloton high-tech stationary bike. Users can participate in live-streamed workout sessions, and women can join a Facebook group for Peloton moms.

Inside Chepucavage's traditional, colonial-style home, a Peloton occupies most of a largely empty room next to the living room. "Peloton has changed the way I work out," the banking executive told me. "I don't have to get in the car and go to the gym."

Chepucavage prefers to ride her stationary bike at 4:50 a.m. two mornings a week. Her children have fun playing nearby when she instead pedals before their bedtime. "If I'm doing the weight section, my kids . . . get the weights and they start doing [the work-out] with me."

Emily Chardac, another second-wave mother, lacked any fitness regimen during her four years at Guggenheim Partners, a global money manager. When we spoke, the thirty-four-year-old executive had a toddler and two school-age children. She was the second highest human resources officer at Guggenheim.

We reconnected in January 2020, right after Chardac quit her high-powered post to become a full-time HR consultant. She said she had resigned because she hated coming home feeling depleted, drained, and directionless. "The guilt was mostly self-imposed. 'What example am I giving my children?' I wasn't proud of the answer."

Being self-employed gives Chardac greater control over her schedule. With blocks of time that she reserved for staying fit, she attended Pilates, yoga, and ballet-style classes during the inaugural week of her consulting career.

"My clients are paying me for my expertise and balanced [work-and-family] approach. So I need to care for myself in a new way," she noted. "When I live my life authentically, I'm hoping that the guilt is a fleeting thought."

Number 6: Streamline Your Priorities

Time is an especially precious commodity for working mothers. While a busy Home Depot vice president, Stacey Tank somehow also found time to serve on five nonprofit boards. Her trick? She effectively invented a twenty-five-hour day.

You feel as though you gain that mythical hour by "streamlining everything that can be streamlined," she suggested during our interview. "Just be superefficient at the stuff that matters less so that you can spend time on the things that matter more."

Tank carefully organizes her daily routine to minimize unnecessary stress and duplicated efforts. She assembled a digital photo folder of her business outfits, matched with appropriate shoes and jewelry. A glance at the suitable combinations enables her to pack quickly for her frequent business trips.

She even bought a special towel that's guaranteed to dry hair 70 percent faster. She now spends three minutes blow-drying her long brown hair rather than the previous fifteen minutes.

In Tank's opinion, devising brutally efficient tactics resembles a game. Winning the game creates extra time with her two sons—and reduces her feelings of guilt.

Number 7: Take Strategic Breaks

Several executives overcame working-mother guilt by taking sabbaticals from their high-octane spots. Jane Stevenson, the Korn Ferry vice chair, took a year off in 2009 so she could develop deeper ties with eighth grader Emily and fifth grader Jonathan. She was then a partner and top biller at Heidrick & Struggles International, a rival executive search firm. She ran its biggest practice, which recruited chief marketing officers. "I was definitely burning the candle at three ends," she said.

I asked Stevenson why she had taken a sabbatical at a time of tremendous professional accomplishments during her late forties.

"Everyone said, 'Kids don't like you once they get to a certain age,'" she replied. "And so I didn't want to miss my window."

But from a career standpoint, "it was a very scary decision," she conceded. "I was panicked." Just before her sabbatical commenced,

Heidrick & Struggles insisted that she commit to generating $1 million of revenue while she was away.

Stevenson, a devout Seventh-Day Adventist, prayed for divine guidance before she signed the onerous agreement. "I just needed to do this [sabbatical]. It was like a calling," she recollected. "I said, 'Lord, you know how I got to this point. I don't know how this is going to work. But I'm going to sign this because I'm taking this year [off] and I'm just stepping out in faith that it will work out.'"

During her sabbatical, she generated leads for more than $2 million of revenue—without placing a single business development call. When corporate clients approached her about possible fresh search assignments, she directed them to relevant colleagues. "The work that I'd done all my life paid off," she noted.

Among other things, the protracted work break allowed her to be Jonathan's classroom mother and a chaperone for Emily's weeklong class trip. "I would never in a million years trade that year. It was the best year of my life," she observed. She recommends a sabbatical as a smart strategy for working moms to ditch their guilt.

Stevenson's sabbatical epitomized her version of work/life sway. She "taught me how to play full out," her grown daughter told me. That means "giving both my all at work and at home."

Upon hearing Emily's words, the usually unflappable Stevenson choked up. Being all you can be "is really what my whole life's been about," she said, fighting back tears. "You can do more than you think you can. But you have to be willing to live with the choices you make."

A multimonth sabbatical isn't available for everyone, of course. Yet even a brief strategic break, such as taking a day's or a week's vacation to host playdates at your house with youngsters of stay-at-home moms who assist you during child care crises, could prove worthwhile.

Number 8: Practice Sway Every Day

Living with your choices guilt free may require taking a strong stance in support of your work/life principles. Alexis DiResta took such a stance in 2012. The thirty-two-year-old mother was being wooed to join a small manufacturer of cosmetics as its vice president of product development.

The senior role would pay her $30,000 more than she was then making. Because she knew she wanted a second child, she asked the owner of the family business about its maternity leave policy.

"I don't have a formal maternity leave policy. But I'll give you my word you would have three months," he promised DiResta.

"Well, why don't you have a formal policy?" she inquired.

"Because I can't do it for everybody," the owner responded.

The fact that there was an informal benefit limited to high-ranking mothers deeply rankled DiResta. "I would be talking out of both sides of my mouth if I said that I, as an executive, deserve this [leave] and this person who's an assistant does not," she explained to me. "That's really not what I stand for."

DiResta laid out that rationale in her letter declining the company's job offer. She described her discomfort over compromising her belief in maternity leave policies and her dedication to serving as a role model for other young women. "The most important thing to me is that the person I am perceived to be matches the person that I truly am," her letter stated.

She stuck to the same principles years later during job interviews after she left Estée Lauder, the cosmetics maker: she told would-be employers that her two kids are her number one priority and she would leave the office to handle any urgent family crisis.

She has led a new division of Away since fall 2019. The travel products company honored her family priorities and let her work from home about twice a week. Unfortunately, she got laid off in September 2020 due to the pandemic-driven downturn.

For Jerri DeVard, a meaningful test of her work/life principles occurred in the early 1990s, when an important work meeting was set for the same time as her daughter's appearance in a preschool play. The Pillsbury marketing manager felt special to be invited to a meeting conducted by an influential executive.

"I thought, 'Oh, my God, this meeting is so important. I'm going to miss my daughter's play,'" she said. "I remember being up all night, just riddled with guilt [and] wondering how I was going to tell her."

She lost sleep for another couple of nights. The day before Brooke's play, she changed her mind. She decided to skip the Pillsbury meeting because "I couldn't not be there for her." Her boss, a working dad, supported her choice.

Attending the preschool event persuaded the manager to no longer value herself solely based on job criteria such as titles. "Work was important, but it wasn't my life," noted DeVard, who later became an executive vice president of Office Depot. She left in March 2020.

Number 9: Support the Stay-at-Home Dad

A father who stays home with his children looks like a guaranteed cure for working-mother guilt. However, this cure works only if a Power Mom doesn't micromanage him and demonstrates her genuine appreciation.

Consider Bonny Lee, the SiriusXM Radio vice president. Born in Hong Kong, she and her parents immigrated to the United States when she was two. She obtained her first part-time job at age fourteen and got her first executive role in 2013 when SiriusXM hired the HBO financial planning manager.

Her husband, Sam, quit his job as an Ernst & Young strategy consultant in June 2018. He has since stayed home with their school-age offspring. At first, "he was definitely very sensitive about the fact that he's not working and [feared] that I would . . . start bossing him around like he was the help," she said during our interview.

Sam's fears proved realistic. One evening after dinner, for instance, Lee reminded him to wash a dish that had held raw meat. "It must have sounded like I was ordering him around to do stuff," she said. "He blew up at me."

Lee now hesitates before she complains about his performance as a stay-at-home dad. Nevertheless, "this is a very real issue that we continue to battle."

Melanie Healey, the P&G veteran, is extremely grateful that her husband, Bruce, ended his insurance industry management career in 1998 to start caring for Nick and Jackie. The consumer products giant had just relocated her and her family from Brazil to Venezuela. With that promotion, she oversaw its feminine care products business for Latin America.

Bruce soon became "the best stay-at-home dad ever," Healey said. "For me, it was obviously a huge sense of relief."

He maintained that crucial role after P&G named Healey North American general manager for those products and transferred her to the United States. In 2009, she took charge of the entire North American region.

Healey considers Bruce, whom she met in eighth grade, to be just as much of a mom as she is. They regularly celebrated Mother's Day together when their offspring were young; she encouraged them to wish him "Happy Father's Day" on her holiday.

"I had a partner who cared enough to give up an amazing career to stay home and raise two wonderful kids," she said gratefully. "Too few men have the courage to do this still."

Number 10: Accept Your Imperfections

Executive mothers often dumped their guilt by accepting their imperfections at home and in the office. For several first-wave women, the journey of self-discovery lasted years.

"If you expect perfection, you will let yourself down on both fronts, and you will never be happy," warned Michele Buck, the Hershey chief. Yet she didn't feel completely comfortable with her imperfections until she reached the corner office at the major candy maker. "If you're good enough to reach the [corporate] pinnacle," she said, "I guess it's okay to not be perfect."

Mindy Grossman attempted to be a perfect mother while running Nike's global apparel business. She did so because "the only way I could keep my life together was [by] controlling it and having it as structured as possible," she explained.

Her pursuit of perfection didn't work perfectly, either. She once flew home from Portland and immediately started straightening up her Manhattan apartment—at 1:00 a.m. "You're finally home, and this is what you are doing?" Neil demanded angrily.

Similarly, Grossman believed that she could counteract her frequent Nike-related absences from Lizzy by taking her daughter along on cool international business trips, such as to the Tour de France and the World Swimming Championships. "I thought I was being inclusive, and it was a way to spend more time together," the fast-talking executive recalled. "In retrospect, I would [have] carved out more alone time not affiliated with business."

Her grown daughter said that she also would have liked more private time with her mom during those trips. "I chose not to work in order to not have to make those choices," added Lizzy Grossman-Sirgey, a stay-at-home mother who delivered her own daughters in 2017 and 2019.

"I promise you that we will never go more than three weeks without seeing one another," Grossman told her daughter before the new
grandmother accepted the highest spot at WW International. The
CEO of the diet-and-wellness business kept her word. In addition,
she typically talks to her daughter between five and eight times a
day. Three encounters are mealtime video chats.

"Are you trying to make up for the time you missed with Lizzy in
the past?" I asked Grossman.

"There's probably a little bit of that," she conceded. In hindsight,
"it's not about perfection." Instead, she said, "it's about being there
when you need to be there"—and not beating yourself up when you
can't.

Fab'rik's Dana Spinola unsuccessfully sought to be the perfect
business leader. Though she wanted to stay close to her colleagues
and professional contacts, she amassed a whopping 300,000 unread
emails. "It was just three hundred thousand emails of guilt," she admitted. "I owed people things that I couldn't really deliver because
I was drained myself."

She suffered such severe burnout that coworkers forced her to
take a sabbatical in September 2017. She returned gradually, starting in early 2018. She switched to being chief visionary officer, a
less taxing assignment in which she can pace herself better. Every
Sunday night, she maps out the next week on a dry-erase board by
listing her nonnegotiable commitments for work and family in red
ink. She marks her negotiable obligations in green.

Spinola stopped aiming for perfection after she realized that although she's not great at certain things, she is really good at other
things. Working moms like her once expected that they would
emerge as the "do-it-all" generation, she pointed out. Though it is
clearly an unrealistic goal, at least "our generation is . . . open to
the conversation. We are asking the [work/family] questions," she

noted. "And I'm no longer hiding in my closet taking conference calls, making sure that the man on the other end of the call doesn't hear that I have a child."

I was saddened that both waves of Power Moms felt working-mother guilt. It was further evidence of why American society should treat employed parents better. On the other hand, I was heartened by the clever gambits that executive mothers have crafted to shed their guilt feelings. They have designed weekday Mama Days with their offspring, managed mundane tasks with hyperefficiency, arranged private time for themselves, and enthusiastically supported their stay-at-home spouses.

Second-wave women such as Spinola, Hamilton, Tank, and Di-Resta have gone far beyond the prior wave through their laser focus on reducing working-mother guilt. The extent of this generational divide will emerge in the coming chapter. I'll explore what Power Moms believe they got right or wrong about working parenthood—plus their views on the other generation.

11

Now and Then

I felt isolated at critical turning points during my pursuit of working motherhood. This scary sentiment initially hit me in my late twenties, when my *Wall Street Journal* boss sounded me out about becoming a U.S. bureau chief.

The promotion would make me the first female chief of a *Journal* bureau. But I declined the opportunity, partly because Mike and I were hoping to start a family soon. The role of manager mom struck me as totally unworkable—especially since I knew no manager moms at my employer.

I experienced a similar sense of isolation after the *Journal* approved my uncommon four-day schedule in late 1983. I spent every Friday with our youngsters for the next three years. Yet I couldn't educate my colleagues about the joys of a shortened workweek because I was afraid to disclose my special deal.

Like many baby-boom women back then, I thought I had to play the part of a lone ranger on the job. I now see that I missed a chance to improve the work and family lives of *Wall Street Journal* women by advocating decades ago for more female managers and an official policy about reduced schedules.

Hindsight is 20/20, of course. That was why I asked Power Moms to reveal their memorable accomplishments and shortcomings as working parents. Both waves also shared observations about how their prior or subsequent counterparts had excelled and fallen short.

Trailblazing boomers typically foundered because they lacked female mentors with kids, involved husbands, and supportive employers. "You were kind of out there on your own, forging your own way as an executive mom," recalled Peggy Daitch, a former vice president of the magazine publisher Condé Nast and mother of two grown progeny.

There was no way we could change workplaces ourselves, added Beth Comstock, the first female vice chair of GE. "We needed to ask for more help [and] never should have felt guilty about it."

Genevieve Roth, the ex–*Glamour* executive, believes that the prior generation's reluctance to request help with their mothering burdens frequently hindered their advancement. The anxiety "led to a lack of shared support systems among moms," the thirty-eight-year-old founder of Invisible Hand told me. Roth operates differently. She prefers to hire moms for key jobs at her social impact agency because "I've never met anyone as efficient as a working mother."

Executive moms such as Roth reap the fruits of their forerunners' hard labor—along with more sophisticated technology, egalitarian social attitudes, and employers keen to treat working parents better.

Comstock said that the younger women she counsels seem to be much calmer mothers because they "feel like they got it together." Yet even those moms haven't figured out work/life sway completely free of guilt. "I see that a lot," the GE alum went on. "They're supposed to be able to do all these things," but social media make things worse for them by promoting online images of perfectly balanced lives.

Here are six ways that executive mothers from each generation view the differences between now and then.

Now: Technology Works for You, Not the Other Way Around

These days, "you still worry just as much," observed Kat Cole, the youthful senior leader of the restaurant franchiser Focus Brands. A child care crisis delayed her arrival for our interview at an Atlanta café where Muzak played softly. She had entrusted her toddler, Ocean, to a temporary nanny due to the sudden death of her regular nanny's mother.

Cole grabbed her buzzing smartphone midway through our breakfast. "Your son is still asleep. Shall I wake him up?" the substitute nanny had texted. It was around 8:45 a.m.

Cole instantly switched screens to view peaceful Ocean in his crib via a photo from her baby monitor's webcam. "What time did he go to sleep?" the forty-year-old executive murmured to herself. "Oh, the camera says, '8:19 a.m.'"

That was all the first-time mother needed to know. "You can wake him up at 9:45," Cole texted her temporary caregiver. Ubiquitous access to the latest technology "makes you less afraid of the unknown," she explained to me. "We communicate with nannies real time."

Cole rattled off a litany of useful apps, including a website that identifies qualified babysitters nationwide and online support groups for new mothers that offer "immediate destressing." Compared with Power Moms twenty years ago, "the amount of access to information and resources is radically different [today]," she said.

"That access . . . allows me to believe that I can continue to live life with a child or multiple children relatively unchanged."

Cole gave birth again in August 2019 and returned to her high-level position three months later.

Technology also strengthens the bonds between Laura Chepucavage and her four kids. Although the Bank of America executive must leave for work by 5:30 a.m., she can participate in their weekday morning lives through video chats. She reserves fifteen minutes at 8:00 a.m. on Mondays, Tuesdays, and Thursdays for her FaceTime sessions with each child from a soundproof booth in her Manhattan office.

"Hey, Bo, did you brush your teeth?" she likes to ask her oldest son, who was born in 2010. "What are you wearing today? Did you pack your homework?"

Technology has further empowered the latest wave of Power Moms by minimizing their conflicts with their spouses over running the household. Couples keep things fair by "using project-management apps designed for the workplace to divvy up and track domestic to-dos," the *Wall Street Journal* reported in November 2019. "Using digital task trackers has been a marital game-changer."

Employed mothers in the United States depend on technological solutions to time-consuming tasks more than European ones do, according to the sociologist Caitlyn Collins. Her conclusion emerged from conversations with 135 such moms in the United States, Sweden, Germany, and Italy.

Wealthier American mothers "used grocery delivery services, online shopping, housekeeper and babysitter finding services, smartphone apps, and shared calendars to manage their family's complex schedules and to-do lists," Collins said in her 2019 book, *Making Motherhood Work: How Women Manage Careers and Caregiving*.

However, the present wave's extensive adoption of high-tech solutions has a dark side. That's evident from the brouhaha over Care.com, the largest U.S. online marketplace for child care. Several executive women I met had recruited nannies through the popular website. In 2019, the *Wall Street Journal* reported that Care.com did limited vetting of its caregivers, occasionally with tragic results. Some caregivers had police records.

The *Journal* investigation documented how the company, with about 35 million members in more than twenty countries, largely left it up to families to figure out whether a listed caregiver was trustworthy. Care.com didn't conduct complete background checks, verify the credentials of caregivers, or vet the day care centers listed on its website, the newspaper stated. Its CEO soon resigned, and Care.com was sold in February 2020 to IAC. In July 2020, Care.com agreed to pay $1 million in civil penalties and restitution to settle allegations over misrepresented background checks and auto-renewed subscriptions without getting customers' approval.

Lindsay Kaplan, a cofounder of Chief, the private club for female leaders, fears that technology may harm her fellow current-generation mothers for a different reason. "It provides a false sense of what being a true parent is—which is the quality time that you are just reading a book to your kids [or] under the covers playing 'Hide from the Monster,'" she pointed out. "Those are things that no app can give you."

Meanwhile, boomer executive moms fear that technology excessively tethers their latest cohorts to their jobs. "You have to use technology to your advantage," Jerri DeVard suggested. "If you're always responding [fast], then people expect that." The then Office Depot executive practices her preference: before going to sleep, she places her cell phone on her bedside nightstand. It is turned off.

Now: Power Moms Push Hard for Coparenting

Happy couples evolve into happy new parents if they split child-rearing duties proactively, experts say. Younger pairs tend to embrace this idea. There are significant changes taking root in American homes, "thanks to the more egalitarian attitudes of the millennial generation. I see working parents today doing a better job than I did," Sue Shellenbarger commented in 2020 after almost thirty years as the *Journal*'s work-and-family columnist.

Certain contemporary executives I met purposely picked a partner who appeared committed to involved parenthood. Take Julie Smolyansky, the Lifeway Foods CEO. When she and Jason Burdeen fell in love, they decided that they eventually wanted to have children. She said she had sensed that her future domestic partner would be a good nurturer, and that perception had contributed to "my choice to have kids with him."

Burdeen relinquished his gemology career with a family jewelry business in order to stay home when the first of their two daughters was an infant. "He's a really good nurturer," Smolyansky reported. "He has learned how to make great braids." He even lets their girls polish his nails!

Burdeen rejoined the workforce as an artist manager in 2017. Toiling from home part-time, "he still can be there for the girls," the forty-three-year-old CEO remarked during our interview. Smolyansky likes her generation's positive view of "men taking on [parenting] roles that were traditional for women."

Despite their intolerance of laid-back dads, some Power Moms encounter ingrained popular assumptions that they should be the primary parent merely because they're women. The stereotype forces mothers "to justify the balance between work and parenting," lamented Katie Ioanilli, a senior vice president of Ralph Lauren Corporation, a luxury lifestyle company.

She ran into this outdated attitude after taking maternity leave for her elder son in 2015. Ioanilli was then a partner at a major public relations firm and married to an investor relations specialist. "My husband is a Power Dad," the thirty-three-year-old Brooklyn resident boasted as we gobbled shrimp salads at a noisy Manhattan eatery.

Yet when the first-time mom resumed work, female and male acquaintances pestered her with the same question: "How do you do it?" Their implied pigeonholing of working mothers flabbergasted her.

"If 'it' means being a mother and having a career, then I don't do that independently," Ioanilli replied. "I have a network of people who help me," including a husband and a nanny. The Ralph Lauren executive delivered her second son in 2017.

Now: Mothers Aid Other Mothers at Work

Several present-generation women transformed a personal parenting problem into a broader corporate solution that benefited their associates with children. Meaghan Schmidt exemplifies this approach.

I previously described how traumatic miscarriages had prompted her launch of an employee resource group for parents at AlixPartners, the global consultancy where she is a managing director based in New York. She subsequently spearheaded its adoption of breast milk shipments for traveling mothers—based on her own difficult experience.

Schmidt commuted long distance to a California client during the summer following the 2015 birth of her second son. She flew home every Friday, lugging forty pounds of her breast milk and ice packs through airports. To her dismay, flight delays spoiled the milk and leaking milk inside her suitcase ruined her clothes.

Schmidt, the head of the parents' resource group, proposed that AlixPartners pay to ship staffers' breast milk home at the end of business trips. She lobbied for the change months ahead of her third maternity leave in December 2016. Knowing she would soon bear her last child, she told me, "I was kind of paying it forward for the next wave of AlixPartners mothers."

Schmidt became a "guinea cow" for a pilot project, shipping milk home from an AlixPartners conference in June 2017. Not long after, her employer rolled out the perquisite companywide. In September 2018, the firm took an unusual further step: it extended the subsidized shipments to nursing wives of consultants who accompany them on company trips or lack the perk at their own workplace.

Then: Baby Boomers Bulldozed Trails

First-wave executive mothers overcame numerous obstacles, often serving as influential examples for the current cadre and their adult daughters. These women's breakthrough stints in upper management eradicated much of the stigma that once stymied the professional progress of working moms.

A seasoned manager mom at Jet.com gave considerable support to Sumaiya Balbale, who intended to keep nursing her seven-month-old son after joining the start-up in September 2014 at age thirty-three.

But the novice chief marketing officer felt awkward pumping

breast milk in the solitary unisex bathroom at the online retailer's small office in suburban New Jersey. Male engineers in its open loft space could hear her loud pump. "What the hell am I doing?" mused Balbale, an observant Muslim whose hijab covers her hair.

Her discomfort subsided when she began to report to an older female executive. The newly hired boss was a proud working mom who spoke freely at work about how her high school-age children were a core part of her life. "They didn't take away from her leadership," Balbale recalled. "She became a very great role model" for juggling work and family.

Inspired by her boss, Balbale came to view motherhood as "part of what makes you good at what you do." She also embraced transparency about her parenting choices. Walmart acquired Jet.com for $3.3 billion in 2016 and installed Balbale as a vice president of its U.S. unit. The executive left the giant retailer in February 2019 and joined Sequoia Capital the following year.

Looking back, certain boomer trailblazers wish they had forged closer connections with their daughters years ago. Beth Comstock had high hopes of spending more time with six-year-old Meredith after she landed a corporate vice presidency at GE headquarters in 1998. She relocated her family to a nearby Connecticut suburb.

"Great news! My office is going to be fifteen minutes from where we [live]," Comstock announced to Meredith that summer. "I'm going to be able to come home and have lunch with you."

But Comstock got very busy with her challenging new GE role. "I never once made it home for lunch," she confessed. Meredith was attending New York University when her parents sold their Connecticut home in 2011. "I'm going to miss having you home for lunch," she deadpanned to her mother.

Comstock urges younger executive moms to avoid offering a commitment to their children that they cannot fulfill. "It matters to your kids." More than a decade later, Meredith was "still waiting for me to come home and have lunch with her," she said sadly. "It breaks my heart for both of us."

The GE veteran also wishes that she had educated Meredith and her elder daughter, Katie, about why her management career meant so much to her. If the girls had witnessed their mother lead a GE staff meeting, she feels, "they would have seen me as a different person." Nowadays, Meredith better appreciates her mother as a different person because the aspiring actress is Comstock's executive assistant.

Another prior-generation business leader sometimes didn't connect well with her young daughter's emotions. Stephanie Sonnabend traveled extensively while she advanced to the apex of Sonesta International Hotels Corporation, a hotel chain. Her husband frequently accompanied her on the trips. A live-in nanny took care of Antonia, born in 1987, and their son, Nick, who arrived two years later.

Antonia gave me a detailed account of her childhood separation anxiety, caused by her mother's heavy travel. "I would feel sick to my stomach all the time" she was out of town, Antonia said. Nor did the girl always feel comfortable with her nanny. "We changed nannies way too often," she explained. "I felt like I had to take care of my brother and protect him."

One Saturday when she was around five years old, Antonia begged her mother to apply for a job at the grocery store where they were shopping. "You could be home every night, and you would not have to travel," the child said.

"Well, I've got a really interesting job that I really like," Sonnabend responded.

How did Antonia's plea affect you? I asked the former Sonesta CEO at a restaurant near her grown daughter's apartment in Hoboken,

New Jersey. "It made me sad again to realize that it was really upsetting to her that I was traveling a lot," she said, choking up.

Yet years elapsed before she realized how often Antonia had endured anxious stomachaches during the executive's travels. "It wasn't like she was telling me that she was feeling sick," Sonnabend pointed out.

Antonia disagrees. She contends that her mom knew about her childhood stomachaches—but didn't know that the pain worsened when Sonnabend was out of town. In high school, Antonia was diagnosed with irritable bowel syndrome. The disorder "is highly connected to anxiety," she said.

Now married, Antonia Cohen is an upper middle manager at American Express. She refuses to travel more than 25 percent of the time for the major financial services company. She took her first business trip as a parent eleven months after having a baby in June 2018. "I don't want my son to have the lifestyle that I did growing up," she declared.

Her strict travel limitations mean that "I likely will never be a CEO. I am totally fine with that."

Then: Bootstrappers Trod Lonely Paths

The initial generation of Power Moms stuck to their self-help philosophy because they faced risks expressing their work/life concerns at the office. Reminding men in senior management "that you had a family might have made them think less of you professionally," observed Meredith Bodgas, the *Working Mother* editor.

The scarcity of manager moms aggravated their conundrum. They tried to solve problems on their own because they saw themselves as an island, recollected Hope Neiman, the chief marketing officer of Tillster, the digital commerce company for the restaurant industry. "You didn't have somebody else who was experiencing the same thing [so that] together you could come up with some rationale that made sense."

Neiman wishes that the tiny sorority of boomer executive mothers had attempted to aid one another in managing their careers and kids. She thinks their combined efforts could have enabled them to maintain their sanity and stand together for change. But "sometimes," she conceded, "you were alone."

The Walt Disney Company recruited the thirty-nine-year-old marketing maven in 1995 for a new division. At the time, Neiman's daughter was nearly three. The big entertainment company had a reputation for being a family-friendly business.

The opposite proved true for Neiman. "It was probably one of the least family-oriented [employment] experiences I've ever been in," she remembered. Every vice president in her division was a guy— except for her. And none of the female divisional managers below her level had youngsters.

In 1998, two senior Disney women without children separately recommended that Neiman make a terrible decision. "Those female executives said I should not have any 'daily family obligations,'" she told me. "My husband should stay home with our daughter if I wanted to advance at Disney."

Her husband, an investment banking professional, had no interest in being a stay-at-home dad, however. The female executives' outrageous proposal shocked Neiman, persuading her to quit Disney not long afterward.

She's happy to see how much the world of work has improved for women since 1998. The tremendous camaraderie among employed moms today "is probably the single biggest thing and the single best thing in [that] generation," she asserted.

Then: Raising Feminist Sons Was a Payoff

There's an additional reason GenX executive mothers find their dual roles easier than their predecessors did: many boomers raised boys right—by educating them about the importance of treating women fairly. Their adult sons smash the mold of traditional parenting at home and oppose sexism at work.

Dorrit J. Bern, the former CEO of Charming Shoppes, feels proud that her three sons are now great fathers who usually feed their kids breakfast while their wives dress for work. "Would that have happened without [their] working mother?" the sixty-eight-year-old executive wondered during our chat. "I don't think so."

Morgan Dewan unexpectedly reaped the benefits of one executive mom's wise parenting. The Turner Sports unit at Time Warner promoted Dewan to vice president in 2016, months before she had her first son at age thirty-three.

The following year, she attended an Atlanta business meeting with nineteen male executives and middle managers. Their catered meal was running late. A Turner executive vice president familiar with Dewan's title repeatedly asked her, "When's lunch going to get here?"

"I don't know. I'm as hungry as you are," she repeatedly answered. Because Dewan was the only woman in the room, the EVP insisted that she go check on everyone's missing meal.

A colleague who is the son of a female executive abruptly cut him off. "Just because she's a woman doesn't mean she knows where lunch is," he said. "This isn't her meeting."

The unhappy higher-up silently marched out of the room to locate their food. An aide finally wheeled in their lunch. Once the session ended, Dewan profusely thanked her rescuer. "Your words rang ten times as clear as mine," she told him.

"That [demand] was ridiculous," he replied. "I am sorry."

His intervention demonstrated the power of a man "sticking up for a woman in a situation of bias," Dewan said. In particular, sons of manager moms "are the most progressive [and] the most supportive."

I would say the same about our grown son. I see multiple signs that we raised Dan right. He and his wife hold executive roles while they purposefully coparent their three offspring. They alternate staying home with a sick child, for example.

During a 2019 family vacation, Dan comforted his fussy, almost one-year-old daughter by lining her portable crib with one of his sweaters. His familiar scent comforted the baby, and she fell asleep immediately. The sweater tactic had worked equally well when his son and elder daughter had been infants.

Dan suspects that men in his generation feel guilty if they don't try "to be as involved in their kids' lives as their spouse." But to be an involved dad, "you have to give something up," he told me. "I have a small number of hobbies." His comments echoed portions of my 1980 *Wall Street Journal* essay about combining a career with rearing him.

In 2013, Dan was a senior Democratic staffer in the Minnesota House of Representatives when he received two months off with full pay following the birth of his son and his wife's resumption of work. He worried about possible career damage from his leave.

"It was pretty unusual for a House employee to take paternity leave," he recalled. When he took seven weeks off to care for his second daughter in 2018, he was a senior leader of a Minnesota state agency. The paid benefit had been renamed "parental leave" and extended to all state government employees.

"The most important part of paid leave for both parents is what it says to the workforce about who is in charge of raising children," he emphasized. "We all are."

Paid parental leave for new parents is gaining popularity but remains relatively rare. About 27 percent of U.S. employers offered the perk in 2019, up from 17 percent in 2016, according to a survey of 2,763 human resources professionals by the Society for Human Resource Management. It expects that employers will continue to expand paid parental leave.

The expansion will further boost the careers of GenX executive mothers, who already enjoy more advanced technology, involved spouses, and egalitarian social attitudes. We've come a long way from the boomer era, when Power Moms fought hard to advance their ambitions. They usually blazed trails alone because they lacked supportive male bosses and female mentors with kids.

Yet we lack answers to several urgent questions about the future of working mothers and fathers. When will employed moms no longer be asked "How do you do it all?" What might accelerate societal shifts that would alleviate parents' tough trade-offs between job and family? And why don't U.S. employers better assist their staffers with children? My final chapter provides an in-depth look at four big businesses with cutting-edge approaches against the backdrop of the United States' unfinished agenda for working parents.

12

Making Work Workable
for Parents

Pregnant for the first time, I was delighted to hear that the *Wall Street Journal* gave ten weeks of paid maternity leave. My delight quickly disappeared.

Corporate policy required that I stop working four weeks ahead of my due date. I complained to my boss, who agreed to ignore the ridiculous rule.

I worked until the day before Dan's 1979 birth, took the full maternity leave, and returned to the *Journal*'s Washington bureau. Four of the five other *Journal* women who bore babies around the same time decided to quit, however.

Decades later, the picture is definitely improved for new parents at Dow Jones. The News Corp unit that publishes the *Journal* has provided twenty weeks of paid parental leave since 2018. Primary caregivers enjoy the benefit, irrespective of their gender. *Journal* moms and dads routinely return to its newsrooms following their breaks for childbirth, adoption, or foster care.

The challenge of creating work/life sway for U.S. parents has eased dramatically on multiple fronts beyond companies' recent extension of paid leave to new fathers. The private-sector practice will likely spread further amid a rising wave of governmental requirements.

By early 2020, eight states plus the District of Columbia had enacted legislation requiring paid family leave for an individual's new baby, own illness, or sick family member. They are New York, New Jersey, California, Rhode Island, Oregon, Connecticut, Massachusetts, and Washington. A small payroll tax increase, paid by employees and employers, finances the mandates.

Nationwide, U.S. law guarantees only unpaid leave. But new legislation effective in October 2020 provides twelve weeks of paid parental breaks to civilian federal staffers.

The wider availability of paternity leave has positive repercussions for mothers at home and work. During 2019, "men were roughly as likely as women to take leave when they became new parents," McKinsey and Lean In reported in their study of 329 American companies.

Highly involved dads create a virtuous circle of fathering, noted the journalist Amy Westervelt in *Forget "Having It All": How America Messed Up Motherhood—and How to Fix It*. Such fathers "are more likely to advocate alongside women for [workplace] policies like flextime and family leave."

Men in nations with paid parental leave help manage their households long after they resume work. Research has demonstrated that they "continue to perform 2.2 more hours of domestic work per week than men living with children in countries not offering that time," the clinical psychologist Darcy Lockman stated in her book *All the Rage: Mothers, Fathers, and the Myth of Equal Partnership*.

In addition, more women serve on boards of directors in nations where fathers enjoy generous paternity leave, according to a survey of 21,980 companies in ninety-one countries. Women with fewer child care burdens "can build the business acumen and professional contacts necessary to qualify for a corporate board," the 2016 paper said. Businesses tilted toward gender parity in the boardroom or management increase their market value and competitive advantages, numerous studies have shown.

Employed U.S. parents also benefit from the striking progress in flexible work arrangements. About 42 percent of employers permitted part-time telecommuting in 2019, a sizable spike from 31 percent in 2016, according to polls by the Society for Human Resource Management.

Some second-wave executive moms I interviewed regularly use their part-time telecommuting option. For example, Tatyana Zlotsky handled her American Express duties from home on Wednesdays and Fridays. Nearly half of the company's U.S. staffers telecommuted during a portion of the week before the coronavirus pandemic. She subsequently left American Express to become chief marketing officer of A Place for Mom, an assisted-living referral service.

The 2020 coronavirus pandemic forced millions of Americans to work from home full-time. But many individuals employed by restaurants, bars, and hotels couldn't do so. More than 77 percent of professional, scientific, and technical service jobs can be performed remotely—compared with only 3 percent of jobs in food services and lodging, the *Wall Street Journal* reported in April 2020. Women dominate the food service and lodging industries.

No wonder that working parenthood remains an exhausting solo sport for U.S. women in many other respects. Sheryl Sandberg summarized why. "We still need to make work work for parents, and it needs to be reframed as an issue that's not just for mothers but for fathers," Facebook's chief operating officer told the *Wall Street Journal* in 2020. Sandberg wrote the bestseller *Lean In: Women, Work, and the Will to Lead.*

Fathers are less likely than mothers to take their full amount of newborn leave, largely due to stereotyped perceptions about manly roles. One-third of men believe that taking the time off could jeopardize their position, a 2016 Deloitte survey of one thousand employed U.S. adults found. Caregiving dads also confront financial worries and inadequate managerial support, concluded a 2019 survey of 2,966 Americans conducted for Better Life Lab, a research and policy group.

Anne Weisberg, a boomer Power Mom, cites other evidence of the slow progress. Perks for working mothers, such as breast milk shipments, aggravate pressures to be constantly available for their jobs, she suggested in a *New York Times* opinion piece. Ideal employees shouldn't be "ones who get on a plane on a moment's notice, even with a nanny in tow, but the ones who figure out how to conduct the meeting without having to travel," she wrote. The current director of the women's initiative at Paul, Weiss penned her essay while senior vice president of the Families and Work Institute, a New York think tank.

"We have seen very little progress toward redefining the ideal worker," concurred the feminist legal scholar Joan C. Williams. Too many men define "their moral worth and their manliness through their [heavy] schedules," the director of the Center for WorkLife Law at the University of California Hastings College of the Law complained to me.

There also are concerns about the sustainability of reduced-hour alternatives, which appeal to working parents. Employers' frequent failure to implement flexibility consistently means it may be cut "because of manager discretion or larger economic vicissitudes," warned the sociologist Pamela Stone. She raised the issue in the 2019 book she coauthored, *Opting Back In: What Really Happens When Mothers Go Back to Work*.

Indeed, only 19 percent of 1,583 white-collar professionals with access to some flexibility could participate in so-called structured flexibility programs, concluded a 2018 survey by Annie Dean and

Anna Auerbach, co-chief executive officers of Werk Enterprises. Their start-up promotes workplace flexibility through "people analytics" software. The tool uncovers workforce data and insights so Werk clients, mainly Fortune 2000 companies, can fix their flexibility gaps.

Dean and Auerbach contend that structured flexibility efforts should cover six distinct options, including minimal work-related travel and the freedom to unexpectedly leave the office for a few hours. Yet businesses significantly underdeliver across every type of flexibility, they pointed out in a *Harvard Business Review* article.

The pair launched their enterprise in 2016 as a job board for women interested in high-level positions with built-in flexibility. They have now broadened their focus. They encourage work fluidity by documenting the productivity gains that a company gets from revamping its corporate culture.

"Flexibility is the fundamental defining change to make it possible for working parents to succeed," Dean asserted during our interview. "You can't work like you don't have children or parent like you don't have a job."

Several major U.S. corporations are changing their cultures because they recognize this new reality. I interviewed executives at four such companies whose innovative approaches propel the success of working parents and the business. These big employers landed on *Working Mother* magazine's 2019 list of the 100 Best Companies plus that year's separate tally of the fifty best companies for dads.

American Express Coaches Bosses and Parents

An American Express vice president named Andrew R. Johnson arranged my interview with Tatyana Zlotsky. But he was absent on the balmy spring afternoon when I arrived at its Manhattan head-quarters near the Ground Zero memorial.

Johnson had just begun five months of paid parental leave with his first baby. Several new fathers at his level or higher had recently taken long breaks from the charge card giant. The male executives' lengthy leaves highlight how well American Express serves the needs of its U.S. employed parents. In 2017, the company enlarged paid parental leave to twenty weeks—plus up to eight weeks more for birthing mothers.

Parenting breaks previously lasted just six weeks for primary caregivers and two weeks for secondary caregivers. The limited ben-efit implied that "fathers are less valuable caregivers than mothers," American Express stated in an outline of the company's past and revised parental perks. Even today, "society hasn't made it totally acceptable for dads to be home for an extended period," observed David Kasiarz, the company's executive vice president of colleague total rewards and well-being.

That's why American Express gives frontline bosses temporary-replacement allowances to fill staffing gaps caused by parental leaves. Training prepares supervisors to manage the rest of their team during those protracted absences. Leaders as high as execu-tive vice president divulge their working-parent problems during regular fatherhood breakfasts attended by both genders.

"We wanted to overcome objections to the increased parental leave," Kasiarz explained during our interview.

American Express also holds support chats for new or soon-to-be fathers where they discuss preparing for and returning from pa-ternity leave. A *Wall Street Journal* reporter attended a headquar-ters session. Rajeev Subramanyam, a senior executive who took five months off following his son's 2017 birth, addressed male associates at that support session. "Your career is a long road. This is just a blip," he assured them.

To further increase paternity leave usage, American Express mounted posters of men and babies in elevator banks and other communal areas of its U.S. offices. "Future Dads, don't miss these moments," one poster read. Below a picture of a father cradling a sleeping infant, the caption added, "Take up to twenty weeks parental leave. You both deserve it."

The result? "A majority of dads are taking all or some of the paid parental leave," Kasiarz told me.

An additional U.S. perk that American Express inaugurated in 2017 is the new-parent concierge. Staffers can receive personalized assistance while planning a family, during parental leave, and upon their return. They can rely on the 24/7 concierge service for as long as they wish, Kasiarz said.

A growing number of businesses arrange parenting coaches, in person or online. Consultant Barbara Palmer, the founder of Broad Perspective Consulting, has signed up about a dozen tech companies and law firms for her new-parent program, "Your Fourth Trimester."

"The name is not perfect for men," she conceded. Nevertheless, eager fathers who want to be highly involved in their children's lives are looking for support, she said. She counsels them about issues such as working-father guilt.

Babies at Bain Conferences

In 2018, I stepped inside a large hotel ballroom crammed with hundreds of female management consultants who work for Bain &

Company. Most had journeyed from distant countries to attend its global women's leadership conference in Washington.

I was even more impressed when I peeked into an adjacent room. Infants sprawled on colorful blankets or dozed in strollers, watched closely by their caregivers. New mothers had to walk only a short distance from the conference ballroom whenever they wanted to breastfeed or play with their babies.

The unusual setup isn't new for Bain. More than a decade ago, the management consultancy started reserving infant care space for new moms at women's leadership forums. It later extended the arrangement to its training meetings, held multiple times a year.

The special rooms enable new parents to access Bain's full gamut of training and networking, remarked Julie Coffman, a partner and former chair of its Global Women's Leadership Council. The firm covers caregivers' conference travel costs if the Bain consultants they serve cannot afford the expense.

The internal reaction "has been incredibly positive," reported Melissa Artabane, the director of Bain's global diversity and inclusion programs. "New moms see this as a signal that Bain invests in the whole person and recognizes that thriving professionally requires an integration of priorities at work and home."

No one objected when several female consultants and their infants mingled with Bain senior executives during a breakfast at the 2019 women's leadership forum. Instead, Artabane quipped, the babies "were some of the most popular attendees."

No new father has brought his infant and caregiver to the babies' space at a Bain training event. But dads do use the company's array of flexible schedules, which the firm commenced decades ago. Thirty percent of the company's employees have used or are using a flex model, according to Russ Hagey, the firm's worldwide chief talent officer.

Alternatives include job sharing, client assignments with little travel, six-month "externships" at other employers, and part-time roles with a variety of schedules. "We continue to invest behind truly flexible working models that address some of the demands that come with parenthood," Coffman said. For the first time in 2019, Bain ranked among the ten best companies in *Working Mother*'s overall lineup.

Johnson & Johnson Helps Parents Worldwide

Johnson & Johnson earned *Working Mother*'s number one ranking for 2019. That initially surprised me, as the maker of Tylenol and other iconic health products offers a relatively modest eight weeks of gender-neutral parental leave.

I subsequently learned that new J&J parents anywhere in the world can take the paid time off. The global business employed about 132,000 people in sixty countries as of late 2019.

"In my experience, the number of U.S. companies of that size who operate globally and have the same parental leave policy around the globe is exceptionally small," said Amy Beacom, the founder and CEO of the Center for Parental Leave Leadership. "You could count them on your hands, possibly even one hand."

Some smaller businesses are much more generous than J&J. Etsy, for example, gives all its employees twenty-six weeks of paid parental leave. But the online crafts marketplace had only 1,209 people on its worldwide payroll in September 2019.

J&J globalized fully paid parental leave in 2017, three years after introducing the benefit in the United States. A couple of its other perks designed for new mothers operate worldwide as well.

The company began a global breast milk shipment program in 2016 because "our moms travel globally," said Peter Fasolo, the company's chief human resources officer. Among J&J women, he pointed out, "the vast majority are working moms—even at the most senior level." It has also supplied nursing mothers with private lactation space in corporate facilities everywhere for at least twenty years.

Worldwide parental perquisites reflect J&J leaders' strong interest in retaining employees for the long term and their belief in work/life sway. "It's not about balancing work and family life," Fasolo stressed. "It's about integrating work and family life."

PwC Eases the Strains on New Moms

PwC, the U.S. arm of a global professional services company, pioneered parent-friendly practices long before most other U.S. employers did. For instance, in 2008, it created the Mentor Moms program, which matched expectant and new mothers with more senior internal counterparts.

At the time, motherhood represented an identity shift that could conflict with a woman's employment, recalled Jennifer W. Allyn, PwC's longtime managing director of diversity strategy, during our interview. Unfortunately, she added, "it's still true today." (Allyn left PwC in 2020.)

Another PwC manager proposed the mentor program after informally counseling younger female colleagues about how to cope with their demanding clients and kids. The manager mom recommended that returning new mothers request the lactation room key before their leave ended—and restart work on a Wednesday so they would feel less overwhelmed.

Allyn was the mother of a ten-year-old daughter when she joined PwC's pilot group of sixty mentor moms. She advised two anxious first-time mothers about the emotional conflicts and tricky logistics of working parenthood. Ahead of her maternity leave, a PwC employee picks a mentor mom from the company's internal database of biographies and photos. The firm's two hundred mentor moms guide their mentees for up to eighteen months.

Another radical move by PwC a decade ago decreased staffers' fears about taking time off: the company exempted new mothers and anyone else off work for at least sixteen weeks from being measured for their annual performance review against peers who stayed on the job that year. The change significantly improved its retention of new mothers, according to a *Wall Street Journal* article that I coauthored.

About 98 percent of PwC women on maternity leave resumed work in 2014, up from 88 percent in 2009. Allyn "thinks the increase reflects the women's realization that their careers are still on track," the *Journal* piece said.

PwC remains a pacesetter in the U.S. race to sweeten parental perks. Complaints by stressed new moms persuaded the firm to establish a "phased return to work" in mid-2018, Allyn told me. New parents work 60 percent of their normal schedule at 100 percent pay for four weeks following their leave.

Roughly 1,600 new moms and dads—36 percent of whom are new dads—took advantage of PwC's phased return through early February 2020. Participants report that their gradual restart "gave them a cushion to figure out new schedules and to adapt to a new child care situation," a PwC spokesperson said.

Though not a novel concept, a phased return typically involves a reduced salary. About 79 percent of *Working Mother*'s 100 Best Companies in 2018 offered some kind of phase-back policy, the magazine reported. But almost all paid part-time wages for parents' part-time hours.

Another exception to that partial pay practice exists at Rent the Runway, the clothing rental start-up run by Jennifer Hyman. The younger Power Mom gives new parents full-time pay if they toil two days a week for two months after they return. Rent the Runway employees "transition back to work in the way that's most flexible for you," Hyman said.

Within the client-focused PwC, however, Allyn found it hard to win acceptance of shortened parental schedules. "It was a real cultural shift," she commented. "Inertia is a real barrier when employers want to do things differently for working parents."

The Unfinished Agenda for Working Parents

"Working parents—men and women—need a better support structure from society at large, too." I advocated that sweeping solution in my 1980 *Journal* essay about my difficulties balancing motherhood with a career. "We need to elect union representatives and public officials who can translate these intensely personal issues into political action," I stated. "But so far, there is no recognized constituency of employed mothers and fathers."

Despite their formidable numbers, contemporary working parents have yet to form a widely recognized constituency. That may explain why Congress has failed to enact paid family leave funded by employers across the country.

In February 2020, President Donald Trump backed a federal bill that would let new parents pay for leaves through their early collection of certain future child tax credits. Trump acted weeks after the Business Roundtable wrote to him and congressional leaders endorsing legislation that would make paid family leave available "to as many working Americans as possible." The group represents the chiefs of companies with more than 15 million workers.

"The [present] business climate is very different," observed Katie Bethell, the founder and executive director of Paid Leave for the United States, a nonprofit advocacy group that seeks paid family leave.

But the narrow legislation endorsed by Trump doesn't protect parents' jobs or provide a new funding source to pay them during their leave, a *New York Times* analysis stated. "Opponents of the bill fear it would end momentum for paid family leave—without actually achieving it," the *Times* said.

In response to the coronavirus pandemic, Congress adopted temporary legislation that gave certain employees as much as twelve weeks of family leave at two-thirds of their normal pay to care for a youngster whose school or child care facility was closed. The measure was limited in scope and duration. It didn't apply to all employers and was due to expire at the end of 2020.

Even without more extensive congressional action, U.S. businesses keen to attract and keep younger people will likely accelerate their commitment to those with kids. Millennials value extra paid parental leave to a greater degree than does any other generation, the 2016 Deloitte poll found. And 77 percent of all adults told the pollsters that the amount of such leave could sway their choice of a new workplace.

Similar findings emerged from subsequent surveys. About 32 percent of U.S. workers with caregiving responsibilities left a job because they couldn't balance their work and family duties, according to a 2019 study by two Harvard Business School researchers. Such turnover was even higher among people aged twenty-six to thirty-five.

"Perhaps counterintuitively, more men than women said they had left a job because of family responsibilities," noted a *Wall Street Journal* article about the Harvard research. But businesses don't realize the impact of caregiving on staff performance, the study authors said in their report. "Companies incur millions of dollars of hidden costs due to employee turnover, loss of institutional knowledge, and temporary hiring."

A To-Do List for U.S. Employers

How else should U.S. businesses assist moms and dads in their employ? For openers, big companies should take stakes in the burgeoning flurry of start-ups whose apps, gadgets, products, and services cater to parents of young children. During the last six years, investors have poured $500 million into enterprises that play in "the new mom economy," and this market segment is worth $46 billion, *Forbes* estimated in 2019.

The mother of invention for those young companies is often motherhood. Sandra Oh Lin, a first-wave Power Mom, typifies the trend. She runs KiwiCo, a subscription-based vendor of children's activity kits. By spring 2019, the business she had cofounded in 2011 had shipped 10 million kits and was generating more than $100 million in annual sales.

KiwiCo inspires kids "to grow their creative competence, build their problem-solving skills, and hopefully feel empowered to change the world," Lin said. We chatted in a lime green conference room at its single-story headquarters in Mountain View, California. Whether a KiwiCo kit contains a science experiment or an engineering project, "we're kind of transforming play," the forty-four-year-old CEO went on.

Lin immigrated to the United States from South Korea as an infant. She earned an undergraduate chemical engineering degree and a Harvard MBA. After stints at Procter & Gamble and elsewhere, she led a multibillion-dollar operation for eBay. She left the e-commerce giant in 2010 in order to explore fresh opportunities, possibly with a smaller company. She had no intention to launch a business, however.

Lin invented the concept of KiwiCo while spending time with her two children during her job search. "I was starting to do these hands-on activities with my kids because I was home," she remembered. She disliked dragging youngsters under four years old from store to store to buy materials for their activities, which included making globes of ice from frozen balloons.

KiwiCo "was born out of personal need," she said. Nor were her needs unusual. "A lot of busy, well-intentioned parents . . . want enriching activities for their kids." KiwiCo staffers, most of whom are women, have developed product lines for children ranging from newborns to adolescents.

The start-up turned profitable in 2016, the year Lin gave birth for the third time. "He was actually my fourth child," she joked. "Kiwi is my third."

Lin said she raised just over $10 million for her venture, and KiwiCo has sufficient capital to fund further growth. Some small firms providing services for employed parents are beginning to attract buyers. Werk was acquired in March 2020, for example.

Other tactics could turn working parenthood into a truly team sport, spurring a more equitable distribution of domestic labor. Countries such as Iceland and Sweden pursue this goal by pressuring men to take part in their widely available paternity leave.

"Ninety percent of Icelandic fathers choose to use rather than lose their dedicated paternity leave," said Pamela Stone, the sociologist, in her 2019 book. "Swedes allocate separate and nontransferable amounts of paid leave to mothers and fathers in the same household, thereby introducing incentives for fathers to use it or lose it."

U.S. companies with paid parental leave could move in the same direction by normalizing the practice. Facebook already does. The social media giant urges bosses to ask expecting fathers and mothers "when"—rather than "if"—they intend to take their four months of paid parental leave, the *Wall Street Journal* reported. Mark Zuckerberg, its founder and chief executive officer, took two months off after the birth of each of his daughters.

U.S. businesses should also promote more mothers into upper management and showcase their achievements, suggested Betty Spence, the president of the National Association for Female Executives. Up-and-coming women would see "that they can reach senior leadership and have families."

A 2019 study of 3,038 U.S. professionals by the association and Working Mother Research Institute explored why so few women have reached the executive suite. Among the biggest obstacles cited by female professionals was their perception that being a senior leader is incompatible with having a family.

"It's shocking that women are still saying this," Spence told me. "You'd think [things] would have changed by now."

In my opinion, powerful mothers could have the greatest impact on improving the lives of working parents. They can wield influence through their elevated professional status, political authority, or personal wealth. I recognized that potent weapon during my close encounters with eighty-six executive moms from the present and prior generations.

I won't forget the meaningful workplace changes driven by contemporary business leaders such as Meaghan Schmidt at AlixPartners, Katia Beauchamp at Birchbox, and Jennifer Hyman at Rent the Runway.

Hyman's championship of parenting parity goes beyond fully paid phased returns. "Part of my job as a CEO is to make the men here take their full paternity leave," the pregnant cofounder explained when we met. Encouraged by Hyman, the chief technology officer of her company took his twelve weeks of paid leave. His 2017 decision strengthened the acceptability of new fathers' taking significant time off for a newborn. "Before him, it was scattered," Hyman recollected. But "there's not been a single man post him that hasn't taken full paternity leave."

Nor will I forget the trailblazer chief executive officers from the boomer generation. Women such as Michele Buck at Hershey, Betsy Holden at Kraft, and Andrea Jung at Avon Products made substantial strides on behalf of employed parents and provided clear career road maps for their daughters to follow.

Aida Sabo is an equally memorable member of that cadre. She wielded considerable clout in weighing an offer to be vice president of diversity and inclusion at Parexel, the drug research firm. At the time the vice president of diversity and inclusion at the health care services company Cardinal Health, she wanted to replicate the Engaging Men program that she had successfully introduced there. Men had learned to bolster women's progress through such actions as organizing informal alliances with male coworkers at Cardinal.

"I won't come here unless I can do this [program]," Sabo told Parexel. The company accepted her demand. Engaging men as partners of change became her top Parexel initiative.

But does engaging men on behalf of women alter their view of sharing responsibilities at home? I wondered during my interview with Sabo.

"I see men shedding tears of joy and sadness because they see the opportunity . . . for them to use the privilege they have to help change our environments at home and at work," she replied passionately. "They want to see a different future."

Mothers in charge of national governments are shaping a different future, too. We've come a long way since 1960, when the tiny nation now called Sri Lanka broke the global gender barrier by electing a female prime minister. The mother of three rose to power a year after the assassination of her husband, who had been its prime minister.

In 2018, New Zealand's prime minister took six weeks off from her job to give birth and care for her daughter. The male partner of Jacinda Ardern is their baby's primary caregiver.

Thirty-four-year-old Sanna Marin became the youngest prime minister in Finnish history late the following year—when her daughter was a toddler. In February 2020, Marin's government unveiled a new policy to equalize paid leave for parents by granting each nearly seven months off. Finland planned to replace gender-based allowances that gave mothers about four months of paid leave and fathers half that amount.

A Bold Vision for the Future

Wealthy moms wield equally enormous clout to shake up the status quo, especially for working women with kids. That's part of an ambitious game plan designed by Melinda Gates. She and her husband, Bill, the tech titan, have three kids and are worth billions of dollars. She founded Pivotal Ventures, an investment and incubation company.

Melinda Gates has committed $1 billion to expanding U.S. women's power and influence through her business. One priority will be "dismantling the barriers to women's professional advancement," she vowed in a *Time* magazine essay. "Even though most women now work full-time (or more), we still shoulder the majority of caregiving responsibilities."

She ended her October 2019 essay with an upbeat outlook about removing inequities that hold women back: "Americans are no longer willing to accept the glacial pace of change—and I feel lucky to be alive at a time when we no longer have to."

We are also lucky to be alive at a point when younger manager moms attain breakthroughs on the job and at home that the prior generation never imagined. It's now easier for women with kids to reach top management because they enjoy significant support from their involved spouses and empathetic employers.

And consider this: we live at a time when a woman could soon walk on the moon for the first time. NASA has announced plans for such a breakthrough mission during this decade.

Ideally, the American astronaut won't disrupt her historic lunar stroll by anxiously texting her child's nanny because moms like her will no longer worry about work/life conflicts. That even greater feat will be one small step for a woman—and one giant leap for womankind.

Acknowledgments

It takes a village to raise a child, as Hillary Clinton wisely wrote in her 1996 book.

It takes many villages to write a book about raising children in a household with an executive mother. I was lucky to have many villages, populated by an array of acquaintances and relatives.

I'm thankful that eighty-six Power Moms chose to tell me about their struggles and triumphs. They painted a memorable portrait of intergenerational progress toward work/life sway. Their achievements will soon propel more mothers into the upper echelons of U.S. business.

I enjoyed extensive support from Hollis Heimbouch and Rebecca Raskin, my HarperCollins publishers, and steady encouragement from Karen Gantz, my literary agent. Yale Fisher, my retinal specialist, introduced me to Gantz. Equally important, he saved much of my deteriorating vision.

Family members played pivotal parts in giving birth to this book. My parents, Betty and Irv Lublin, encouraged my colorful creative writing from an early age. Mom served as an especially powerful role model of working motherhood. During much of my childhood, she toiled as a Sunday school teacher and occasional public school substitute. I greatly admired her ability to teach full-time while raising four offspring aged four to sixteen years old in 1965. She was the first employed mom I ever heard utter the infamous words "I don't know how I did it." She passed away as I put the finishing touches on my manuscript in spring 2020.

My grown children, Abra and Dan, also greatly inspired me. Her eye-opening insights about our relationship enriched my encounters with baby-boomer executives and twenty-five of their adult daughters. Abra's battle with an incurable and painful genetic disorder prompted me to add the chapter called "Power over Pain."

Dan, her older brother, is a feminist-minded father who twice took paid paternity leave to care for a newborn. His initial one in 2013 made him a pacesetter at his office. He was a senior leader of a Minnesota state agency when he took his latest leave in 2018. He and his wife, a corporate attorney, are highly devoted to coparenting their three kids.

My loving husband and soul mate deserves my deepest gratitude. Mike tirelessly toiled alongside me throughout this protracted project. He cheered me up when my spirits waned, fixed endless tech snafus, and deftly edited every chapter of the manuscript. His smart revisions and patience with my prickly ego produced the book that you are now reading.

"Don't make a big deal about me in the acknowledgments," Mike implored. Too late, life partner. I just did.

Interviewed Executive Women

Fifteen of the eighty-six women—or 17 percent—are a current or past CEO of a public company. They are denoted by asterisks.

First Wave

Wendy Abt, CEO of WPA

Cheryl A. Bachelder, former CEO of Popeyes Louisiana Kitchen*

Mary L. Baglivo, former CEO of the Americas for Saatchi & Saatchi

Joanna Barsh, former senior partner at McKinsey & Company

Carol Bartz, former president and CEO of Yahoo! and Autodesk*

Dorrit J. Bern, former CEO of Charming Shoppes*

Cathie Black, former president of Hearst Magazines

Diane M. Bryant, chair and CEO of NovaSignal and a former senior executive of Alphabet and Intel Corporation

Michele Buck, CEO of the Hershey Company*

Sheila Buckley, senior vice president of Dstillery

Beth Comstock, former vice chair of General Electric Company

Peggy Daitch, former vice president of Condé Nast

Jerri DeVard, former executive vice president of Office Depot

Virginia Gambale, former executive at a Deutsche Bank unit

Laurie Ann Goldman, former CEO of New Avon

Lynn Zuckerman Gray, founder and CEO of Campus Scout and a former executive of Lehman Brothers Holdings

Mindy Grossman, CEO of WW International*

Melanie Healey, former group president, North America, of Procter & Gamble Company

Penny Herscher, former CEO of FirstRain and Simplex Solutions*

Betsy Holden, former co-CEO of Kraft Foods*

Annalisa Jenkins, biotech entrepreneur and former CEO of PlaqueTec

Kerry Jordan, former chief operating officer of D'Orazio Capital Partners

Andrea Jung, former CEO of Avon Products*

Margaret Keane, CEO of Synchrony*

Merrilee Kick, CEO and founder of Buzzballz/Southern Champion

Ellen Kullman, CEO of Carbon and former CEO of DuPont*

Melanie Kusin, vice chair of Korn Ferry

Alexandra Lebenthal, former CEO of Lebenthal & Co.

Challis Lowe, former highest human resources officer at Beneficial
    Corporation, Ryder System, and Dollar General Corporation

Lisa Mann, chief marketing officer of Raines International and former
    president of the Global Nutrition Group at PepsiCo

Nina McIntyre, chief marketing officer of ETQ

Hope Neiman, chief marketing officer of Tillster

Martha Olson, former senior executive at Warnaco Group

Jane Parker, CEO of InterbrandHealth, a unit of Omnicom Group

Denise Ramos, former CEO of ITT*

Aida Sabo, vice president of diversity and inclusion at Parexel
    International Corporation

Jana Schreuder, former chief operating officer of Northern Trust
    Corporation

Laurie Siegel, former chief human resources officer of Tyco International

Stephanie Sonnabend, former CEO and president of Sonesta
    International Hotels Corporation*

Pernille Spiers-Lopez, former global chief human resource officer of
    IKEA Group

Anne Stevens, former CEO of GKN and Carpenter Technology
    Corporation*

Jane Stevenson, vice chair of Korn Ferry

Johnna Torsone, executive vice president and chief human resource officer at Pitney Bowes

Anne Weisberg, women's initiative director at Paul, Weiss, Rifkind, Wharton & Garrison

Second Wave

Genevieve Aronson, North American vice president of communications at Nielsen Holdings

Sumaiya Balbale, chief marketing officer of Sequoia Capital and former vice president of a U.S. unit of Walmart

Katia Beauchamp, cofounder and CEO of Birchbox

Mithu Bhargava, senior vice president of NCR Corporation

Janelle Bieler, senior vice president at the U.S. arm of the Adecco Group

Nancy Bong, head of private bank channel of VanEck

Emily Chardac, former global human resources officer at Guggenheim Partners

Laura Chepucavage, managing director of Bank of America

Kat Cole, chief operating officer and president of North America for Focus Brands

Morgan Dewan, vice president of content partnerships at Turner Sports, a media firm owned by AT&T

Alexis DiResta, former division head at Away and former executive at Estée Lauder Companies

Lauren Fanning, assistant general counsel of Freeman Company

Annie Granatstein, executive vice president of Edelman

Vanessa Hallett, worldwide head of photographs and deputy chairman, Americas, at Phillips

Mary Hamilton, a managing director of Accenture

Malena Higuera, general manager of L'Oréal's Dermablend Professional division

Sarah Hofstetter, president of Profitero and former president of Comscore

Ling Hu-Kramer, chief transformation officer at Bridgewater Associates

Jennifer Hyman, cofounder and CEO of Rent the Runway

Katie Ioanilli, senior vice president of Ralph Lauren Corporation

Lindsay Kaplan, cofounder of Chief

Bonny Lee, vice president of finance at SiriusXM Radio

Sandra Oh Lin, cofounder and CEO of KiwiCo

Marissa Mayer, cofounder of Lumi Labs and former CEO of Yahoo!*

Ann Miller, vice president of Nike

Kathy O'Sullivan, partner at Ernst & Young

Alison Rand, senior director, head of design operations of InVision

Genevieve Roth, founder and president of Invisible Hand

Danielle Scalzo, partner at Willkie Farr & Gallagher

Meaghan Schmidt, managing director of AlixPartners

Clara Shih, CEO of Hearsay Systems

Julie Smolyansky, executive chair and former CEO of Lifeway Foods*

Dana Spinola, founder and chief visionary officer of fab'rik

Melanie Steinbach, former U.S. chief people officer of McDonald's and
    its former chief talent officer

Stefanie Strack, CEO of VIS Holdings and former vice president of Nike

Jennifer Stybel, leader of caregiving program strategy at Pivotal
    Ventures and former vice president of FreeWill

Anjali Sud, CEO of Vimeo, a unit of IAC

Inhi Cho Suh, general manager and vice president of IBM

Stacey Tank, vice president of Heineken and former vice president of
    Home Depot

Caroline Tsay, cofounder and CEO of Compute Software

Heidi Zak, cofounder and CEO of ThirdLove

Tatyana Zlotsky, chief marketing officer of A Place for Mom and former
    vice president at American Express Company

Interviewed Adult Daughters of First-Generation Executive Moms

Daughter	Mother
Emily Abt	Wendy Abt
Antonia Cohen	Stephanie Sonnabend
Katie Curran	Johnna Torsone
Charlotte Diamond	Alexandra Lebenthal
Gabriella Garbasz	Joanna Barsh
Samantha Gladis	Jane Parker
Emily Gray	Lynn Zuckerman Gray
Elysabeth Grossman-Sirgey	Mindy Grossman
Alison Harvey	Cathie Black
Jackie Healey	Melanie Healey
Melanie Herscher	Penny Herscher
Olivia Jenkins	Annalisa Jenkins
Megan Keane	Martha Olson
Maggie Kullman	Ellen Kullman
Sine Lopez	Pernille Spiers-Lopez
Candice Lowe-Swift	Challis Lowe
Arielle Mann	Lisa Mann
Martha Meguerian	Mary Baglivo
Emma Nosofsky	Laurie Siegel
Kate Bachelder Odell	Cheryl Bachelder
Avery Rowe	Melanie Kusin
Alex Sarkowsky	Hope Neiman
Sara Shaker	Sheila Buckley
Emily Stevenson	Jane Stevenson
Jennifer Zechman	Anne Stevens

Notes

INTRODUCTION

xii The percentage of women: Rachel Thomas, Marianne Cooper, Gina Cardazone, et al., "Women in the Workplace 2020," McKinsey & Co., September 30, 2020, 8.

xx That's especially the case: Kathleen L. McGinn, Mayra Ruiz Castro, and Elizabeth Long Lingo, "Learning From Mum: Cross-National Evidence Linking Maternal Employment and Adult Children's Outcomes," *Work, Employment and Society*, April 30, 2018.

1: HARD WORK FOR WORKING MOTHERS

1 "Our society has failed": Joann S. Lublin, "Questions a Woman Asks Herself," *Wall Street Journal*, January 2, 1976.

2 "white women typically left": Nina Banks, "Black Women's Labor Market History Reveals Deep-Seated Race and Gender Discrimination," Working Economics Blog, Economic Policy Institute, February 19, 2019.

2 By 1920, African American women: Amy Westervelt, *Forget "Having It All": How America Messed Up Motherhood—and How to Fix It* (New York: Seal Press, 2018), 72.

2 "The U.S. government": Ibid., 114.

3 exceeded 40 percent by 1966: Joann S. Lublin, *Earning It: Hard-Won Lessons from Trailblazing Women at the Top of the Business World* (New York: HarperCollins, 2016), 16.

3 Economists estimate that: Ibid., 15.

3 "The recent expansion of parental benefits": Vanessa Fuhrmans, "Female Factor: Women Drive the Labor-Force Comeback," *Wall Street Journal*, March 1, 2019.

4 "has the least generous benefits": Caitlyn Collins, *Making Motherhood Work: How Women Manage Careers and Caregiving* (Princeton, NJ: Princeton University Press, 2019), 1.

6 Men who actively care for: Jennifer L. Berdahl and Sue H. Moon, "Workplace Mistreatment of Middle Class Workers Based on Sex, Parenthood, and Caregiving," *Journal of Social Issues* 69, no. 2 (June 12, 2013): 341.

7 "the first to provide": Shelley J. Correll, Stephen Benard, and In Paik, "Getting a Job: Is There a Motherhood Penalty?," *American Journal of Sociology* 112, no. 5 (March 2007): 1297–1339.

8 Those mothers earned 10 percent less: Paula England, Jonathan Bearak, Michelle J. Budig, and Melissa J. Hodges, "Do Highly Paid, Highly Skilled Women Experience the Largest Motherhood Penalty?," *American Sociological Review* 81, no. 6 (December 2016): 1161–89.

9 "workism": Derek Thompson, "Workism Is Making Americans Miserable," *The Atlantic*, February 24, 2019.

10 "What holds women back": Robin J. Ely and Irene Padavic, "What's Really Holding Women Back?," *Harvard Business Review*, March–April 2020, 58–67.

10 "believe they get fewer": Bright Horizons, *Modern Family Index 2018*, January 2019, 7.

10 the proportion of polled women: Ibid.

10 "the motherhood penalty": Ibid., 6.

13 "This is when parents": Claire Cain Miller and Jonah Engel Bromwich, "The Unstoppable Snowplow Parent," *New York Times*, March 17, 2019.

14 "believed that autism": Deborah Tannen, *You're Wearing That? Understanding Mothers and Daughters in Conversation* (New York: Random House, 2006), 43.

14 About 74 percent of parents: Kevin Quealy and Claire Cain Miller, "When Parents Jump In Even When You're 28," *New York Times*, March 13, 2019.

2: HIGH POTENTIALS WITH HIGH HOPES FOR MOTHERHOOD

34 paternal postpartum depression: Peggy Drexler, "It's OK for Parents to Feel Ambivalent About Their Children," *Wall Street Journal*, June 22, 2019.

35 "I didn't realize juggling": Joann S. Lublin, "What Should a Mother Do About Her Career?," *Wall Street Journal*, March 21, 1980.

37   "from employees who are": Liz Morris, Jessica Lee, and Joan C.
      Williams, "Exposed: Discrimination Against Breastfeeding Workers,"
      Center for WorkLife Law, University of California, Hastings College of
      the Law, January 2019, 4.

38   "At week five": Joann S. Lublin, *Earning It: Hard-Won Lessons
      from Trailblazing Women at the Top of the Business World* (New York:
      HarperCollins, 2016), 141.

3: WHEN WORK AND FAMILY COLLIDE

42   I consider applying: Joann S. Lublin, "Alas! Countdowns to
      Bedtime," *Wall Street Journal*, January 14, 1986.

42   "increased psychological strain": Tarani Chandola, Cara L. Booker,
      Meena Kumari, and Michaela Benzeval, "Are Flexible Work
      Arrangements Associated with Lower Levels of Chronic Stress-
      Related Biomarkers? A Study of 6025 Employees in the UK Household
      Longitudinal Study," *Sociology* 53, no. 4 (August 1, 2019): 779–99.

43   "found themselves marginalized": Pamela Stone, *Opting Out?: Why
      Women Really Quit Careers and Head Home* (Berkeley: University of
      California Press, 2007), 19.

58   "high-powered men": Anna North, "What a CEO Mom's Viral
      Nanny Ad Says About Gender, Work, and Power," Vox, January 27,
      2020.

61   "you feel can be": Marisa LaScala, "The 'Nanny Stigma': It's Time to
      Get over It," *Working Mother*, June 1, 2016.

4: TRIALS AND TRIUMPHS OF DOMESTIC LABOR

64   "I don't like the way": Joann S. Lublin, "Fear & Mowing in
      Suburbia," *Wall Street Journal*, May 10, 1977.

64   "the raising of their children": Arlie Hochschild, *The Second
      Shift: Working Families and the Revolution at Home* (New York: Viking
      Penguin, 1989), xv.

64   "there is no known": Francine M. Deutsch, *Halving It All: How
      Equally Shared Parenting Works* (Cambridge, MA: Harvard University
      Press, 1999), 4.

64   She also cited other studies: Ibid., 3.

66   "biology, cultural mandates": Darcy Lockman, *All the Rage: Mothers,*

Fathers, and the Myth of Equal Partnership (New York: HarperCollins, 2019), 16.

67   "often has higher earnings": Claire Cain Miller, "What Same-Sex Couples Reveal About Modern Parenting," *New York Times*, May 17, 2018.

70   Yet no working father: Lockman, *All the Rage*, 8.

71   "studies in the last decade": Ibid., 41.

78   "The social costs": Emily Huddart Kennedy and Julie A. Kmec, "Is There an 'Ideal Feeder'? How Healthy and Eco-friendly Food Consumption Choices Impact Judgments of Parents," *Agriculture and Human Values* 36, no. 4 (December 2018): 137–51.

83   "It is harder to sell": Elizabeth Emens, *Life Admin: How I Learned to Do Less, Do Better, and Live More* (Boston: Houghton Mifflin Harcourt, 2019), 59.

83   "to be not just parents": Bright Horizons, "Modern Family Index 2017," December 2017, 1.

84   "That's because in our culture": Eve Rodsky, *Fair Play: A Game-Changing Solution for When You Have Too Much to Do (and More Life to Live)* (New York: G. P. Putnam's Sons, 2019), 31.

84   "Women are taking on": Eve Rodsky, "Everyone Is Home Right Now, but Who's Doing all the 'Home' Work?," *Harper's Bazaar*, March 26, 2020.

5: BEING ALWAYS ON DOESN'T ALWAYS WORK

88   "the workday's boundaries": Matthew Kitchen, "Far from the Madding Co-workers," *Wall Street Journal*, October 6, 2018.

89   Those with the most workplace telepressure: Larissa K. Barber and Alecia M. Santuzzi, "Please Respond ASAP: Workplace Telepressure and Employee Recovery," *Journal of Occupational Health Psychology* 20, no. 2 (April 2015): 172–89.

89   "This helps widen": Sue Shellenbarger, "Many Companies Say They're Family Friendly. But It Often Isn't the Case," *Wall Street Journal*, October 11, 2019.

98   "to explore whether": Leslie A. Perlow, *Sleeping With Your Smartphone: How to Break the 24/7 Habit and Change the Way You Work* (Boston: Harvard Business Review Press, 2012), 10.

98   "The cycle of 24/7": Leslie A. Perlow and Jessica L. Porter, "Making Time Off Predictable—and Required," *Harvard Business Review* 87, no. 10 (October 2009): 102–09.

98   Bandwidth, a telecom company: Kelsey Gee, "Phones, Apps Make Sunday the New Monday Morning," *Wall Street Journal*, July 8, 2019.

6: MAKING ROOM FOR CAREERS AND KIDS

102   "Mommy Day": Joann S. Lublin, *Earning It: Hard-Won Lessons from Trailblazing Women at the Top of the Business World* (New York: HarperCollins, 2016), 145.

108   The tiny firm grew: Alexandra Wolfe, "Sara Blakely of Spanx: Smooth Operator," *Wall Street Journal*, October 11, 2013.

112   "It is likely": Titan M. Alon, Matthias Doepke, Jane Olmstead-Rumsey, and Michèle Tertilt, "The Impact of COVID-19 on Gender Equality," NBER Working Paper No. 26947, April 2020, 17.

112   "While women carry": Ibid., 24.

7: MY MOTHER, MY COACH

122   "to not only rethink": Amy Westervelt, *Forget "Having It All": How America Messed Up Motherhood—and How to Fix It* (New York: Seal Press, 2018), 150.

122   research shows that they're less: Kevin Quealy and Claire Cain Miller, "When Parents Jump In Even When You're 28," *New York Times*, March 13, 2019.

122   "are questions that shape": Terri Apter, *You Don't Really Know Me: Why Mothers and Daughters Fight and How Both Can Win* (New York: W. W. Norton, 2004), 21.

122   "wants her mother": Ibid., 241.

127   "an urge to exaggerate": Ibid., 21.

130   "The business skills": Pamela F. Lenehan, *My Mother, My Mentor: What Grown Children of Working Mothers Want You to Know* (Bloomington, IN: Archway Publishing, 2015), 131.

133   "The best": Dana Spinola, *Love What You Do: A Plan for Creating a Life You Love Filled with Passion and Purpose* (Austin, TX: Fedd Agency, 2018), 12.

136   Only two female heads: Emma Hinchliffe, "Former DuPont CEO

Ellen Kullman Takes Over 3D-Printing Startup Carbon," *Fortune*, November 21, 2019.

8: BETTER MOM, BETTER BOSS

145 "Working moms are": Bright Horizons, *Modern Family Index 2018*, January 2019.

145 "suggests a potential shift": Ibid.

145 More than half: Marcus Noland, Tyler Moran, and Barbara Kotschwar, "Is Gender Diversity Profitable? Evidence from a Global Survey," Working Paper 16-3, Peterson Institute for International Economics, February 2016, 2.

150 "I am a person": Joann S. Lublin, *Earning It: Hard-Won Lessons from Trailblazing Women at the Top of the Business World* (New York: HarperCollins, 2016), 111.

153 "Our warehouse, customer service": Jennifer Y. Hyman, "Equal Benefits for All Employees," *New York Times*, May 7, 2018.

153 "I have a deeper": Ibid.

9: POWER OVER PAIN

162 Dembe documented this link: Allard E. Dembe and Xiaoxi Yao, "Chronic Disease Risks from Exposure to Long-Hour Work Schedules over a 32-Year Period," *Journal of Occupational and Environmental Medicine* 58, no. 9 (September 2016): 861–67.

168 "to be that vulnerable": Emma Hinchliffe, "11 Female CEOs and Founders on What It's Really Like to Have a Baby While Running Your Company," *Fortune*, August 14, 2019.

10: DITCH WORKING-MOTHER GUILT

175 another forty letters: Joann S. Lublin, *Earning It: Hard-Won Lessons from Trailblazing Women at the Top of the Business World* (New York: HarperCollins, 2016), 144.

177 "Recent research exploring": Eve Rodsky, *Fair Play: A Game-Changing Solution for When You Have Too Much to Do (and More Life to Live)* (New York: G. P. Putnam's Sons, 2019), 76.

179 After the nanny agreed: Lublin, *Earning It*, 153.

181 "forming a tight-knit group": Amy Westervelt, *Forget "Having It All"*:

How America Messed Up Motherhood—and How to Fix It (New York: Seal Press, 2018), 37.

11: NOW AND THEN

198 "using project-management apps": Julie Jargon, "Honey-Do List Goes Digital," *Wall Street Journal*, November 6, 2019.

198 "used grocery delivery services": Caitlyn Collins, *Making Motherhood Work: How Women Manage Careers and Caregiving* (Princeton, NJ: Princeton University Press, 2019), 241.

199 The *Journal* investigation documented: Gregory Zuckerman and Dave Sebastian, "IAC to Buy Care.Com in $500 Million Cash Deal," *Wall Street Journal*, December 20, 2019.

200 There are significant changes taking: Sue Shellenbarger, "The Challenges That Working Mothers Still Face," *Wall Street Journal*, January 3, 2020.

12: MAKING WORK WORKABLE FOR PARENTS

212 "men were roughly as likely": Jess Huang, Alexis Krivkovich, Irina Starikova, et al., "Women in the Workplace 2019," McKinsey & Company, October 15, 2019, 34.

212 "are more likely to advocate": Amy Westervelt, *Forget "Having It All": How America Messed Up Motherhood—and How to Fix It* (New York: Seal Press, 2018), 253.

212 "continue to perform": Darcy Lockman, *All the Rage: Mothers, Fathers, and the Myth of Equal Partnership* (New York: HarperCollins, 2019), 219.

212 "can build the business acumen": Marcus Noland, Tyler Moran, and Barbara Kotschwar, "Is Gender Diversity Profitable? Evidence from a Global Survey," Working Paper 16-3, Peterson Institute for International Economics, February 2016, 13.

213 More than 77 percent: Harriet Torry, "Coronavirus Pandemic Deepens Labor Divide Between Online, Offline Workers," *Wall Street Journal*, April 3, 2020.

213 "We still need to make": Sue Shellenbarger, "The Challenges That Working Mothers Still Face," *Wall Street Journal*, January 3, 2020.

214 "ones who get on a plane": Anne Weisberg, "What Flying Nannies Won't Fix," *New York Times*, August 24, 2015.

214 "because of manager discretion": Pamela Stone and Meg Lovejoy,

Opting Back In: What Really Happens When Mothers Go Back to Work (Berkeley: University of California Press, 2019), 185.

215 Dean and Auerbach contend: Annie Dean and Anna Auerbach, "96% of U.S. Professionals Say They Need Flexibility, but Only 47% Have It," *Harvard Business Review*, June 5, 2018.

217 "Future Dads, don't miss": Vanessa Fuhrmans, "As More New Dads Get Paternity Leave, Companies Push Them to Take It," *Wall Street Journal*, July 11, 2018.

221 "thinks the increase reflects": Nikki Waller and Joann S. Lublin, "What's Holding Women Back in the Workplace?," *Wall Street Journal*, September 30, 2015.

221 About 79 percent: Barbara Frankel, "How Phase-Back Programs Are Making It Easier than Ever for Moms to Return to Work After Baby," *Working Mother*, September 19, 2018.

222 "Working parents—men and women": Joann S. Lublin, "What Should a Mother Do About Her Career?," *Wall Street Journal*, March 21, 1980.

223 "Opponents of the bill": Claire Cain Miller, "Why Few Democrats Clapped for Trump's Call for Paid Family Leave," *New York Times*, February 6, 2020.

224 "Perhaps counterintuitively": David Harrison, "Employers Need to Address 'Caregiving Crisis,' Study Finds," *Wall Street Journal*, January 16, 2019.

224 "Companies incur millions": Joseph B. Fuller and Manjari Raman, "The Caring Company: How Employers Can Help Employees Manage Their Caregiving Responsibilities—While Reducing Costs and Increasing Productivity," Harvard Business School, January 2019, 2.

224 During the last six years: Tanya Klich, "The New Mom Economy: Meet the Startups Disrupting the $46 Billion Millennial Parenting Market," *Forbes*, May 10, 2019.

225 "Ninety percent of Icelandic fathers": Stone and Lovejoy, *Opting Back In*, 190.

226 "Swedes allocate separate": Ibid., 189.

226 The social media giant: Fuhrmans, "As More New Dads Get Paternity Leave, Companies Push Them to Take It."

229 "dismantling the barriers": Melinda Gates, "Here's Why I'm Committing $1 Billion to Promote Gender Equality," *Time*, October 5, 2019.

Selected Bibliography

Apter, Terri. *You Don't Really Know Me: Why Mothers and Daughters Fight and How Both Can Win.* New York: W. W. Norton, 2004.

Bachelder, Cheryl. *Dare to Serve: How to Drive Superior Results by Serving Others.* San Francisco: Berrett-Koehler, 2015.

Balswick, Judith. *Mothers and Daughters Making Peace: The Most Intimate, Tangled, Beautiful, and Frustrating Relationship Shared by Women.* Ann Arbor, MI: Servant Publications, 1993.

Barsh, Joanna. *Grow Wherever You Work: Straight Talk to Help with Your Toughest Challenges.* New York: McGraw-Hill Education, 2017.

Chiquet, Maureen. *Beyond the Label: Women, Leadership, and Success on Our Own Terms.* New York: HarperCollins, 2017.

Collins, Caitlyn. *Making Motherhood Work: How Women Manage Careers and Caregiving.* Princeton, NJ: Princeton University Press, 2019.

Comstock, Beth. *Imagine It Forward: Courage, Creativity and the Power of Change.* New York: Penguin Random House, 2018.

Deutsch, Francine M. *Halving It All: How Equally Shared Parenting Works.* Cambridge, MA: Harvard University Press, 1999.

Emens, Elizabeth. *Life Admin: How I Learned to Do Less, Do Better, and Live More.* Boston: Houghton Mifflin Harcourt, 2019.

Hochschild, Arlie. *The Second Shift: Working Families and the Revolution at Home.* New York: Viking Penguin, 1989.

Lacy, Sarah. *A Uterus Is a Feature, Not a Bug: The Working Woman's Guide to Overthrowing the Patriarchy.* New York: HarperCollins, 2017.

Lenehan, Pamela F. *My Mother, My Mentor: What Grown Children of Working Mothers Want You to Know.* Bloomington, IN: Archway Publishing, 2015.

Lockman, Darcy. *All the Rage: Mothers, Fathers, and the Myth of Equal Partnership.* New York: HarperCollins, 2019.

Lublin, Joann S. *Earning It: Hard-Won Lessons from Trailblazing Women at the Top of the Business World.* New York: HarperCollins, 2016.

Perlow, Leslie A. *Sleeping with Your Smartphone: How to Break the 24/7 Habit and Change the Way You Work*. Boston: Harvard Business Review Press, 2012.

Rodsky, Eve. *Fair Play: A Game-Changing Solution for When You Have Too Much to Do (and More Life to Live)*. New York: G. P. Putnam's Sons, 2019.

Ruddick, Sara. *Maternal Thinking: Towards a Politics of Peace*. Boston: Beacon Press, 1989.

Smolyansky, Julie. *The Kefir Cookbook*. New York: HarperCollins, 2018.

Spinola, Dana. *Love What You Do: A Plan for Creating a Life You Love Filled with Passion and Purpose*. Austin, TX: Fedd Agency, 2018.

Stone, Pamela. *Opting Out?: Why Women Really Quit Careers and Head Home*. Berkeley: University of California Press, 2007.

———and Meg Lovejoy. *Opting Back In: What Really Happens When Mothers Go Back to Work*. Oakland: University of California Press, 2019.

Tannen, Deborah. *You're Wearing That? Understanding Mothers and Daughters in Conversation*. New York: Random House, 2006.

Tassler, Nina, ed. *What I Told My Daughter: Lessons from Leaders on Raising the Next Generation of Empowered Women*. New York: Simon & Schuster, 2016.

Westervelt, Amy. *Forget "Having It All": How America Messed Up Motherhood—and How to Fix It*. New York: Seal Press, 2018.

Index